D1249604

Resolving Conflict
Strategies for Local Government

Edited by
Margaret S. Herrman

NORTH CHICAGO
PUBLIC LIBRARY

303.69
RES

International
City/County
ICMA
Management
Association

PRACTICAL MANAGEMENT SERIES
Barbara H. Moore, Editor

Resolving Conflict
Balanced Growth
Capital Financing Strategies for Local Governments
Capital Projects
Current Issues in Leisure Services
The Entrepreneur in Local Government
Ethical Insight, Ethical Action
Hazardous Materials, Hazardous Waste
Human Services on a Limited Budget
Local Economic Development
Long-Term Financial Planning
Managing for Tomorrow
Managing New Technologies
Pay and Benefits
Performance Evaluation
Personnel Practices for the '90s
Police Practice in the '90s
Practical Financial Management
Productivity Improvement Techniques
Shaping the Local Economy
Strategic Planning for Local Government
Successful Negotiating in Local Government
Telecommunications for Local Government

The Practical Management Series is devoted to the
presentation of information and ideas from diverse
sources. The views expressed in this book are those of
the contributors and are not necessarily those of ICMA.

Library of Congress Cataloging-in-Publication Data

Resolving conflict: strategies for local government/edited by
    Margaret S. Herrman.
        p.   cm.—(Practical management series)
    Includes bibliographical references.
    ISBN 0-87326-071-6
    1. Conflict management. 2. Municipal government.
    3. Local government. I. Herrman, Margaret S., II. Series.
    JS155.R47 1995
    303.6′9—dc20   94-16815
                                                            CIP

Copyright © 1994 by the International City/County Management Association, 777 North Capitol Street, N.E., Washington, D.C. 20002. All rights reserved, including rights of
reproduction and use in any form or by any means, including the making of copies by any photographic process, or
by any electronic or mechanical device, printed or written
or oral, or recording for sound or visual reproduction, or for
use in any knowledge or retrieval system or device, unless
permission in writing is obtained from the copyright
proprietor.

Printed in the United States of America.
9897969594
54321

Resolving Conflict:
Strategies for Local Government

The International City/County Management Association is the professional and educational organization for appointed management executives in local government. The purposes of ICMA are to enhance the quality of local government and to nurture and assist professional local government administrators in the United States and other countries. In furtherance of its mission, ICMA develops and disseminates new approaches to management through training programs, information services, and publications.

Managers, carrying a wide range of titles, serve cities, towns, counties, councils of governments, and state/provincial associations of local governments throughout the world. These managers serve at the direction of elected councils and governing boards. ICMA serves these managers and local governments through many programs that aim at improving the manager's professional competence and strengthening the quality of all local governments.

The International City/County Management Association was founded in 1914; adopted its City Management Code of Ethics in 1924; and established its Institute for Training in Municipal Administration in 1934. The Institute, in turn, provided the basis for the Municipal Management Series, generally termed the "ICMA Green Books."

ICMA's interests and activities include public management education; standards of ethics for members; the *Municipal Year Book* and other data services; urban research; and newsletters, the monthly magazine *Public Management*, and other publications. ICMA's efforts for the improvement of local government management—as represented by this book—are offered for all local governments and educational institutions.

Foreword

Conflict can arise about almost anything—from the schedule for lunch breaks to the choice for chief of police; from the timing of organizational changes to the siting of subsidized housing. But whatever the dispute, managers need a positive outlook and sharp skills to facilitate a successful resolution. Having a positive outlook means recognizing conflict as a natural aspect of any relationship. Conflict is not a dead end but the beginning of a process in which issues and needs can be clarified, understanding increased, and collaboration fostered.

Resolving Conflict: Strategies for Local Government takes a close look at practical strategies to help ensure a satisfactory outcome to conflict. It explores fundamental aspects of conflict resolution, including the role of leadership, the impact of diversity, and changing definitions of governance and public participation. The book also offers a variety of approaches to the task of intervention: techniques for determining whether to intervene, screening consultants, avoiding deadlock, and coping with difficult disputes are covered in detail. As both organizational life and governance become more participatory, managers find themselves searching for innovative methods to facilitate participation. *Resolving Conflict: Strategies for Local Government* explores a wealth of participation strategies, including consensus-based problem solving, small-group processes, workshops, and open houses. Finally, the volume examines the systems approach to conflict resolution, in which the emphasis is on proactive, comprehensive mechanisms for uncovering conflict and dealing with it before it becomes destructive.

This book is part of ICMA's Practical Management Series, which is devoted to serving local officials' needs for timely information on current issues and problems.

We wish to thank Margaret S. Herrman, who compiled the volume; the authors who contributed original material; and the individuals and organizations that granted ICMA permission to use their material. Finally, we wish to thank Barbara Moore and Sandy Chizinsky Leas for their editorial guidance.

William H. Hansell, Jr.
Executive Director
International City/County
Management Association

About the Editor and Authors

Margaret S. Herrman is a Senior Public Service Associate with the Vinson Institute of Government, the University of Georgia. Dr. Herrman helps cities, counties, and human resource agencies in Georgia, as well as federal and state agencies, to facilitate and mediate public policy decisions; improve functioning, especially through assessments and training that enhance problem resolution capacities; implement mediation programs; and empirically assess the needs of high-risk children and youth.

In the early 1980s, Dr. Herrman created the National Conference on Peacemaking and Conflict Resolution. She organized and chaired the first two conferences, served as executive director until August 1987 and chaired the board of directors until February 1989.

From 1984 to 1986 she served on the Dispute Resolution Task Force of the Carter Center of Emory University. She has facilitated/mediated large group decision making for over twenty years and has mediated court- and agency-referred cases since the early 1990s. She is also trained to mediate in farmer/lender disputes, divorce, and difficult domestic/family conflicts.

Dr. Herrman is author or coauthor of fifteen articles and/or monographs on collaborative problem solving, the impact of divorce, occupational choices of women, and deviant behavior. She has also authored or coauthored over thirty-five technical reports. Finally, she has contributed to over fifty professional meetings, often as keynote speaker, plenary speaker, session organizer, or conference organizer.

She earned a Doctor of Philosophy degree from Emory University and a post-doctorate from the University of Georgia.

Lorenz Aggens is a facilitator, mediator, trainer, and program consultant for public and private organizations, assisting in the management of public policy conflict and interorganizational disputes.

Frederick W. Allen is Director of the Office of Strategic Planning and Data, Environmental Protection Agency, Washington, D.C.

Geoff Ball of Geoff Ball and Associates, Los Altos, California, has worked for more than twenty years as a master facilitator, trainer, and conflict manager with a diverse client base.

Ozzie Bermant is director of the Concordia Systems Group and has provided mediation and conflict management training in a variety of settings, including federal agencies, local government, and higher education.

Susan Carpenter, former director of the Program for Community Problem Solving, Washington, D.C., has spent the past twenty years designing and managing programs to achieve consensus, resolve controversies, and develop goals and visions related to public issues at the local, state, and national level.

Desmond M. Connor is an applied sociologist with an international practice in preventing and resolving public controversy for government agencies or corporations with new projects, programs, or policies.

Gerald W. Cormick is a principal in The CSE Group, an organization that provides dispute settlement and relationship management services, and senior lecturer in the Graduate School of Public Affairs at the University of Washington. His mailing address is 15629 Cascadian Way, Mill Creek, Washington 98012.

Vincent T. Covello is director of the Center for Risk Communication at Columbia University and president of the Society for Risk Analysis (affiliation at the time of writing).

James L. Creighton, president of Creighton & Creighton, Inc., and past president of the International Association of Public Participation Practitioners, has been a consultant in public involvement, risk communication, and social impact assessment for more than twenty years.

Arthur Turovh Himmelman, founder of The Himmelman Consulting Group in Minneapolis, Minnesota, is a consultant whose practice is focused on the design and facilitation of multisector, community-based collaboration.

Steven Kelman is a professor of public policy in the John F. Kennedy School of Government, Harvard University (affiliation at the time of writing).

Bruce Levi is counsel of The North Dakota Consensus Council, Inc., a private, nonprofit corporation established in 1990 to provide forums and assistance to public and private leaders and citizens as they establish basic agreements regarding major issues of public structure, service, and policy.

Roger M. Schwarz, an organizational psychologist specializing in organizational change and conflict, serves on the faculty of the Institute of Government at the University of North Carolina at Chapel Hill (affiliation at the time of writing).

Larry Spears is executive director of The North Dakota Consensus Council, Inc.

John M. Stafford is the founder of JMS Associates, an organizational consulting and training firm located in Martinez, California.

Dr. David Stiebel is a University of California statewide lecturer and a specialist in municipal dispute resolution in Fairfax, California.

Andrea Williams is a consultant in the field of leadership and collaboration focusing on issues of diversity and gender and is based in Denver, Colorado.

Douglas H. Yarn is the in-house attorney-mediator for the American Arbitration Association and Senior Associate with the Southeastern Negotiation Network, a program of the City Planning Department at the Georgia Institute of Technology.

Contents

Introduction

Margaret S. Herrman

Conflict is an expression of incompatibility: It exists when the actions of one person or group block or redirect the actions of another person or group.[1] If the conflict surfaces—in other words, if both sides decide to take the conflict on—one of four outcomes is possible: (1) you win, and your rival loses; (2) your rival wins, and you lose; (3) the two of you compromise, and both of you lose to some degree; or (4) you put your combined energies into an integrative solution, and both of you win to some degree.[2]

Historically, the American public—including public officials—has favored the first outcome, feared the second, and chosen the third only as a last resort. Until the 1980s, outcome 4 was rarely considered an option.

Most of us have learned through observation and experience that conflict brings about either partial or total loss. Thus, our strategies for dealing with conflict are based not on seeking a cooperative resolution but on protecting ourselves against loss. Given the experiences of most people—lessons learned from parents in childhood, from the competitive atmospheres of school, sports, and the marketplace—it is not surprising that the guideposts we follow when working out conflict rarely lead to win/win solutions. It is the rare lesson that illustrates the path to mutual gain. Specifically, this volume looks at what you might do, who to involve, how to proceed, and when to act in a variety of situations and circumstances.

In this brief introduction, I will (1) explore the origins of conflict in organizational life; (2) describe which conflict resolution strategies lead to losses and which to gains; and (3) explain how the materials in this volume can support your efforts to deal with conflict at various levels and in various settings.

Organizations and conflict

Government entities—agencies, programs, departments, commissions, or policy bodies—are like any other organization: they employ individuals who are connected by a variety of relationships and devoted to the task of transforming inputs into outputs. In the case of government, fiscal resources, constituent support, and political leverage are transformed into public services.

For this transformation process to be effective, a number of conditions must exist:

1. Goals or desired outputs must be clearly defined.
2. A high level of consensus regarding goals needs to exist.
3. People must cooperate to achieve goals.
4. People must understand how to act with each other. In other words, roles or jobs must be well defined, along with expectations for behaving (e.g., reporting to work, routing paperwork, producing documentation).
5. Support technologies must be available to people doing the work (e.g., computers, vehicles, machinery).
6. The management process must integrate human and technical resources into a total system focused on goals.[3]

Given these conditions, it is clear that people working in organizations do not function independently: they rely on each other—and often on outsiders—to ensure the transformation of inputs to outputs. And given this interdependence, organizations are environments rife with the possibilities for conflict even under the best of circumstances.

Finally, while government entities share characteristics with other organizations, public accountability adds pressure and even more potential for conflict. For example, government officials, like officials in all organizations, cope with a variety of conflicts, from personnel grievances to interdepartmental warfare and interorganizational disputes. But accountability expands the sphere of interdependency beyond what is typical for private-sector businesses and many not-for-profit agencies. Public officials must deal regularly with angry constituents—who in some measure are "the boss"—and participate in highly visible public confrontations over complex policy issues.

A view of conflict

There is no question that a high probability of conflict is part of your professional life. Your first, and perhaps most basic, choice concerns how you view conflict: Is it as an ally or an enemy? Just as we associate conflict with loss, we also associate it with negative feelings like anxiety, tension, fear, and anger. These enculturated responses may shift over time, but most of us still prefer that things run smoothly, without any fuss or bother. In an organizational setting, this preference may mean viewing conflict as an enemy, believing conflict to be a sign of dysfunction, and attempting to suppress, avoid, or tightly "manage" conflict.

On the face of it, it seems logical to avoid what can be painful; but conflict is as fundamental to the human condition as breathing or blinking. How do you avoid breathing or blinking? Suppressing, avoiding, or tightly managing conflict is at best impractical and at worst damaging to the fabric of relationships, especially where people are highly interdependent. In the long run, these strategies carry an awful price.

Resolving Conflict: Strategies for Local Government offers a slightly different perspective: the authors encourage you to view conflict positively, more as a mutual problem to be resolved than a contest to be won or lost. Consider these comments from Johan Galtung, a leading theorist in the field,

> If you cannot remove conflict from life, why not adjust your thinking about it? If you can't beat it, join it. Why not try and see conflict as the salt of life, as the big energizer, the tickler, the tantalizer, rather than a bothersome nuisance, as a noise in a perfect channel, as disturbing ripples in otherwise quiet water? Why not treat conflict as a form of life, particularly since we all know that it is precisely during the periods in our lives when we are exposed to a conflict that really challenges us, and that we finally are able to master, that we feel the most alive.[4]

Conflict is not an evil but a necessary force that, like a wonderful spice, enhances our functioning, whether we are in pairs, in groups, in offices, or in communities.

When we view conflict positively, we expand our choice of strategies for dealing with it. One of the goals of this book is to expand the range of choices. In the next portion of this introduction, I'll consider some of the common strategies for dealing with conflict, paying particular attention to those that are the focus of the book.

Actions, reactions, and outcomes

Figure 1 displays common responses to conflict in their simplest forms. As the figure indicates, we tend to swing between flight

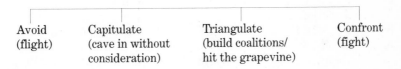

| Avoid (flight) | Capitulate (cave in without consideration) | Triangulate (build coalitions/ hit the grapevine) | Confront (fight) |

Figure 1. Four basic responses to conflict.

(avoiding the situation) and fight (openly confronting the issue), with capitulation and triangulation (bringing in allies) in between. Flight, or avoidance, is our most common reaction when faced with a conflict, but sometimes avoidance is not possible, and we are forced to look for other options. A second common reaction is simply to cave in to someone's demand for change. Oddly enough, some people cave in simply from habit, because they don't want to invest energy in scouting out ramifications of a decision to change. Most people don't realize they are courting failure by responding this way, because they associate capitulation with being "nice."[5]

Triangulation is yet another way of working through a conflict.[6] Triangulation occurs when direct confrontation is too painful or too risky: when you can't keep doing what you are doing, you don't want to cave in, and you can't really avoid the issue. Under these circumstances, you may start talking to people either inside your group (if a safe confidant exists) or outside your group (if safe coalitions exist beyond your unit) for at least two reasons: First, you may bring others in as a sounding board or as a source of expert knowledge; perhaps your allies will offer potential solutions for the difficult situation.[7] Second, you may seek emotional support or personal validation by shifting your allegiance from the old relationship to a new one.

The fourth and final option is to confront the situation openly. Although this is the "fight" response, you will see in Figures 2 and 3 that "fighting" can take a range of forms, each carrying more or less potential for winning or losing. Interestingly, studies of conflict behaviors indicate that confrontation is the least common response. We usually try the other three responses first, turning to confrontation only after other avenues have been exhausted.

Figure 2 takes the varieties of response a little further by showing when we are likely to encounter a loss and when we can anticipate a winning solution. From the figure, it is clear why we don't like to engage in conflict: With the exception of a few of the nonviolent confrontational strategies, most of our reactions either guarantee loss, are highly associated with loss, or are ambiguous enough to carry a fairly high probability of loss. Avoidance, for example, usually brings loss both for you and for the other person, unless the relationship can be easily replaced.[8] At the opposite extreme, violent confrontation also carries the threat of loss.

Capitulation and triangulation are risky responses because the outcome is hard to predict. For example, a quick decision to change is associated with winning only if your current activity, policy, or management strategy is not working and a new way of doing things is not very risky. Otherwise, caving in is highly associated with failure.[9] Outcomes associated with triangulation are similarly am-

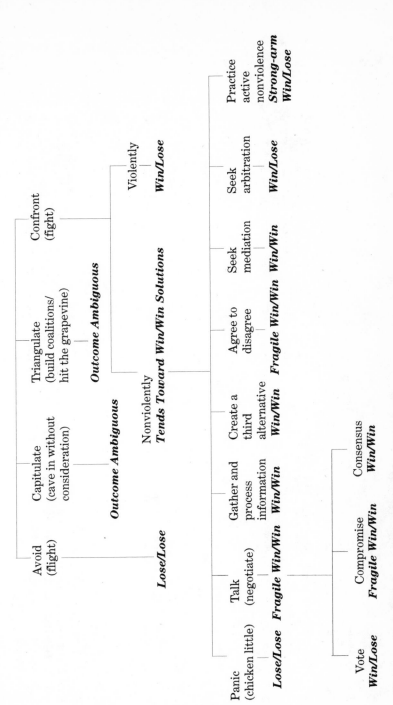

Figure 2. Responses to conflict and possible outcomes.

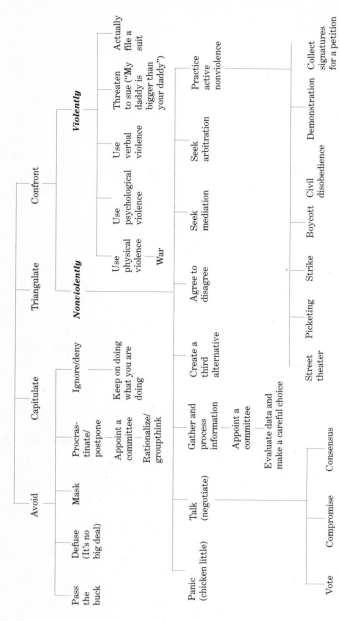

Figure 3. Responses to conflict: expanding your options. Source: Based in part on Kathy Bickmore, Prill Goldthwait, and John Looney, *Alternatives to Violence: A Manual for Teaching Peacemaking to Youth and Adults* (Akron, OH: Peace GROWS, Inc.: 1987; Leon Mann and Irving L. Janis, "Decisional Conflict in Organizations," in Tjosvold and Johnson, eds., Productive Conflict Management (New York: Irvington Press, 1983); and Claude M. Steiner, *The Other Side of Power* (New York: Grove Press, 1981).

biguous. Triangulation moves you away from the immediate heat of a conflict, but the move actually prevents you from addressing underlying problems. In fact, triangulation often shifts the locus of the fight to different relationships or sectors in an organization, making the fundamental issues even harder to resolve at some later time. Although you may gain valuable insight into a problem by talking it over with others who may suggest good strategies, until you confront the offended or offending parties the conflict will simply fester.

Figure 3 specifies some of the actions associated with avoidance as well as with nonviolent and violent confrontation. The figure does not by any means include all possible options: Many more actions or reactions could be listed; indeed, the list would expand dramatically if we took it out of the context of Western, English-speaking culture.

Before defining the options and processes that stand at the heart of this volume, it might be important to note what this book does not cover. First, avoidance is not typically considered a good conflict resolution strategy. Although avoidance is effective for dealing with stranger-to-stranger conflicts, avoidance of conflict in ongoing interactions only increases the chances of repeated and gradually escalating cycles of conflict.

Second, although other volumes use the term *conflict management,* I feel that the phrase can too easily be used to describe techniques for evading or suppressing conflict, including quick-change strategies, triangulation, and violent confrontation.

Resolving Conflict: Strategies for Local Government concentrates instead on a set of strategies noted in Figure 3: gathering and processing information, creating multiple alternatives, formal mediation, and negotiations that fall under the heading of consensus strategies.

In *Resolving Conflict: Strategies for Local Government,* Steven Kelman's "Cooperationist Institutions in Public Policymaking" lays out a way of thinking about conflict in government organizations. Kelman urges government leaders to create forums or to use existing forums for the face-to-face dialogues necessary to any win/win strategy. Geoff Ball's "What Works When: Matching Leadership Style to Conflict Type" demonstrates that a leadership style chosen on the basis of the specific conflict can increase the chances of a successful outcome. A number of articles, including Andrea Williams's "Resolving Conflict in a Multicultural Environment," John Stafford's "Managing Conflict in Law Enforcement Agencies," David Stiebel's "Want to Resolve a Dispute? Don't Ask!" Ozzie Bermant's "The Seven Deadly Syndromes of Dispute Resolution," Roger Schwarz's "Ground Rules for Effective Groups," Gerald Cormick's "Crafting the Language of Consensus," and Vincent Covello and Frederick Allen's "Seven Cardinal Rules of Risk Communication," provide specific tips on how to move win/win strategies to fruition. Since effective communication lies at the heart of a successful approach, several of these articles examine spoken and written communication styles that either facilitate win/win solutions— or that enhance the risk of failure. In addition, the principles and approaches described in these articles apply to virtually any category of win/win scenario, including consensus, information gathering and analysis, and mediation.

Although Douglas H. Yarn, in an unpublished lexicon of alternative dispute resolution processes, includes more than twenty pages of definitions of mediation, mediation classically involves a third-party neutral in a range of roles such as problem solver, process consultant, meeting facilitator, convener, and ultimately, communication conduit for problem resolution. The precise form of mediation can vary considerably—from very informal and private sessions that involve two protagonists in a single, forty-five-minute meeting to multiforum interventions lasting six months or longer and involving a team of mediators. My article, "Finding Help," offers a decision format to help you decide, first, whether seeking a mediator makes sense; and second, who the right mediator might be for a particular dispute.

Susan Carpenter's "Solving Community Problems by Consensus" provides an overview of complex, mediation-based processes for multiparty problems. Desmond Connor's "A Generic Design for Public Involvement Programs" is another look at facilitated public involvement processes. Lorenz Aggens's "The Samoan Circle: A Group Process for Discussing Controversial Subjects" is a classic description of a highly functional approach to conducting politically sensitive meetings. James Creighton's "Designing and Conducting Public Meetings," a companion to both the Aggens and the Connor articles, provides invaluable information on meeting formats as well as process suggestions to help ensure the success of conflict resolution interventions involving the public.

Since the late 1980s, more and more public officials and professional mediators have come to realize that there are advantages in creating and institutionalizing systems to provide win/win forums and support on an ongoing basis. Four articles discuss how such support systems can be developed. Arthur Turovh Himmelman's "Communities Working Collaboratively for a Change" focuses on collaboration, a theme that is beginning to surface in a number of sectors including human services, planning, and public-private partnerships. Himmelman creates a vision of potentials and strategies for making them happen. Ozzie Bermant's "A Proactive Approach to Organizational Conflict" and Douglas H. Yarn's "Developing a Comprehensive Internal Dispute Resolution System" offer insights into creating effective dispute resolution systems within a government setting. Finally, in "Unlocking Gridlock: Establishing a Regional Network of Local Consensus Councils," Bruce Levi and Larry Spears suggest the need for regional as well as internal support systems. The authors provide an insightful look at one state's successful efforts to address major regional pubic-policy disputes on an ongoing basis.

1. Based in part on Morton Deutsch, *The Resolution of Conflict* (New Haven: Yale University Press, 1973), 2.
2. Suggested by Henry C. Metcalf and L. Urwick, eds., *Dynamic Administration: The Collected Papers of Mary Parker Follett* (New York: Harper, 1940).
3. Based in part on Dean Tjosvold and David W. Johnson, "Introduction," in Dean Tjosvold and David W. Johnson, eds., *Productive Conflict Management* (New York: Irvington Press, 1983), 2.
4. Johan Galtung, *Essays in Peace Research, 1975–1980* (Copenhagen: Christian Ejlers), vol. 3, p. 501.
5. See Leon Mann and Irving L. Janis, "Decisional Conflicts in Organizations," in Tjosvold and Johnson, *Productive Conflict Management.*
6. An excellent article on triangulation in a government context is Kenwyn W. Smith, "The Movement of Conflict in Organizations: The Joint Dynamics of Splitting and Triangulation," *Administrative Science Quarterly* 34 (1989): 1–20.
7. See Chapter 7 of Irving L. Janis and Leon Mann, *Decision Making: A Psychological Analysis of Conflict, Choice, and Commitment* (New York: Free Press, 1977).
8. See William L. F. Felstiner, "Avoidance as Dispute Processing: An Elaboration," *Law and Society Review* 9, no. 4 (1975): 695–706.
9. See Janis and Mann, *Decision Making.* In groups or bureaucracies, the mere speed of change can provoke disaster if people are not adequately prepared for it.

PART 1

Laying the Groundwork

What Works When: Matching Leadership Style to Conflict Type

Geoff Ball

Many facilitators feel that openness in communication is *always* the best process. Yet, mediators, having dealt with situations in which substantial mistrust exists as a precursor to their being called in, feel that open communication early in the process often makes things worse. Political leaders focus on winning elections and building coalitions of constituencies around self-interest. Community organizers see few people interested in working to bring about needed changes and focus on generating hope and empowering the powerless. How do these different styles and perceptions fit together? Who is right?

In a report for the League of Women Voters written about 1968, a Baptist theologian, Tex Sample, presented his concerns about the League's involvement with the War on Poverty. Sample noted that the League's style was one of open, facilitative, interactive communication. He believed that if the League began to work with inner-city neighborhoods and retained that style, they would in fact hinder rather than help those neighborhoods.

He observed that six people could go to City Hall and demand that the garbage be picked up on a regular basis in their low-income neighborhood. They could allege that they had 6,000 people in back of them all organized to dump garbage on the City Hall steps. But if the League observer, speaking openly and honestly, said "Well gee, there really were only 23 people at the meeting and I'm not sure how many other people would be interested in working together," the City Hall folks would pat the organizers on the head and say, "Thank you very much. We will get back to you real soon,"

Reprinted by permission from *Vision/Action* March 1992. This article was originally entitled "What Works When—Types of Leadership Needed to Resolve Conflict."

and then do nothing, knowing full well that there are no political consequences, no real reason for shifting the way they do business or for really working to solve the garbage collection problem.

So if open communication is not the (only) approach to this kind of situation, what else is needed, and how do I as intervener or participant think about it? Sample developed a multi-level model in response to this question. His work provided the basis for the development of the "What Works When" framework.

The "What Works When" framework

This framework posits that there is not one single kind of effective leadership pattern in a complex conflictual situation; that very different kinds of leadership behaviors, strategies and objectives are needed; and that these differences may necessitate shared leadership.

This framework provides a map that guides the choice of leadership style in a conflict situation; it relates leadership style to the perceptions and emotions of those involved. Further, it provides a rationalization of the role of power in consensus building and legitimizes relative equality of power as a precondition for collaborative work in which the interests of the parties are significantly affected. The framework can be used to understand the dynamics of conflict and devise processes that match the situation—rather than forcing the situation and the people into the leader's process.

The "What Works When" framework is shown in Figure 1. It embeds four leadership styles into a framework that relates prevailing feeling to communication style to leadership needed to outcome. The framework can be entered at any of the four levels: Inspiration, Confrontation, Negotiation or Facilitation. Lower levels are the foundation for the higher levels. A process of conflict resolution can advance up the levels and fall down to a lower level when the foundation previously laid is not strong enough. Viewed conceptually, the process "spirals" up the framework.

Let me put words to the diagram. Where there is apathy, there is likely to be *no* communication focused on changing the situation. Inspirational leadership can transform people's beliefs about what is desirable, create a positive vision in people's minds and lead to hope. Where there is hope, there is a comparison between what is and what might be—between the current reality and the desired vision. The gap may seem insurmountable. In a powerless community there is apt to be a feeling of fear or anxiety associated with even daring to hope openly. Communication is distorted and misleading. Confrontational leadership challenges this perception of lack of power. It enables people to learn that they have power. The developing power of one group can evoke suspicion in other groups, especially when these different groups are in conflict. What are *they* going to do?

Given this suspicion, group members are likely to be guarded in their communications with people outside their group. Yet, if the conflict is to be resolved, they will need to engage with these outsiders. Negotiation leadership transforms suspicion into a sense of justice. Through effective negotiation each group comes to feel it has been treated justly and it becomes more likely that trust will exist across group boundaries. With trust comes open communication. With trust as the prevailing emotion and with open communication, facilitation leadership can enable everyone to work effectively and efficiently together to everyone's mutual satisfaction.

This framework assumes that successful leadership at one level *transforms the state of the situation* to a new state in which a new style of leadership is needed. But it does not preclude the possibility that a given level may be revisited more than once in a complex controversy.

An application of the framework to a conflict situation

The following example uses the framework to bring order to a chaotic situation.

A suburban high school, desegregated under court order, had one-third (not the same one-third) of the students absent one or more periods each day. It had a highly principled, highly intelligent,

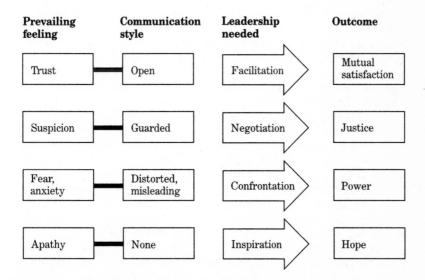

Figure 1. The "What Works When" framework.

Lincolnesque principal who was not an effective administrator; independent teachers who had not worked together; and a student body drawn from the full economic spectrum and with the widest range of preparation for and interest in school.

When I was asked in as an intervener, the human relations specialist for the school district indicated that there were a small number of teachers who felt that there was some possibility of resolving this difficult situation. A number of issues had surfaced: a loss of teacher confidence in the principal's administrative capabilities, the very high rate of absence previously mentioned, and interracial conflict, which was the reason the human relations specialist had been called.

The levels of leadership

Inspirational leadership level. Most teachers at the school described the situation as hopeless. There was little or no effective communication among the faculty as a whole—mostly grousing, grumbling, and complaining. I met with a small group of teachers who wanted to construct some way of mobilizing the school. Together we planned a collaborative process to address school issues. Following a substantial amount of work with this leadership group, we initiated a process. The leadership group talked with other teachers and I talked with the principal and other administrators. Enough people found hope to agree to start the process.

Confrontational leadership level. Assessment interviews showed that some of the faculty and staff feared retaliation. Comments were made like "Don't tell him anything; they'll get even." Some of the communication was both indirect and distorted. Yet, issues emerged from the interviews. We held a meeting of all 125 teachers and the four administrators for the school to select the issue on which to focus.

In this charged meeting, both sides demonstrated a willingness to confront each other and, to some extent, the situation—that is, to exercise power. The teachers were able to raise their issues, including whether they wanted to seek removal of the principal. The principal had asserted his authority to punish individual teachers who were unwilling to engage in a process to resolve the conflicts and address the problems.

Both the administration and the teachers realized they had power, but power limited in its exercise. While the principal could censure individual teachers, he could not get full support for solutions to address the school's problems. While the teachers could undermine the solutions, they could not move *as a school*, without the support of the principal.

Negotiation leadership level. Two groups, each of which has power, will eye each other with suspicion. "What is the other group going to do? Perhaps we need to talk with them so we can find out—but don't tell them too much." We negotiated ground rules and understandings regarding how the work on a solution was to be used. At this point we had only a modest sense of possibility of a just outcome, but enough to move to the top level.

Facilitation leadership level. With a sufficient sense that the process might lead to a just result, teachers began to trust the process and to communicate more openly about the problem selected to work on—the absence of one out of three students one or more periods every day.

The teachers engaged in problem solving. Options were developed and maps were created of the proposed system. The details of a preferred alternative emerged. The solution demanded teachers take on new responsibilities. The attendance office was clogged with nearly 500 students needing to get their absence permits signed each morning. Only if teachers became involved in monitoring attendance would the system have a chance of working. This proposed solution was presented to the full faculty.

Back to the confrontational level. We dropped down to the confrontation level. It was at this time that one teacher stood up and said, "I will never monitor the attendance of students in other teachers' classes. If I had to go to those classes, I'd cut too. I think they are terrible teachers."

At this time the framework became even more useful to me. Holding the framework in my mind helped me understand that dropping to the power level was legitimate and that when vital interests were threatened it was natural for people to react confrontively. The framework helped me respond appropriately. Without the framework in mind I might have seen this attack as violating the ground rules for facilitation. Instead I understood the need for this confrontive action to take place and to be acknowledged.

A week later the outraged teacher totally reversed her position. She said, "I think this is a terrific plan. It will cut noise in the hall, reduce vandalism, increase our ability to provide a good learning environment for our students." When I asked her what had changed her mind, she said that she figured out a way to monitor the attendance of the students in other teachers' classes *without having it interfere with her teaching.* She had discovered a way to accomplish the plan without compromising her commitment to quality teaching.

We continued moving back and forth between facilitation levels and confrontation levels as the various groups raised issues, had their power acknowledged and their interests addressed. Finally, in the later stages of the process, issues came up that required trade-offs—issues regarding who was going to do how much of what—zero sum or distributive bargaining in the language of negotiation.

At this point in the process, a power leader emerged to engage in negotiations with the administration. This was a person who had been identified to me as a leader of the teachers' union, a strong teacher advocate, a person willing to confront the administration. These power leaders came to the table and, through negotiations, allocated work to roles in a way that people eventually felt was fair. It started out in an atmosphere of mistrust and suspicion and, at the same time, with acknowledgment of the power of both of the groups. Communication was guarded. But, bit by bit, with the intervener serving as mediator, we were able to arrive at a trade-off that was felt to be fair and just.

Implications and action principles

How does this framework help, beyond providing a descriptive set of categories that allow us to map a process? It suggests some rather specific things. For example, Hans Spiegel, while evaluating Model Cities programs, noticed that inspirational and confrontational leadership was relatively easy to develop. These leaders brought neighborhoods together and people began to have the sense of their own power. City halls faced with this threat also mobilized their power. *However, what tended to be lacking were people in both groups skilled in negotiation and facilitation.* As a result, when the Model Cities neighborhood leaders came together with the folks from City Hall to figure out how the garbage was to get picked up, it was often true that neither side moved to the upper two levels in the framework. Instead they made threats and allegations—confrontational tactics—and went back to punishing each other. They were never able to get above the dividing line between confrontation and negotiation.

In some cases confrontational leaders were able to hand over negotiation to a different person who was not so identified with the tactics of confrontation, but more skilled at working things out. In these cases good solutions did emerge and progress was made.

Negotiation and facilitation leaders are, in personality and style, often different from people who are good at inspiration and confrontation. The community organizer Saul Alinsky may be an outstanding exception. From reading his books it appears to me that he was capable of working at any of these four levels. While he is best known for inspirational and confrontational leadership, it seems clear he was an extremely effective negotiator and understood the value of collaborative problem solving and facilitation when appropriate. Thus, the success of Alinsky and the failure of so many of his adherents is perhaps related to their hearing only part of Alinsky's message, not understanding how important negotiation and facilitation skills are to the eventual outcome.

The inability to get above the level of confrontational leadership in order to engage in negotiation or facilitation can result from several things: lack of negotiation leadership, a confrontational leader unwilling or unable to shift leadership style or allow others to take the appropriate leadership role, or inadequate development of the foundation on which the higher levels rest.

On the other hand, those people who understand the importance of negotiation and facilitation and yet shy away from power politics and away from being inspirational may be led by the framework to build the foundation on which negotiation and facilitation rest when significant interests are at stake.

Conclusions

The "What Works When" framework suggests the need to ensure that in any complex situation where key interests of different parties are at stake, there are leaders for each of the various interest groups who *collectively* have the abilities needed for inspiration, confrontation, negotiation, and facilitation leadership.

We see from the framework that at various stages in the process, leadership may need to shift from one person to another—either because it is unlikely that any one person will have all the leadership skills for all four levels or because the "other side" will be unwilling to negotiate or be open and trusting with the confrontational leader. If this shift in leadership styles does not take place, it is likely that the conflict will not be reconciled to mutual satisfaction, and that the conflict will be stalemated or settled coercively. Finally, the framework suggests that those who favor open communication need to consider that there are situations in a real-world process when open communication can do real disservice to one or more parties in the situation.

Resolving Conflict in a Multicultural Environment

Andrea Williams

Managing conflict is difficult enough when it involves people with the same backgrounds, from the same or similar cultures, who are motivated by the same underlying values. Most organizations, including local and regional government entities, now face conflict that crosses cultures. Managing conflict involving a cultural dimension requires both a mastery of basic conflict management principles and an understanding of the cultural issues.[1]

When we travel to a foreign country, we *expect* to encounter a different culture. When we stay at home, we expect everyone to be operating from the same basic cultural values and beliefs. If that were ever true in the United States, it is true no longer. The makeup of the United States population is changing, both in terms of demographics and attitude. Today, one in four people in the United States identifies as Hispanic or a person of color.[2] However, statistical averaging mutes the significance of the trends: for example, in California, Anglos now make up just 58% of the population. States and regions that are below the national average in population diversity are experiencing many of the same changes, but at a slower rate. By the middle of the twenty-first century, a majority of the U.S. population will consist of Hispanics and people of color.

As important as increasing demographic diversity is the changing attitude of nontraditional groups. Originally aspiring to blend into the Eurocentric cultural base, many groups are now maintaining their cultural traditions and values with pride, regardless of conflict with traditional Anglo culture.[3] The change in attitude—reflected in dress, style of interaction, use of language, and celebration of holidays—applies both to groups long active in our governmental processes and to more recently arrived cultural groups.

The combination of these two trends—changing demographics and changing attitudes—requires government entities to become more sophisticated in dealing with cultural issues and with the conflicts arising from them. The choice is not whether to notice and respond, only how.

Defining culture

When we define culture, we often think, for example, of art, language, food, and dress, but we have also come to understand that values are an integral part of culture: e.g., individual autonomy or collective community, competition or cooperation.[4] Cultural values shape the way people in a given culture perceive the world. If we perceive and identify ourselves as part of a specific group and look to that group as a source of values, that group is a culture.[5]

No one definition of culture or list of different cultures is inclusive enough. For example, the federal government coined the term *Hispanic* to describe the population of Spanish-speaking people in the United States. Yet there are as many as a hundred different cultures encompassed by that label. Although they speak a common language, the cultures of Cuban-Americans and Mexican-Americans are not especially similar.

Cultural identities and values may be based on one or more of the following differences:

- Race (e.g., Native American, African-American)
- Ethnicity (e.g., Irish, Italian)
- Gender (male, female)
- Socioeconomic class (e.g., upper, middle, lower-middle, underclass)
- Religion (e.g., Muslim, Catholic)
- Country of origin (e.g., Russia, Cuba)
- Geographic region (e.g., the American South, the Midwest).

Taking this broad view of culture and cultural identity allows us to realize that there are many groups with varying cultural norms. In some instances, the values espoused by one cultural tradition are not compatible with those of another culture: for example, some cultures assign rights equally to men and women, while others place the male or the female in the dominant legal position.

Cultural assumptions

Conflict may arise between people of different cultures when a similar issue would create no conflict between people of the same culture. This occurs because people assign greatest importance to different values, and fashion their behavior to honor those values. At the same time, people "read" observed behavior as they would in the context of their own culture.[6] For example, in some cultures it is a sign of disrespect to suggest alternatives to an older, more senior colleague. If an employee who held that value reported to a supervisor from the Anglo culture—which values youth over age, aggressiveness over cooperation, and innovation over everything—the employee's respectful behavior would be interpreted as showing little initiative, self-confidence, or commitment. In other words, the supervisor would be likely to read the behavior in the language of his or her culture.

When we consider "diverse" cultural perspectives, we may think only of cultural traditions that *differ* from Anglo culture. One lesson of cultural awareness is that Anglo culture is just one of many cultures in the expanding American multicultural community. Anglo culture needs to be explained not only to those who do not share the same tradition, but also to the Anglos themselves, who take their behavior and perspectives as an absolute norm. The values are so ingrained that Anglos often have difficulty describing the precepts of their culture: for example, observers of Anglo culture often remark on its bias toward action, whereas Anglos tend not to recognize that bias or to be aware that other cultures are more contemplative.

Identifying cultural conflicts

How can we know whether a conflict is affected by cultural differences? We first have to understand the dimensions of conflict in general.

Every conflict has at least two dimensions: *content* and *relational*; effective conflict resolution deals with both factors.[7] The con-

---

Cultural patterns

What we take for granted as acceptable may differ from the patterns accepted by other cultural groups. For example, in one local government, a group of women responding to a request for proposals submitted a lengthy and complete written proposal. When they arrived for the interview portion of the evaluation process, they were subjected to a fast-paced interchange in which a panel of knowledgeable government officials fired questions at them. The women came from a culture in which business relationships are based on personal relationships, and they were baffled by a procedure that prohibited them from having a casual conversation with the officials before being called upon to "perform." Their proposal was excellent, but the respondents' discomfort with the standard procedure prevented the evaluators from seeing its worth.

tent dimension is the substance of the dispute, and is usually the focus of discussion and negotiation. The relational dimension is an emotional need for an intangible such as security, acknowledgment of achievement, or respect. Disputants may or may not be aware of their own—or the other party's—relational needs.

Interpersonal conflict between people from different cultures has a third, deeper dimension—a clash of cultural values. Whereas content and relational needs tend to "belong" to the individual, the cultural dimension reflects a more general pattern; it determines the parameters of what is important and what appropriate interaction looks like. Intercultural conflict is usually about who the individuals are as people: how they think, how they see things, their values and traditions—their very identity. The conflict is taken personally and seriously. Resolving a conflict involving such emotionally charged issues tests any conflict resolution process.

The three dimensions of a cross-cultural dispute can be likened to an underwater volcano: the peak—a small island—is analogous to the content aspect of the dispute, the part that can be seen and that receives most of the attention. The relational dimension is just below the water's surface, surrounding and upholding the island. The cultural dimension is like the base of the volcanic mountain: the foundation underpinning the entire structure. It is unseen, unmoving, stable—and critical to the shape and formation of the overall structure.

When the volcano erupts, there is an explosion; we see the small island tremble, heat up, and become overrun with molten lava, just as we would see intense discussion about, for example, which days should be official city holidays. Although we see and hear only the content piece, the personal emotional stake of the person and his or her cultural beliefs and traditions are integral to understanding and resolving the full dispute—just as knowing how the entire volcanic mountain functions is essential to knowing what created the eruption. The source and strength are at the base, but it tends to be ignored; most of the attention is given to the fireworks occurring at the surface.

Although there is no sure procedure or symbol to alert us, cross-cultural conflicts often contain certain indicators.

First, if the individuals or groups in conflict are from different cultures, the dynamics may be more complicated than they would be in the case of a conflict over a specific substantive issue fueled only by the emotional needs of the people or groups involved.[8] In examining a conflict, the concept of culture should be taken in its broadest meaning: differences in perspective arising from gender, social class, education, or background (e.g., region of origin, urban or rural upbringing) are as likely to create the cultural character of a disagreement as are differences in religion, race, ethnicity, or country of origin. Moreover, these factors do not operate independently: our cultural identities and the associated values create complex mosaics within each of us, and the combinations of different strands of cultural identity can spark a conflict. Any one of the specific differences might be manageable, but in combination they create a complex set of expectations of how to act and how others should respond that causes a cultural confrontation. Nevertheless, differences along just one cultural dimension may be sufficient to create a cultural clash. A man and a woman, both from the Northeast and with similar educational and social backgrounds, may be locked in conflict because of their perceptions of gender roles.

Second, if more traditional conflict resolution processes fail to resolve the conflict, this is an indicator that the conflict may have a cultural aspect.[9] Attempting to understand both content and relational needs—and helping the parties accept that effective resolution will come about only when the relational as well as the content needs are addressed—often leads to a fairly swift, creative solution to the conflict. However, if focusing on the emotional aspect of the dispute does not resolve it but only seems to heighten the tension, a deeper cultural issue may be creating the friction.

A third sign of a cultural component is repeated conflict (often over what do not seem to be particularly significant content issues) or conflicts that are more emotionally explosive than the problem would reasonably warrant (e.g., whose fault it was that a report

---

Cultural provocations

The actions of one cultural group may be perceived as a provocation by another group, even though the first group is unaware of the cultural implications of its action. In 1991, the City of Kenai, Alaska, was planning a celebration of the 200th anniversary of the landing of the first Russian fur traders in 1791. When plans for the celebration were announced, the Kenaize Indian Tribe protested. The Dena'ina Athabascan Indians, their ancestors, had lived in the region for a thousand years. The Kenaize resented the implication that civilization did not exist until 200 years ago, when the Russians settled the coast. In response to the objection, a broader coalition of interests was assembled to plan for the year-long celebration. The native culture became the foundation of the celebration, and the volunteer organizing group was expanded to include native community leaders. The celebration's lasting achievement was the completion of the Kenai Bicentennial Visitors and Cultural Center to house the region's artifacts and historical data. What began as a cultural clash ended with an enhanced appreciation of the region's legacy.

was not delivered on time). Seemingly unrelated substantive controversies can mask conflict about basic values and acceptable behavior. Until the cultural dimension is explicitly acknowledged and discussed and the parties involved state their beliefs, traditions, and needs, any resolution will be temporary and superficial.

Resolving cultural conflicts

Cross-cultural conflict resolution begins with determining whether the conflict includes a cultural dimension. In a multicultural environment, three approaches are available to minimize and resolve the inevitable conflicts:

1. Personal interaction: probing for the cultural dimension
2. Learning about other cultures
3. Altering the organization's procedures and systems.

Probing for the cultural dimension. When signs of cultural conflict become apparent, the first step is to acknowledge that the conflict involves a cultural dimension: It is critical to obtain agreement from all people involved that a cultural conflict might or does exist.[10] The second step is an agreement that the parties are willing to work on the conflict, including its cultural component. This does not foretell the outcome of the dispute or commit the parties to taking or giving up any particular position; it is merely an agreement to work on the controversy. The third step is to work on the conflict in a systematic phased process.[11]

Phase 1: Describe the offending behavior. This first phase requires each party to articulate clearly exactly what it is about the other's behavior or attitude that is causing the conflict for them. We often assume that the other person's concern is exactly what we would be concerned about if we were in his or her position. When cultural values are involved, the other's motivations may be wholly different from ours, maybe even unimaginable to us. We must ask for and then listen carefully to a description of the conflict as the other party sees it.

Phase 2: Gain cultural understanding. The second phase is to understand how the conflict-creating conduct is viewed *within* each culture. Only by releasing our assumptions about what specific behaviors must mean can we uncover their meaning in another culture and discover the clash of cultural values and traditions. We are not being asked to agree with the perceptions of other cultures, only to understand them in their own terms. As we probe cultural differences, we learn that some beliefs and values are shared among cultures, but expressed differently. We also learn that some values are not shared. Seeing the clash allows us to move toward resolution of the specific conflict, although not of the larger cultural differences.

Phase 3: Learn how the other culture would address this situation.   The third phase is to seek an explanation of how each culture would expect someone to act in this situation. If the problem had occurred within one culture, how would it be handled? In this phase, we move from a description of general cultural values to their application to particular situations. We do not have to adopt a culture's way of responding to the situation, but knowing what it is enhances our understanding.

Phase 4: Create an acceptable solution.   The fourth phase of creative problem solving requires the most energy. The resolution may

---

Cultural awareness vs. stereotyping

Respecting cultural differences while avoiding stereotyping is the principal challenge of functioning appropriately and effectively in a multicultural environment. Stereotypes are preconceived notions that we embrace despite conflicting experience.[1] The stereotype can be negative (e.g., "Hispanics are lazy"), or it can be positive (e.g., "fat people are jolly"). As our population becomes increasingly diverse, many articles have been written and programs created to assist people in comprehending that diverse groups have diverse perspectives. The risk (and perhaps even the reality in some instances) is that old, largely negative stereotypes will be replaced with new ones that may be less negative, but that still oversimplify the cultural beliefs and values of the groups they are meant to describe.

We are all products of our environment, and it is neither practical nor realistic to ask us, in the spirit of cultural diversity, to encounter each new person without preconceived notions. Notions of what to expect from members of certain groups have been embedded in us subtly and subconsciously, if not deliberately. Cultural awareness is an effort to

1. Identify the preconceived notions we hold, regardless of their source
2. Learn *not* to respond and react to others on the basis of those preconceived notions
3. Develop a broader understanding of the values and traditions of people whose cultural backgrounds differ from ours
4. Use that general understanding of other cultural perspectives to inform—but not shape—the interaction with an individual or group

be obvious, once the conflict is clarified. In some disputes, the conflict does not involve core values but a misreading of the other's behavior; those conflicts can be resolved through increased understanding. When positions do stem from core values, difficult work is required to forge a collaborative solution to a common problem. In some cases the parties may adopt the resolution traditional in one culture; more often, the resolution will require flexibility from one or both parties in crafting a solution not typical in either culture.

Learning about other cultures. A second approach is to anticipate cultural conflicts by learning about other cultures. We cannot know enough about all cultures in our country or region to anticipate potential cultural sensitivities in all interactions. Yet we can learn something about the principal cultures with which we come

---

5. Be prepared to discard our expectations if the values and behaviors displayed by the person or persons in the interaction do not flow from the cultural norms of their cultural group *or*
6. Be prepared to respond to others in a way that shows respect for a cultural norm (e.g., showing deference to age, establishing a personal relationship in conjunction with a growing business relationship) if the values and behaviors displayed by the person or persons in the interaction do reflect a cultural norm.[2]

In dealing with cultural values, individual differences must also be recognized and respected. For example, Anglos are culturally described as rational and analytical,[3] and African-Americans are culturally described as expressive and emotional.[4] However, the individuals involved in a particular conflict may not manifest the characteristics of their cultural group. Raising awareness that conduct may be culturally influenced allows those involved to delve into culture as the *possible* basis of misunderstanding, but the misunderstanding may not have cultural roots. Conflict between people of different cultures does not automatically arise from cultural differences or from the fact that the individuals adhere to the values of their cultural group. Awareness of the cultural dimension and the conflict it may engender simply provides an additional avenue for conflict resolution.

1. Gordon W. Allport, *The Nature of Prejudice* (Reading, MA: Addison-Wesley, 1990), 191; Mark Snyder, "Self-Fulfilling Stereotypes," in Paula S. Rothenberg, *Race, Class, and Gender in the United States*, 2nd ed. (New York: St. Martin's Press, 1992), 325–31.

2. R. Roosevelt Thomas, Jr., *Beyond Race and Gender* (New York: American Management Association, 1991), 25.

3. Janet E. Helms, *A Race Is a Nice Thing To Have* (Topeka: Content Communications, 1992), 13.

4. Thomas Kochman, *Black and White Styles in Conflict* (Chicago: University of Chicago Press, 1981), 43–62.

into contact. We do not want to learn stereotypes: people are unique and do not all express their cultural values in the same way. Nevertheless, learning basic traditions and styles of interaction helps us recognize the cultural dimension.

The objective of this education is to understand the cultural roots of existing conflict or to gain sufficient awareness to anticipate or avoid potential conflict. While we are unlikely to become experts in the cultures of others, we will feel more at ease asking about their cultural traditions, and we may learn enough to develop a genuine feeling for other traditions. In future conflicts, the resolution process would begin on a firmer basis of trust and respect.

There are a variety of ways to gain greater knowledge and understanding. Knowledge about specific cultures can be acquired through training programs available from many professional trainers and consultants. Employee or community groups can also stage programs. Asking individuals in the organization or the community to lead the study of their traditions builds a foundation to facilitate improved communication and conflict resolution. Cultural education can also take place through general reading or in one-on-one discussions with people from different cultural backgrounds. Information about another culture sought with an open and nonjudgmental attitude fosters understanding and enriches the relationship between the participants.

Finally, we can learn about cultural traditions by extracting lessons from past encounters. Many cultural conflicts are settled and then forgotten, but if we discuss past conflicts with other individuals or in groups in which several cultures are represented, we can develop general concepts for use in future interactions. If a specific conflict arises we might say, "Do you remember the situation with . . . ? Do you think this is similar?"

Another aspect of the educational process is to understand our own cultural maxims. This gives us a framework for discussing issues with others and for understanding similarities and differences between our culture and those of others. Because we live in our own cultures, we often have difficulty identifying their compelling values.

Altering organizational practices and procedures. The third approach to cultural conflict resolution requires system change to eliminate inherent cultural bias. Cultural conflict may arise because the system reflects the traditions and values of one culture. Instead of addressing the conflict each time the situation occurs, we can alter procedures to take other cultural perspectives into account. For example, most of our organizational systems stem from an Anglo model that exalts precision, competitive performance, and arm's length transactions, but some cultures perceive relationship-building as integral to any interaction. Flexible procedures can be developed that would make all who participate more comfortable.

Conclusion

Conflict is not inherently bad; it depends on the outcome. If the result is alienation, gridlock, or violence, then conflict is harmful. But conflict can have advantageous consequences—increased awareness; creation of more options; identification of a better solution, product or decision; and stronger support for a decision as a result of increased participation.

Changing demographics are giving more visibility to the many cultural groups in our country. Rather than shed or conceal them and assimilate into the Anglo culture, many groups are now retaining their cultural beliefs and behaviors and demanding that they be respected by others. We must learn about each other's cultures, and we must be sensitive to conflicts growing out of clashes of cultural values. These conflicts can be resolved only if the cultural dimension is directly and openly addressed.

Notes

1. Larry A. Samovar, Richard E. Porter, and Nemi C. Jain, "Intercultural Communication Problems and Guidelines," in *Understanding Intercultural Communication* (Belmont, CA: Wadsworth Publishing, 1981).
2. Statistics in this paragraph are from "Beyond the Melting Pot," *Time*, 9 April 1990, 28–29.
3. R. Roosevelt Thomas, Jr., *Beyond Race and Gender* (New York: American Management Association, 1991), 7.
4. Edward T. Hall, *Beyond Culture* (New York: Doubleday, 1976), 85–103; Taylor Cox, Jr., *Cultural Diversity in Organizations* (San Francisco: Berrett-Koehler, 1993), 48–58.
5. Cox, 108, 142.
6. Marc Robert, *Managing Conflict from the Inside Out* (San Diego: University Associates, Inc., 1982), 59–60.

7. Deborah Tannen, *You Just Don't Understand* (New York: William Morrow, 1990), 32; Roger Fisher and William Ury, *Getting to Yes* (New York: Penguin Books, 1983), 30–33.
8. L. E. Sarbaugh, "Some Boundaries for Intercultural Communication," reprinted in John Stewart, ed., *Bridges Not Walls* (New York: McGraw-Hill, 1990), 390–393.
9. See Robert for a practical discussion of how conflict manifests itself and alternatives for dealing with it effectively.
10. These steps apply the tested model of collaborative decision making in communities to conflicts in which the diversity is based less on interests than on culture.
11. See generally Larry A. Samovar and Richard E. Porter, *Communication between Cultures* (Belmont, CA: Wadsworth Publishing, 1991).

References

Gray, Barbara. *Collaborating: Finding Common Ground for Multiparty Problems.* San Francisco: Jossey-Bass, 1989.
Gudykunst, William B. *Bridging Differ-ences: Effective Intergroup Communication.* Newbury Park, CA: Sage Publications, 1991.
Kochman, Thomas. *Black and White Styles in Conflict.* Chicago: University of Chicago Press, 1981.

Loden, Marilyn, and Judy B. Rosener. *Workforce America: Managing Employee Diversity as a Vital Resource* Homewood, IL: Business One Irwin, 1991.

Robert, Marc. *Managing Conflict from the Inside Out.* San Diego: University Associates, Inc., 1982.

Schaef, Anne Wilson. *Women's Reality: An Emerging Female System in a White Male Society.* New York: Harper and Row, 1981.

Stewart, Edward C. *American Cultural Patterns: A Cross-Cultural Perspective.* Yarmouth, ME: Intercultural Press, 1972.

Tannen, Deborah. *You Just Don't Understand: Women and Men in Conversation.* New York: William Morrow, 1990.

Cooperationist Institutions in Public Policymaking

Steven Kelman

The topic of this article is the choice of institutions for dealing with political conflict. In particular, I contrast institutional forms that I characterize as adversarial and (to use a neologism I will justify shortly) cooperationist. My approach is avowedly iconoclastic. There is considerable literature criticizing the use of adversary institutions in public-policy conflict resolution.[1] The literature typically criticizes adversary institutions for creating delays and for doing little to encourage the parties to feel responsibility for the results of the process.

I shall take a different tack, evaluating the impact of adversary and cooperationist institutions on the encouragement of "public spirit." By "public spirit" I mean not any substantive set of policy prescriptions, but rather a certain disposition among participants in the political process—the disposition to take serious account of the good of others and not just oneself when acting in public life. Roughly speaking, I regard public spirit as the opposite of self-interest.

By adversarial institutions, I mean those in which there is a division of labor between advocates and decisionmakers. The job of advocates is to present for a third party the strongest possible case for their own point of view. (The third party may be either an individual decisionmaker, as in the administrative process, or multiple decisionmakers, as with Congress or a jury.) Responsibility for actual political choice is then left to the third party. There is no expectation that the parties themselves need come to any agreement.

Adapted from Steven Kelman, "Adversary and Cooperationist Institutions for Conflict Resolution in Public Policymaking," *Journal of Policy Analysis and Management* 11, no. 2 (1992):178–206. ©1992, Association for Public Policy Analysis and Management; reprinted by permission of John Wiley & Sons, Inc.

Cooperationist institutions, in contrast, bring together advocates and government officials in small face-to-face groups to work out conflicts among themselves. In areas of stable, ongoing conflict, such as tax policy or pollution policy, these groups would continue to meet over time and over particular issues. I use the expression "cooperationist" rather than "cooperative" because I want to make clear that participants in the institutions I have in mind will normally be expected to have different initial views on the issues at hand, just as do participants in adversarial institutions. The word "cooperative" suggests more harmony, more initial sweetness-and-light, than characterizes participants in the political process, and therefore I am not using it.

What I am calling "cooperationist" institutions have two features that distinguish them from adversarial ones. One feature involves the procedures for discussion and decision. In adversary institutions, participants talk to a third party. In cooperationist institutions, they talk to each other. In adversary institutions, the third party makes the decisions. In cooperationist institutions, since there is no third party, any decision must come from the participants themselves. A second feature of cooperationist institutions involves the norms for what decision rule the group should apply in making choices. The norm (which, I will argue, partly grows out of dynamics of the group process itself) is that an effort be made to reach a final decision that is acceptable to most or all the participants. This norm distinguishes cooperationist institutions not only from adversarial ones, but additionally from such forms of collective decisionmaking as majority rule (where wide agreement is not necessary), and from formal negotiation (where there is a unanimity requirement and each participant in effect has a veto power over decisions).

The imprecise nature of the norm ("an effort be made," "most or all the participants") is reinforced by the special role of participants in cooperationist groups who are government officials. Political choices with the force of law should be made only by such officials. When officials with the formal authority to make decisions serve as leaders of cooperationist groups that also have nongovernmental members, the norm would be that these officials would be inclined, although not obligated, to endorse decisions with widespread support in the group. If the group cannot come to anything approaching agreement, the government officials may nonetheless proceed to make decisions on their own.

Public spirit and good public policy

I wish to criticize adversary institutions against the standard of their effect on development of public spirit for two reasons. First,

public-spirited participants in the political process are more likely
to produce good public policy than are participants motivated solely
by self-interest. Second, public spirit gives us practice behaving
ethically that we can then apply to behavior in our everyday lives,
allowing government to serve, to use a phrase that goes back to
John Stuart Mill, as a "school" for molding character.[2]

Public spirit and institutional choice

If public spirit is important to achieving good public policy and to
allowing the political system to function as a school for molding
character, then a new challenge for institutional design appears: the
challenge of designing institutions to nurture the presence and to
foster the development of public spirit.

At the base of both public spirit in public life and the disposition
to behave ethically in everyday life is valuing and respecting other
people. When we value and respect others, we take their concerns
into account in deciding how to act, whether in public or everyday
life. This connection proceeds through the logical implications of
what it means to say that one values something: If we value something, we must wish that it will survive and flourish. The central
contention of this article is that cooperationist institutions promote
public spirit by encouraging participants to value and respect others. The institutions change people from how they otherwise would
have been.

Cooperationist institutions do this in two ways. The first way
is simply by setting up ongoing groups and getting the people in
the groups to talk with each other. Crucial to this is that the people
come into the groups from across ideological, regional, or ethnic
boundaries—and are people who might otherwise have little feel
for the humanity of those on the other side of the boundary. One
of the hoariest findings of social psychology research is that institutions that get people sitting down together, especially on an ongoing basis, tend to encourage people to like each other, to derive
emotional satisfactions and rewards from each other. The realization that others are important for giving us satisfaction and rewards slides naturally into the realization that others are important
tout court, since it would hardly make sense for us to derive satisfaction from the fellowship or approval of beings who themselves
were valueless. As the social psychologists David Johnson and
Frank Johnson write:

> There is considerable evidence that cooperative experiences, com-
> pared with competitive ... ones, result in more positive relationships
> among members, relationships characterized by ... mutual concern, friend-
> liness, attentiveness, feelings of obligation to each other, and a desire to
> win each other's support.[3]

The ties with others and realization of the importance of others that cooperationist institutions encourage thus promote development of a concern for others that is at the base of public spirit. The greatest challenge for the development of public spirit in a society is to get people to feel sympathy and understanding for people different from themselves. Cooperationist institutions help with that challenge.

The second way that cooperationist institutions promote public spirit by encouraging participants in those institutions to value and respect others is through the norm that people seek as far as possible to come to agreement. Cooperatively to compromise differences can itself be a statement of respect for others, in this case the opinions of others, and of taking others seriously.[4]

Pressures toward cooperation and agreement grow out of the dynamics of small-group interactions themselves; an operational sign of growth of bonds in a group is development of dispositions toward cooperation and agreement within the group that reflect those bonds. A norm encouraging agreement promotes that further. And successful cooperative experiences promote psychological ties to others in their wake.[5]

In contrast, adversary institutions fail to create any relationship among the parties to a policy disagreement. Participants in adversary institutions are not in any real sense part of a group. They remain separate individuals, physically proximate only in order to argue in front of a third party. They do not talk with each other.

More than that, adversary institutions create a contest in which people compete against each other for the visible prize of a favorable decision by the contest judge. Not surprisingly, such a competitive system creates emotions.

There are several things to be said on behalf of such emotions. For one thing, they are probably natural in the human species, so it is probably hopeless to try to eliminate them. For another, it is undeniable that the urge to be first and best can be a powerful source of individual self-worth and dignity, as well as a potent generator of achievement and accomplishment that benefits society as a whole. We would probably not wish to banish the competitive urge from the human race even if it were feasible to do so.

Nonetheless, competition should not be all there is to life. Competitiveness separates us from other people rather than linking us to them. Competition sets up a situation in which we are dependent for our satisfactions only on our own efforts—and sometimes even on our efforts at the expense of others. It can also encourage us to denigrate others in our minds, rather than valuing them. Like cooperationist institutions, then, adversary institutions also change people, but in the opposite direction, reducing rather than increasing their bonds with others.

The meager empirical evidence that exists on the impact of using mediation to deal with conflicts, mostly involving small claims or other legal disputes, suggests that the cooperationist setting of mediation (where the parties are encouraged to sit down together and work out a mutually satisfactory solution to their dispute) produces a greater appreciation for the human worth of the person with whom one is in dispute than does an adversary trial setting.

A word is also in order about the effect of cooperationist institutions on the willingness of participants to engage in a deliberative mode of collective decisionmaking—to be willing to listen to each other and to change their minds when appropriate. Adversary institutions undercut the inclination to listen to others and to be willing to change one's opinion, since one is supposed to plant one's flag and defend one's initial position to the end. In contrast, cooperationist institutions promote a good environment for listening. For one thing, they get people talking with each other rather than talking to a third-party decisionmaker, which would seem to be a prerequisite for (although no guarantee of) listening. The norm about reaching agreement also makes it more imperative to listen to others so as to make it easier to reach agreement. And public-spirited participants in a group discussion are more likely to be open to change than even a public-spirited judge listening to arguments from adversarial advocates; experiments on opinion-change show that "passive exposure to arguments outside an interactive discussion context generally produces less [opinion] shift than actual participation in discussion."[6] Finally, cooperative rather than competitive settings also promote learning from others. Morton Deutsch's classic experiments showed that students who were graded competitively on the basis of their individual performance in class discussion were less attentive to each other and less influenced by the ideas of others than were those who were graded on the quality of discussion in the group as a whole.[7]

Moving toward cooperationist institutions

What specific changes in the structure of American political institutions are suggested? The basic change is to promote the development of forums in both the legislative and administrative processes where representatives of different points of view can meet together in face-to-face discussions with each other on an ongoing basis.

There can, of course, be no assurance that cooperationist institutions will promote public spirit. Certainly there are many situations, in the context of private negotiations and even public ones, where simply getting people to sit down together to try to work out their disagreements would seem to produce little more than bargaining among self-interested people with more or less fixed views. The more the structure of the group resembles the cooperationist mode as I have described it, the greater the chances for the promotion of the understanding and respect for others that lie at the base of public spirit. In particular, I believe that the presence of government representatives in such groups, even if the groups consist in significant measure of representatives of private organizations, is helpful in encouraging public-spirited norms.

My conclusion, then, is that we ought to give serious consideration to greater use of cooperationist institutional mechanisms in the policymaking process. Presumably, the principal contribution that scholars can make toward increasing the likelihood of experiments with cooperationist institutions occurs in the realm of ideas and the influence of ideas over the course of public decisionmaking. Worries about being labeled "touchy-feely" inhibit us, I think, from thinking about ways that institutional design can encourage our inclination to show concern for others. If this is so, we pay a heavy price for the tyranny of tough-mindedness.

1. Robert Kagan, "Adversarial Legalism and American Government," *Journal of Policy Analysis and Management* 10, no. 3 (1991).
2. John Stuart Mill, "Consideration on Representative Government," in *The Philosophy of John Stuart Mill* (New York: Modern Library, 1961), 420.
3. David W. Johnson and Frank P. Johnson, *Joining Together: Group Theory and Group Skills*, 2d ed. (Englewood Cliffs, NJ: Prentice-Hall, 1982), 163.
4. George Sher, "Subsidized Abortions: Moral Rights and Moral Compromise," *Philosophy and Public Affairs* 10 (Fall 1981):361–372; J. Patrick Dobel, *Compromise and Political Action* (Savage, MD: Rowman and Littlefield, 1990).
5. See Robert Axelrod, *The Evolution of Cooperation* (New York: Basic Books, 1984).
6. David G. Myers, "Polarizing Effects of Social Interaction," in Hermann Brandstatter et al., eds., *Group Decision Making* (New York: Academic Press, 1982), 142.
7. Morton Deutsch, *The Resolution of Conflict* (New Haven: Yale University Press, 1973), 25–27.

Communities Working Collaboratively for a Change

Arthur Turovh Himmelman

Transforming power relations

The purpose of this article is to help transform power relations within and among large public, private, and nonprofit institutions and between such institutions and community and neighborhood-based organizations. This transformation would be based on the realization that, as a nation of growing class, race, and gender divisions, we can no longer ethically condone—nor economically afford—a society in which the values and practices of our public, private, and nonprofit sectors often sustain and even promote such divisions.

The vision of and processes for societal change called for in this article are embodied in a concept called "collaborative empowerment." Just as strategic planning promotes systematic organizational development, collaborative empowerment promotes systematic societal change. It is a planning and organizing method through which community and neighborhood-based organizations can design, implement, and assess problem-solving strategies that increase their self-determination. Collaborative empowerment advocates that those most affected by a collaborative change effort should be full partners in decisions made about it. When all those in a collaborative have substantial ownership, there is a far greater likelihood that its primary purposes will be achieved and sustained.

Multisector collaboration defined

When public, private, and nonprofit organizations collaborate, it is often referred to simply as a "public/private partnership." Unfor-

Copyright 1992, Arthur Turovh Himmelman, The Himmelman Consulting Group, 1406 West Lake, Suite 209, Minneapolis, MN 55408; (612) 824-5507. Adapted and reprinted by permission of the author.

tunately, the nonprofit sector is less likely to be considered as a full partner in collaboration when it is viewed as only a part of the private. When, in fact, all three sectors collaborate, the phrase "multisector collaboration" is a better description. Multisector collaboration is defined as:

> A voluntary, strategic alliance of public, private, and nonprofit organizations to enhance each other's capacity to achieve a common purpose by sharing risks, responsibilities, resources, and rewards.

Sharing risks, responsibilities, resources, and rewards is very central to effective collaboration. Although it is not uncommon to find organizations waiting for others to take risks, and to join with them only if the risk has passed, this kind of behavior is not appropriate for collaboration. Partners stand with, work with, and support each other—especially when risks must be taken. Similarly, collaborative partners share responsibilities for tasks, large and small, that must be accomplished. It is not collaborative to leave the large majority of such responsibilities to relatively few organizational representatives. Shared responsibility is a fundamental principle of collaboration and should be consistently held up as an important value and practice. As for the sharing of resources, it is important to acknowledge that each partner can and should make contributions to the collaborative. This means that resources are best defined very broadly. For example, credibility with and access to neighborhood residents ought to be as important as—if not more important than—financial contributions. People who can provide a narrative history of a community issue from their personal experience should be viewed as making the same quality of contribution as others who may have highly technical research skills to focus on the same issue. And, finally, sharing rewards must be regarded as another key element in successful collaboration. This means that no single organization can take credit for accomplishments because publicity about the collaborative's work acknowledges all partners. Sharing rewards can also mean simply enjoying each other's company or celebrating the achievement of particular goals. Shared celebrations can have very positive benefits for all partners and can make the longer-term viability of the collaborative much stronger.

It is important to emphasize that this definition of multisector collaboration assumes that the organizations involved will make a "good faith" effort to address fundamental issues of concern in a constructive manner. Even with such commitments, however, most collaboratives face numerous and substantial challenges as they attempt to address and resolve differences in viewpoints, power, and trust among their members. Of particular importance is the way that people view and treat each other. If those participating in a collaborative "walk the talk" of enhancing each other's capacity, they will make every effort to share their concerns in ways that allow others to respond without defensiveness. It also means that key decisions about the collaborative would not be made between meetings in private sessions among a few members, nor would people simply withdraw or disappear from the collaborative without providing others with information about the reasons for their departure.

Understanding and practicing multisector collaboration

The approach to multisector collaboration outlined here is, admittedly, very ambitious. It attempts to promote multisector collaboration, particularly in its collaborative empowerment design, as a very broad and comprehensive social change strategy that spans the continuum from social service to social justice. The summary provided below only touches upon the basic elements of this emerging theory and practice of social change collaboration.

Seven elements of multisector collaboration require attention if it is to reach its social change potential. These elements have been identified from extensive participant observer research by the author as well as from theoretical and conceptual insights from this research. They are:

1. Acknowledging the role of adult development, and disparities in maturity levels among individual participants, in fostering or hindering effective collaboration
2. Understanding and responding to cultural differences in values and methods of communication, and the tension between exclusivity and inclusivity
3. Providing opportunities for effective small group interaction, conflict resolution, and group problem-solving
4. Understanding, designing, and facilitating processes in which multiple organizations can communicate and effectively work together
5. Encouraging perspectives and contributions from public, private, and nonprofit organizations, and fostering the most appropriate roles and responsibilities for each organization and sector on particular issues
6. Discussing, assessing, and acting upon common viewpoints about the larger political, economic, social, and cultural context in which multisector collaboration takes place
7. Emphasizing the contributions multisector collaboration can make in encouraging democratic practices within and among organizations and in changing values in the larger society.

The next section of this article describes two processes of multisector collaboration, "collaborative betterment" and "collaborative empowerment," and briefly comments on the transition from betterment to empowerment. It is useful to keep in mind the seven elements of multisector collaboration noted above and to consider how they might be related to collaborative betterment and collaborative empowerment processes.

Multisector collaboration: Betterment and empowerment

As the success of many community-based initiatives suggests, the ownership of any social change process is among the most, if not *the* most, important of its characteristics. There are few more fundamental indicators of whether community initiatives will have long-

---

Collaboration compared with other change strategies

It is important to consider a variety of options for working with others since there is increasing pressure on organizations to find common purposes as financial resources for community needs become more scarce in relationship to such needs. Although both public and private funding sources are emphasizing collaboration, organizations that are not ready for or interested in collaboration should consider other options. The options below are among those used by organizations with common interests.

- *Networking* is defined as exchanging information for mutual benefit. It is the most informal of the inter-organizational linkages and, as a result, can be used most easily. It often reflects an initial level of trust and commitment among organizations and is a very reasonable choice for such circumstances.
- *Coordination* is defined as exchanging information and altering activities for mutual benefit and to achieve a common purpose. Coordination requires more organizational involvement than networking and, given the degree to which both internal and inter-organizational "systems" are poorly coordinated, it is a very important strategy for change. This is particularly true from the point of view of those who find uncoordinated systems very unfriendly yet also regard them as essential for the maintenance of their daily life or longer-term well being. Coordination is most useful when all parties affected by proposed changes share in decisions about their intended consequences as well as in considerations of unintended consequences.
- *Cooperation* is defined as exchanging information, altering activities, and sharing resources for mutual benefit and to achieve a common purpose. Cooperation requires even greater organizational commitments and, in some cases, may involve legal arrangements. Shared resources can encompass a wide variety of

---

lasting benefits. Ownership is also a reflection of a community's capacity for self-determination and can be enhanced or limited depending upon how collaboration is designed and implemented. Two basic ways of designing and implementing multisector collaboration are collaborative betterment and collaborative empowerment. Each has particular effects on community ownership, self-determination, and the long-term sustainability of the collaborative's efforts.

Collaborative betterment begins outside the community within public, private, or nonprofit institutions and is brought into the community. Community involvement is invited into a process designed and controlled by larger institutions. This collaborative strategy can produce policy changes and improvements in program

---

human, financial, and technical contributions, including knowledge, staffing, physical property, access to people, and money.
- *Collaboration* is defined as exchanging information, altering activities, sharing resources, and enhancing the capacity of another for mutual benefit and to achieve a common purpose. Enhancing the capacity of another organization requires sharing risks, resources, responsibilities, and rewards, all of which can increase the potential of collaboration beyond other ways of working together. Because we live in an individualistic and competitive society, collaboration also may challenge both organizational and personal values, beliefs, and assumptions. Those engaging in collaborative relationships view others as partners, not competitors, and seek to enhance their partners' capacity to achieve their own definition of excellence to help accomplish a common purpose.

Collaboration is best used only when other interorganizational strategies cannot achieve mutual goals. Even though collaboration offers the greatest potential benefits, it often challenges traditional values, its processes are complex, and the time it requires can be considerable. Therefore, collaborative processes should be chosen after conducting careful, strategic assessments of their viability and appropriateness for addressing specific issues or circumstances.

It is also important to recognize that, in some cases, confrontation can be useful in a community change process. Confrontation strategies can lead to strong working relationships between neighborhood and community groups and larger institutions once confrontational methods gain the attention of those in power. Some initial confrontations, such as those around the implementation of the Community Reinvestment Act, eventually have led to cooperative or collaborative relationships between large institutions, like banks, and community-based organizations. Those interested in the appropriateness and effectiveness of confrontational methods in community change can find excellent resources to assist them.

delivery and services, but tends not to produce long-term ownership in communities or to significantly increase communities' control
over their own destinies.

Collaborative empowerment begins within the community and
is brought to public, private, or nonprofit institutions. In this context, *empowerment* refers to the capacity to set priorities and control resources that are essential for increasing community self-
determination. An empowerment strategy includes two basic
activities: (1) organizing a community in support of a collaborative
purpose determined by the community, and (2) facilitating a process
for integrating outside institutions in support of this community
purpose. The empowerment approach can produce policy changes
and improvements in program delivery and services. It is also more
likely to produce long-term ownership of the collaborative's purpose, processes, and products in communities and to enhance communities' capacity for self-determination.

In practice, betterment and empowerment processes exist
along a continuum on which they can be seen as approaching or
moving away from the characteristics ascribed to them in this article. Therefore, the models should be used as guides to, and pre-
dictors of, the consequences of particular methods of multisector
collaboration and not as mutually exclusive descriptions. Indeed,
change strategies often should be based on transforming collaborative betterment into collaborative empowerment processes.

Collaborative betterment: Key principles. Most multisector
collaboratives can be classified as betterment processes. In this
way, their processes are similar to those used by large institutions
to deliver most human and educational services and community programs. The collaborative betterment model includes a number of
key principles.

- Large and influential institutions initiate problem identification
  and analysis, primarily within institutional frameworks, assumptions, and value systems.
- Governance and administration are controlled by institutions,
  although limited community representation is encouraged in
  advisory roles. Frequently, groups within the collaborative are
  intentionally separated to give decision-making roles to those
  considered to be in the community's "leadership" and implementation roles to those providing or receiving services.
- Staff are responsible to institutions, and although they seek
  advice from target communities, staff are not directly accountable to them.
- Action plans are usually designed with some direct community

involvement but normally emphasize the ideas of institutionally related professionals and experts.

- Implementation processes include more community representation and require significant community acceptance, but control of decision-making and resource allocation is not transferred to the community during the implementation phase.
- Although advice from the community is considered, the decision to terminate the collaborative is made by the institutions that initiated it.

Collaborative betterment: Key activities. The collaborative betterment model can be illustrated by describing seven of its basic activities. Please keep in mind that the following observations are very brief summaries of highly complex processes and relationships that merit greater attention and discussion.

Activity 1: Initiating institutional discussions. Large or influential agencies or institutions in the public, private, or nonprofit sector initiate discussions, primarily among themselves, to consider problems, concerns, or issues in their community. A strong leader from one of the large institutions often emerges early to give "credibility" to the initiative. Betterment initiatives are usually led by people associated with large corporations or major nonprofits, although in many cases public officials play the same role or jointly share it.

Activity 2: Mutual problem assessment and shared mission. Based on a mutual assessment of the problems, and agreement on sharing responsibility for addressing these problems, these institutions proceed to form a collaborative to address a community problem or problems. Usually, a generally acceptable mission or purpose for the collaborative is also determined at this time. Initial funding for the collaborative is either secured or identified at this point as well.

Activity 3: Planning, governance, and administration. The collaborative begins a planning process to gather necessary data and information about the community problem or issue and to establish a governing and administrative structure. The governance and administration of the collaborative is usually based within one of the large or influential institutions. Although major decision-making is shared by participants, a "lead agency" normally makes key decisions.

Activity 4: Including community representation. Representatives from the community or populations being targeted (either as individuals or as organizational representatives) are invited to join the collaborative. These representatives are always a minority in the collaborative and never have decision-making control. However, the advice of community representatives is sought by the collaborative as it formulates its goals and work plans, and community opinions are often reflected in the decisions made.

Activity 5: Seeking agreements on action plans.   After resolving significant barriers to participation by its members, the collaborative reaches agreement on contributions from its public, private, and nonprofit sector organizations. The collaborative begins to implement its goals through specific action plans. Usually, further representation from the target community or population is sought at this time, and assistance from other large and influential institutions is secured in the implementation of the collaborative's action plans.

Activity 6: Implementing action plans in community settings.   The collaborative implements its action plans in the target community to the degree that the community is prepared to accept them. Collaborative representatives from the target community are asked to play a significant role in implementing the plans. Normally, staff required to implement action plans are drawn from professional fields associated with the large and influential organizations controlling the collaborative. Occasionally, paraprofessionals and community residents are also included as staff.

Activity 7: Concluding the collaborative's work.   Once the action plans have been implemented to the satisfaction of the collaborative's leadership, the work of the collaborative is terminated. The target community has little, if any, control over the continuation or discontinuation of the collaborative's activities except through active confrontation. In addition, the targeted community has limited capacity to continue the work of the collaborative because it has not gained control over decision-making or resource allocation processes used by the collaborative.

Collaborative empowerment.   In this article, it is important to distinguish the collaborative empowerment model, which requires a formally organized collaborative process, from less formalized community-based collaborative approaches. In general, most community-based organizations that engage in multisector collaboration use an informally structured process. The arrangements that community-based organizations make with partners from the public, private, and nonprofit sectors tend to be created only as the process goes along. It is relatively rare for community-based organizations to design a comprehensive process in which their relationships with outside organizations evolve according to an overall collaborative strategy.

In suggesting that community-based organizations might benefit from more strategic and explicitly designed approaches to multisector collaboration, it is also recognized that many informal collaboratives have worked very well. Such collaboratives have been successful at providing employment, economic development, health care, affordable housing, and other human services. The primary purpose in offering the following collaborative empowerment model for consideration is to help communities become even more effective at collaboration, which helps ensure their empowerment as a central part of the collaborative process.

Although used far less often in community problem-solving than the betterment strategy, multisector collaboration based on the empowerment approach appears to be gaining acceptance. This growing acceptance is based, to a large extent, on three factors: (1) Increasing evidence that community-based organizations are taking the initiative in collaborative efforts and can produce outstanding results when involved in shaping a collaborative's agenda; (2) competing and increasing demands on the time and resources of larger public, private, and nonprofit institutions that make it more difficult for them to design, initiate, and implement multisector collaborative betterment processes; and (3) a growing recognition that community efforts that achieve the best results are those which community residents feel are theirs to shape.

Collaborative empowerment: Key principles

- The process is initiated in a community setting and is assisted by community organizing; early discussions focus on assumptions and values.
- Community problem identification includes both data-based trend analysis and narrative examples from community residents. The latter is given equal credibility in considering options for setting priorities.
- Community priorities are reflected by the purpose of the collaborative. Community-based organizations select representatives who negotiate a collaborative with strategically identified public, private, and nonprofit organizations outside the community.
- Negotiations with outside agencies and institutions produce agreements to proceed on a collaborative basis under the purpose established by the community, and within a governance and administrative process in which power is equally shared by the community and outside organizations.
- The governance and administrative structure includes a policy

board, an executive committee, action groups for implementing plans, and staff agreeable to the community to assist the collaborative.

- Substantial attention is given to the balancing of administration/management goals and community participation goals.
- Goals are implemented through action plans fully supported by community residents as well as by representatives from the public, private, and nonprofit institutions from outside the community.
- Commitments to assessment and evaluation in public settings

---

Collaborative empowerment in practice

The practice of collaborative empowerment varies greatly. An excellent illustration of less structured collaborative empowerment processes is the Passport Awarded for Staying in School Plan (PASS Plan) in Passaic and Paterson, New Jersey. Passaic and Paterson are low to moderate income, racially diverse communities, and both have community-based organizations engaged in social change efforts. In the fall of 1986, The Paterson Interfaith Communities Organization (PICO) and the United Passaic Organization (UPO) began working on ways to combat drugs and increase educational and employment possibilities for young people. This work was encouraged by a five-year grant commitment by the Charles Steward Mott Foundation which, in turn, provided funds for regranting through The Community Foundation of New Jersey. In addition to grant funds, The Community Foundation of New Jersey provided technical assistance to the community groups.

PICO and UPO designed their educational program called the PASS Plan after a series of meetings with local banks and corporations and the Paterson and Passaic school systems. A bold, new educational initiative was needed because large numbers of African-American and Hispanic youth in these two cities were not finishing high school. As a result, at a time when New Jersey was creating many new jobs, far too few low-income students or students of color were able to join the labor force. Community residents, taking advantage of the provisions of the Community Reinvestment Act, met with and persuaded key banking leaders to join the community's PASS Plan. The community groups, with the help of the bankers, also secured the involvement of school officials. The PASS Plan includes four key components:

1. Students enter the program during their junior year in high school. They are required to maintain a C or better grade point average, have no more than five unexcused school absences, pass their high school proficiency test exam, and attend all PASS Plan Club meetings with their sponsors/mentors. In return, upon

provide community-based organizations with opportunities for monitoring the progress of the collaborative.

- Community control of resources needed to continue efforts beyond the termination of the collaborative is essential.

Collaborative empowerment: Key activities. Even though the description of the 16 activities that follows is prescriptive, please do not view the collaborative empowerment model as a blueprint that must be followed in every detail. It is best viewed as a plan-

---

graduation, a participating business guarantees students a job with advancement potential.

2. Community representatives or sponsors/mentors are required to attend four days of leadership training (three away in a hotel and another follow-up training day), actively participate in student recruitment, attend and lead group meetings with their students every six weeks, and have at least one personal contact with students every two weeks.

3. Business members are required to support the PASS Plan financially, participate actively as members on the Steering Committee and in the recruitment of students, and make available entry-level jobs with advancement potential to all PASS Plan graduates.

4. Boards of Education/local high schools are required to assist with student recruitment and make assembly time and class time available to adult PASS Plan representatives; maintain student records and make them available to PASS Plan administrators (with parental consent); and participate actively as members of the PASS Plan Steering Committee.

It is important to reiterate that a collaborative empowerment vision includes community-based organizations shaping and facilitating a community change process with larger public and private institutions that normally would dominate community interests. PICO and UPO's vision includes their organizations leading an effort to free young people from drug abuse, gain the confidence and motivation to complete high school, and find employment with a future and/or further educational opportunities upon graduation.

UPO and PICO's vision grew from discussions about the values community people share, their concerns about the problems facing young people in their community, and from forcefully engaging local banks and schools in their discussions and actions. This vision became a community-wide reality that provided hundreds of young people with new opportunities for success and that is broadly shared by students, teachers and other school officials, parents, community activists, business people, and governmental officials throughout Passaic and Paterson.

ning framework open to modifications and improvements appropriate to particular community circumstances and settings.

Activity 1: Discussing assumptions, beliefs, and values.   It is important to begin an empowerment process by being respectful of people and by taking them seriously. One way to do so is by asking community residents and advocates to discuss the assumptions, beliefs, and values that motivate them. Often such discussions easily focus on the idea or importance of community. They also can help prepare people for sharing ideas about community issues and the need and opportunities for community change. Such dialogues also build bonds of trust that are essential for creating the common visions that sustain longer-term and collaborative community change initiatives.

Activity 2: Assessing trends.   In every community there are signs of change that can also be called trends. When discussions suggest that community members share common values about community, and about the need for community change, it is a good time to discuss the trends that affect the community. These trends can be based on stories and narrative examples as well as on empirical data. This activity in the collaborative empowerment process begins to move community members toward a more focused basis for action.

Activity 3: Linking priority issues or problems with opportunities.   The trends that are identified within communities will also reveal issues and problems. In order for a community to take effective action, however, it helps to decide on the specific problems that merit priority attention. Problems identified as priorities for action are best addressed when associated with opportunities and possibilities for change. This also helps provide energy for community change. There may be a need to practice the linkage of problems to opportunities because people often present problems in ways that provide little or no possibility for group problem-solving. If a collaborative effort is to succeed, it must consistently make use of group problem-solving. The development and ongoing practice of this linkage, and of a trust in the group to help solve problems, are vital aspects of collaboration.

Activity 4: Clarifying the community's purpose and vision for collaboration.   Once specific priorities for action are established, community residents can translate them into a mission statement which clearly explains the purpose for forming a community-based collaborative. For example, community residents may decide that increasing and improving health care for young children from low-income families is their top priority. A mission statement calling for action on this priority could be:

To advocate for and implement policies and programs that effectively respond to the comprehensive health care needs of low-income children from infancy to six years old.

The development of a collaborative's mission statement is very important and is a primary way for those participating in its early development to increase their sense of ownership for it. As the collaborative develops, the mission statement may be modified to better reflect a broader consensus about the collaborative's purposes. The mission of a collaborative is also reflective of the vision for collaboration. The vision is an imagined better future that provides strength and energy to the community change process.

Activity 5: Examining what others have done. At this stage in the collaborative's development, it is useful to gather information on how other communities or neighborhoods have designed and organized their collaborative change initiatives on similar topics. If possible, it is always a good idea to actually visit other collaboratives that exist in the community; but if this is not possible, contact should be made by telephone to learn from their activities. The wider the search for what others have done and are doing about comparable concerns, or with similar topics, or through similar collaborative strategies, the better the chances that the collaborative will succeed. Whenever possible, an examination of collaboratives on a national or international level also should be undertaken because there is a growing richness in the diversity of collaborative experimentation.

Activity 6: Organizing a community power-base. The collaborative's mission statement is next shared with as many community members as possible to gain broad support for action. This support becomes formalized when community residents ask community-based organizations to help negotiate the participation of public, private, and nonprofit organizations from outside the community in the collaborative. It is assumed that many community residents will be members of the community-based organizations representing community interests. The relationships of community residents and community-based organizations should reflect shared community visions and a sincere willingness to share the responsibilities of community representation.

Activity 7: Strategically identifying partners. The community organizing committee makes a strategic assessment of which public, private, and nonprofit organizations should be invited to form a

Collaborative roles for local government

The following are among the most common collaborative roles of local government. They are not mutually exclusive; one role often leads to or is integrated into another.

Convener.   Like foundations, large nonprofits, and some corporations, local governments play the role of community conveners on significant issues that may, or may not, result in further community action. The convening role usually includes a highly visible public discussion of community issues. These discussions are often related to data gathering or studies which provide information intended to highlight a common understanding of the issues at hand. Such discussions are important prerequisites for collaborative community problem-solving.

Catalyst.   Local governments may use the convening role to stimulate discussion but may have a longer-term strategy in mind. When local government is catalytic it means that it makes an early and clear commitment to participate in longer-term community problem-solving that begins with an initial discussions of issues. In this way, it uses its considerable influence and resource base to make the collaborative initiative "real" in the minds of various other potential partners who may be waiting for leadership before making their own commitments to an action agenda.

Conduit.   Local governments may serve as conduits for the funding that is essential for collaborative action. For example, many federal grants require a local government to be the "lead agency" in providing grants for local collaborative initiatives. A similar situation occurs when foundations make grants with the condition that a local governmental agency be a lead partner. This stipulation can be very problematic, however, if the local government's conduit role appears to be, or is in fact, a way for it to dominate a collaborative process because of its fiscal role. This can result in conflicts related to power and trust.

Funder.   Local governments may wish to encourage a variety of collaborative activities by funding such activities, either alone or with other funding sources. This is an increasingly common practice but, again, one with complexities. Many recipients of such funding find that funders—local government included—fail to understand that a collaborative is more than a proposal to which many organizations attach letters of endorsement. What must be made clear is that it takes time for organizations to create a well-designed, mutually respectful and trusting collaborative; unfortunately, funders often are not aware of this and, as a result, fail to provide such time.

Technical assistance provider.   Local governments have substantial human and technical resources available to them which can be made available to community-based organizations to assist them in creating and sustaining collaborative efforts. These resources include, among others, data retrieval, new research and information gathering, planning expertise, meeting space, legal opinions, other specific expertise on a wide variety of subjects, access to information and assistance in preparing funding applications, and lobbying assistance. Local government does not have to be a highly visible or formal partner in collaborative efforts to provide many kinds of technical assistance.

Capacity builder. Capacity building is usually part of longer-term local governmental strategy to increase the ability of community- and neighborhood-based organizations to initiate and effectively follow through on problem-solving processes that, to a large extent, community and neighborhood-based organizations can determine. Capacity building would be a primary goal of a local government that chose to encourage empowerment, rather than betterment, strategies.

Capacity building can take many forms but usually includes: (1) acknowledging the important contributions of others; (2) inquiring about and, whenever possible, providing specific requested skill-development opportunities for those interested; (3) being honest and open about motivations and being realistic about what can and cannot be provided in what amount of time; (4) facilitating user-friendly access to resources that normally may be restricted to those with power, status, or money; and (5) sharing risks when others may find themselves in situations that they perceive to be dangerous or threatening to their well-being.

In a collaborative empowerment strategy, local government is not afraid of increasing the power of communities and neighborhoods in relationship to the power that historically was more heavily based in city hall and "downtown" power structures. To the contrary: this strategy proclaims that the primary task of government is to increase power-sharing and community ownership rather than to retain power as a method of control.

Partner. This would appear to be the most obvious role for local government in a collaborative, but, as has been noted, the way that this role is played greatly affects the quality of the collaborative process and the likely outcomes of its activities. If local government plays its partner role as part of a betterment strategy, it may find that it has made progress on key community issues. However, given the limitations of a betterment process in relationship to fully sharing the ownership of the collaborative's activities and outcomes, it may well find its partner role leading to relatively short-term successes. Sustaining the betterment effort may be very difficult, while there is also the real possibility that a collaborative with relatively little power-sharing will elicit strong explicit opposition or meet apathetic responses.

Facilitator. In this role, local government attempts to help make possible collaborative, community problem-solving efforts among nonprofit, business, labor, religious, academic, and other organizations. This can be difficult when local government itself is also a key partner, because the facilitator role may be perceived as another way of adding greater decision-making authority to local government's role. When it works well, however, local government is valued as a source of fairness, encouragement, and as a resource to those who need it in the collaborative process.

collaborative under the community's mission statement. It is important that the community identifies the outside organizations that can best respond to the diversity of the community residents who may be directly affected by the collaborative's primary concern. Once this list is completed, the community organizing committee holds individual meetings with representatives of each of the identified public, private, and nonprofit organizations. These meetings determine which outside organizations will participate in a collaborative addressing the community's mission statement.

Activity 8: Convening and formalizing the collaborative.   Once the viability of a community-based, multisector collaborative is established, the community committee convenes a meeting with all partners to formalize an agreement to work collaboratively on the community's mission statement. At this meeting, all partners are given ample time to comfortably introduce themselves, discuss their motivations for joining the collaborative, share their initial concerns and expectations, and comment on other issues.

To emphasize the empowerment thrust of the collaborative, the representatives of community-based organizations reiterate that they will not negotiate the mission of the collaborative. However, the community representatives express a strong and sincere willingness to share risks, responsibilities, resources, and rewards for all other aspects of the collaborative, including governance, administration, setting goals, determining action plans, and assessing outcomes.

Activity 9: Establishing governance and administration.   After a sufficient number of meetings to eliminate any barriers to a partner's participation, community-based organizations offer a governance and administration plan that includes: (1) a Policy Board; (2) an Executive Committee; and (3) Action Groups. The plan recommends that each person serving on the Policy Board and Executive Committee be an official representative of an organization and have decision-making authority for his or her organization in the collaborative.

The Policy Board meets quarterly to provide overall guidance on the long-term activities of the collaborative and to advocate for policy changes that the collaborative wishes to encourage. The Executive Committee meets monthly between Policy Board meetings to provide ongoing administrative and program guidance. The Action Groups, each convened by a member of the Executive Committee and responsible for a specific goal, meet as needed to formulate specific action plans (objectives/activities) for the collaborative. To encourage broad participation from the community, all Action Groups are open, at any time, to anyone within or outside of the collaborative's formal membership. However, to ensure reasonable administration and accountability within the collaborative's mission and goals, general Action Group plans are approved by the Executive Committee and ratified by the Policy Board.

A Policy Board membership of about 21 is recommended unless strong reasons for a larger board exist. An Executive Committee of 9 to 11 is recommended, including 4 to 5 officers, 3 conveners of Action Groups for three major goals, and 2 to 4 at-large representatives from the Policy Board.

Activity 10: Ensuring shared power.   In forming the collaborative empowerment structure, it is useful to begin with a relatively few community-based organizations negotiating with a small number of institutions from outside the community. This smaller group may first wish to form the collaborative's Executive Committee in order to establish basic ground rules, gain a measure of mutual trust, and formulate initial administrative processes. This Executive Committee can then agree upon the collaborative's goals and establish Action Groups to begin their implementation.

This also allows time for a "culture" of shared decision-making to emerge among the members of the collaborative. This culture could promote values in which power is measured not by how much control one wields, but by how much sharing one can foster. If power is shared rather than controlled, it can also slowly transform the behavior of members who may act in a hierarchical rather than a collaborative manner. The larger and more traditional the institutional partners, the greater the importance of establishing this culture of collaboration.

To emphasize the empowerment nature of the collaborative, a representative of a community-based organization should serve as the chair or as the vice chair of the Executive Committee. These are key positions because, in the collaborative empowerment model, the chair and vice chair of the Executive Committee hold the same positions on the Policy Board. In addition to the chair, the model calls for vice chairs for administration (monitors management and staffing) and program (assists Action Groups), a secretary, and a treasurer as its other officers. Again, all these officers hold the same positions on both the Executive Committee and the Policy Board; therefore, at least two of these officers should come from community-based organizations.

Activity 11: Offering contributions and overcoming barriers.   Once the community-based organizations and institutional partners agree on a governance and administrative structure, they begin discussing both what contributions each member can make in support of the collaborative's mission *and* what barriers exist that might limit such contributions. Whenever possible, the barriers (problems) that make contributions by particular organizations difficult are viewed as problem-solving opportunities for all partners to engage in together. This reinforces the collaborative's "ethic" and operating style and, in a vital way, provides evidence that collaborative efforts can not only enhance the capacities of individual organizations, but can also resolve specific conflicts.

Activity 12: Formulating goals. In the collaborative empowerment model, there are two basic kinds of goals to set: (1) goals that vary widely depending upon the particular mission and issues being addressed; or (2) "generic" goals that are applicable regardless of the mission or issues being addressed. The examples below illustrate how these options could apply to a child care collaborative.

In one case, the collaborative could set goals to: (1) increase the provision of community-based child care centers; (2) improve the integration of diverse child care services; and (3) enhance community participation in the design and implementation of child care services. In another case, the collaborative could choose to set broad, overall or generic goals to: (1) provide research, information, and community education (on child care issues); (2) support program innovations and services that demonstrate improved program delivery (of child care services); and (3) advocate for policy changes (that could improve the health and welfare of children and families).

Collaborative empowerment generic goals focus on: (1) research, information, and community education; (2) program innovations and demonstrations; and (3) policy advocacy and change. The major advantage in using generic goals is that they simplify the collaborative process while, when connected to specific action plans (objectives), they still allow a focus on detailed subject matter.

Activity 13: Linking goals to objectives or action plans. Linking the goals of the collaborative to clear objectives and to implementation strategies (called "action plans" in the collaborative empowerment model) is vital. In this activity, the clarity and specificity necessary to give the collaborative substance and credibility are provided in a way that also emphasizes community participation. Action plans are prepared by a separate Action Group for each goal. Each Action Group is convened by a member of the collaborative's Executive Committee and open to all members of the collaborative and anyone who wishes to join from the larger community.

In the collaborative empowerment model, *all* plans of an Action Group are directly linked to an organization in the collaborative. For example, if an action plan states that a speakers' bureau is to be established to provide community education and information, the objective or activity is linked to a specific organization *in* the collaborative. The organization so identified will then either implement the activity through its own resources alone or, more likely, take responsibility for implementing the activity with both the organization's own resources *and* the help of others.

Again, the convener of each Action Group indicates that periodic reports, to be shared with all members of the Action Group, are expected on each action plan. The Action Group convener provides summaries of these reports, including what progress is being made and what difficulties are limiting success, to the Executive Committee every month and to the Policy Board every three months. The convener's reports to the Executive Committee and the Policy Board provide ongoing communications and serve as a source of recommendations for how the Executive Committee and Policy Board can assist the Action Groups in their efforts.

Activity 14: Implementing plans and securing staffing. In order to increase the involvement and ownership of community members, the collaborative's action plans are continually discussed in both public forums and in informal ways with members of the community to engender their support. In empowerment processes, action plans are not implemented without community support. To ensure good communications, all action plans should explicitly delineate time lines, assessment criteria, and indications of financial requirements whenever possible. It also is helpful if action plans include an assessment of staffing needs, and indications whether staffing needs can be provided within the collaborative or must be met through outside funding. The collaborative's staff should be chosen for their competence and experience, not simply for traditional credentials. Staff members report to the Policy Board quarterly, the Executive Committee monthly, and to the chair of the Policy Board on an as-needed basis.

Activity 15: Evaluating the collaborative. For many reasons, a process as complex as multisector collaboration can be difficult to evaluate. However, if the collaborative process is designed with clear goals and action plans (which can include specific outcomes and time lines), an evaluation plan can be constructed more easily. In the collaborative empowerment model, community-based organizations emphasize the importance of evaluation because it provides for periodic and public monitoring of both the processes and products of multisector, community-based collaboration.

Activity 16: Concluding the collaborative with ongoing capacity. Community representatives negotiate the termination of a collaborative in a manner that can result in increased community self-determination and self-reliance. If possible, the community seeks to retain a combination of financial, human, and technical resources that can be sustained in the community after the collaborative concludes. For example, indicators that a collaborative created to provide affordable housing also empowered a community might include the degree to which: (1) ongoing operating support and better access to development funding packages was secured; (2) technical expertise was increased; (3) reliable linkages between affordable housing and related employment and social services for community residents were created or improved; and (4) more community residents made better decisions about the future of their communities.

Transforming betterment to empowerment collaboration.
When attempting to transform a betterment collaborative into an empowerment collaborative, it is important to consider and discuss the relationship of collaboration to social change and social justice. As has been discussed previously, empowering communities and neighborhoods with the assistance of larger public, private, and nonprofit institutions is not a simple matter of organizational or management techniques. This kind of transformation must encourage and respect a diversity of values and beliefs, and promote shared power to achieve common purposes. When collaboration moves from betterment to empowerment, both large institutions and community organizations are challenged to change their practices.

The transformation of betterment processes into empowerment processes is often quite complicated even if those involved have the best intentions. In large part, this is because institutions transforming a betterment process usually cannot easily secure the confidence and trust of those whom they initially excluded. In addition to overcoming mistrust, the institutions seeking to move toward sharing power and decision-making with community-based organizations also need to redesign their collaborative plans with the active and meaningful participation of community-based organizations.

Even with such difficulties, however, the transformation of betterment into empowerment processes is highly important if collaboration is to lead to significant societal change. It is achievable if organizations are committed to enhancing each other's capacity for a common purpose.

One example of a betterment to empowerment transformation is currently taking place in Hennepin County, the largest county in Minnesota. Hennepin County is a recipient of a multi-year federal (OSAP) grant to reduce tobacco, alcohol, and other drug abuse through a community-wide prevention collaborative. Initially, partly because of the way such federal grants are made, Hennepin County viewed the collaborative (Community Prevention Coalition—CPC) as one of its "projects." However, when community-based organizations were invited to join the CPC, they were not interested in playing the traditional advisory role consistent with a collaborative betterment process. As community-based organizations became more convinced of the possibilities of real power-sharing with Hennepin County, they pushed the CPC to establish governance procedures that include much of the collaborative empowerment model's structure and process. To its credit, Hennepin County now views itself as a partner among equal partners while serving as one of many decision-makers on the CPC Executive Committee, and it strongly supports the CPC's community-based focus.

Local community-based collaboration and national commitments

In closing, this discussion of collaboration must again emphasize that, if community-based collaboratives are given sufficient support, they can turn serious social and economic problems into opportunities for positive social change at the individual, community, and societal levels. As part of this support, we should work to improve collaborative processes that empower community-based organizations so that their ownership both of the processes and products of collaboration will help sustain community change efforts over the long term. In this sense, community-based collaboration can address the social and economic injustices across our nation that increasingly cry out for attention and demand action.

If community-based efforts are to be fully successful, however, new partnerships with the federal government will also have to be created. Because of the magnitude of funding needed to solve our major social problems, local efforts alone can never suffice. Only with the federal government's support can states and local communities adequately meet human needs for health care, child development, education, employment, and affordable housing.

To do this we must make a national commitment to provide for such human needs as the universal benefits of citizenship. We must create a commitment to enhance each other's human capacities, both for our common good as a nation and because of the growing global recognition that we cannot save our fragile planet without a little help from our friends.

PART 2

Approaching Intervention

Finding Help

Margaret S. Herrman

Our culture makes it difficult to seek help by making it hard to admit that we are embroiled in a conflict. Admission of conflict imperils our myth of harmony and feels like an admission of failure. You hear the myth in statements like "We're doing fine here," "Everyone in my department *really* gets along," "This isn't a problem," and "The situation was a fluke; it won't happen again."

Our reluctance to seek help is compounded in political settings, where traditional wisdom equates seeking help with weakness—indecisiveness, lack of vision, or lack of political clout. Because we live in a world that prizes individualism, we are often tempted to handle difficult situations alone. Public officials are often praised by their peers, the media, and the public for decisive actions, but they risk criticism when they turn to process consultants, mediators, citizen panels, or collaborative decision making to devise solutions to thorny problems. Fortunately, as more officials can testify to the value of such alternatives, institutional and public acceptance of these approaches to conflict grows.

Jim Laue, one of the most respected public policy mediators in the United States, has suggested that three conditions are necessary for third-party interventions to be effective:[1] First, parties must be willing to negotiate. Second, a forum that suits all parties must be available—the right place, at the right time, with the right convener, and the right level of visibility. Third, the intervenor must be credible. Without a credible intervener, even brilliantly conceived processes will fail.[2]

This article focuses on a pivotal aspect of the second and third conditions; namely, selecting the right intervener. First, I pose a number of questions to help you think through the implications of intervening in a conflict on your own. The framework for deciding whether to intervene is based on the criteria often used by professional interveners to decide whether and how to involve themselves in a conflict. Second, should you decide that help from someone outside the organization would benefit the resolution process, I offer some suggestions on qualities to look for in an outside intervener. Finally, I provide a list of questions to use in screening potential interveners.

Deciding whether to seek outside help

Regardless of the configuration of a dispute (employee-employee, interdepartmental, interagency, or intrastate), the first step when you are faced with a conflict is to decide whether you are directly involved. If you are involved, you are usually the least able to settle the dispute creatively without some form of third-party help. We are so well trained to fight or flee, to threaten or coerce, that we find it difficult to use more constructive ways to deal with conflict. Typically, it is a third party with no substantive agenda who helps the people directly involved find creative solutions.[3]

If you are not directly involved, you must next decide whether to be a third party or to seek external help. To help you work through this decision, I will pose a number of questions.[4] The first eight pertain to any level of dispute, but are especially relevant when you are faced with disputes between two (or more) employees.

1. Do you or your office have enough power to make meetings happen? If so, can you sustain lengthy face-to-face meetings? Do you have either the institutional authority or personal credibility to bring people to the table several times?
2. If you offer to help resolve a conflict, are you comfortable with the possibility that the parties will reject your proposal?
3. The Montenegrins have a proverb: "The peacemaker gets two-thirds of the blows." Are you comfortable shepherding meetings in which powerful negative emotions swirl around you?
4. Are you experienced in collaborative problem solving processes? Have you been specifically trained to convene meetings (either as a mediator, conciliator, or large group facilitator)? Are your skills comparable to the level of the dispute?
5. According to a Hausa proverb, "If a quarrel gets too hot, pretend it is a game." Do you have either the temperament or sufficient role latitude to step back from the heat of a conflict to analyze the situation as an interesting puzzle?
6. Will your institutional role allow you to sustain neutrality? Neutrality means two things: first, that you don't have an interest in any particular outcome; and second, that you are capable of treating the parties impartially. A combination of in-

stitutional pressures make neutrality difficult to maintain. For example, if the parties fail to reach an agreement and the dispute is channeled to a formal grievance process, administrators in charge of the formal process may seek your advice and input. But by acting as mediator, you have already assured the parties of confidentiality. How will you answer your superiors? In addition, as a manager you have a mandate to support existing policies. Since virtually any grievance invokes policy questions, it is hard to avoid falling back on a policy that favors one party over the other.

7. Can you turn the task of creating solutions over to the conflicted parties? Letting go of solutions is especially hard for managers, who are rewarded for making decisions or upholding policies. If you choose to step into a dispute as a neutral convener, be aware that your organizational instincts will incline you to solutions that meet your organization's needs; but such inclinations are incompatible with the role you are trying to perform.

8. Do you have the time? Facilitating heated discussions between protagonists takes more time than resolving a conflict by dictum or policy. If you agree to facilitate a resolution, you will first spend time in private conversations with the parties. Then you will spend time in several joint sessions, each lasting an hour or two of preferably uninterrupted time.

Now that you have had an opportunity to reflect on your role in interpersonal disputes, let me move on to a second set of questions that apply more particularly to technically complex disputes (land use, noise abatement, regional environmental disputes, multiagency budgetary negotiations, etc.). Even though the second set of questions relates in large measure to "bigger" disputes, you will also see some implications for interpersonal disputes.

1. Do you or your staff have something (data, wisdom born of experience, history from previous negotiations and implementations) that you want to contribute either to deliberations or solutions? If you *do*, you should seriously consider getting outside help. Local government managers have access to a substantial amount of information that may have a direct bearing on public policy negotiations. If it is important to include that information in deliberations, you will want to steer clear of a process manager, convener, or facilitator role. Mixing substantive expert and process expert roles is something like trying to teach a pig to sing: it hurts your ears and it irritates the pig.

2. Will you be perceived as neutral? This looks similar to question 6, but the emphasis is slightly different. There may be times

when you feel you can resist institutional pressures that could pull you off center and you would like to try your hand as a neutral convener. But chances are that your role as a neutral has already been compromised if even one party (or constituency group) *perceives* you or your office as having an agenda or a point of view.

3.   Is this dispute "bigger" than your capacity to facilitate or convene a problem-solving process? Does your office have sufficient resources to convene, facilitate, administer, or manage a complex process that might last a year (or two)? Will resources from other participants, foundations, regional agencies, the state or the federal government need to be pulled in to support a collaborative process? If so, do you have sufficient staff to manage the additional resources?

Once you have reviewed these two sets of questions, you should have a fairly good handle on the risks and rewards involved in trying to convene a resolution process yourself.

On occasion, you may decide that political, financial, or other pressures make it impossible for you to seek outside help, and that you will simply do the best you can on your own. If you do decide to work on your own, just be sure that you are doing it for the right reasons. The risk involved in seeking help is only one reason we sometimes take on more than we can handle; a desire to take on a challenge or earn acclaim are others. We all enjoy acclaim when we do good work, and acclaim is especially valuable in a politicized environment, where the pressure to step in for the glory of a good outcome can be especially tempting. In thinking through your decision, it might be helpful to know that even professional interveners sometimes ask themselves whether they are involved in a project for the right reasons.

Neutrals: Responsibilities, roles, and personal qualities[5]

If you decide that outside help is the best solution for all involved, your task is to select the right intervener. The accompanying sidebar describes some of the types of resources that may be available.

Assume that you have decided that the dispute calls for a neutral convener/facilitator. To assess how equipped any particular consultant is to do the job, you need to understand the three dimensions of the convener's work: responsibilities, roles and skills, and personal qualities. The three sections that follow look at each of these dimensions in detail.

Responsibilities.   As you will see, a few responsibilities can be assumed by government staff, others must be shared, and still others are a necessary part of a convener's work. (Local governments generally try to absorb as much of the cost as possible; that is understandable, but be cautious about what you ask your staff to do. First, they probably already have enough on their plates, and adding to their workload will only ensure that the process will experience delays. Second, remember the importance of neutrality. Sometimes when government offices assume the burden of the com-

---

Choosing a convener

As you begin looking for consultants, you will notice that a variety of services are offered by numerous firms—including law firms; universities; state offices of dispute resolution; other state agencies; local courts; and national, regional, or local nonprofit agencies. If you are in a metropolitan area, the selection of resources may be extensive and bewildering. Rural officials will have a smaller array of local consultants, but even there a few phone calls will reveal numerous possibilities. Several states now maintain statewide lists of certified or registered professionals offering alternative dispute resolution services, and national organizations in dispute resolution and organizational development maintain state-by-state rosters of consultants.

No two consultants are alike. Each offers a different configuration of services, and personal outlooks vary considerably. In going over your various resource lists, consider what you, your agency, and the other parties want to have happen: Do you need advocates, coaches or trainers for negotiation teams, technical consultants or substantive experts, researcher-conflict assessors, process designers, process evaluators, or hearing officers? (Activist-reactivists and enforcers will probably come with the dispute as parties or higher authorities.)[1]

What roles are important to you, and how do you want them played? For example, if you are looking for a hearing officer, do you want that person to gather information about the dispute and then decide? If so, you are looking for a judge (public or private). Do you want a person to deliver an opinion that the parties take under advisement or that goes to a high power? If so, you may be looking for a special master, a case evaluator, or an arbitrator. Do you want the consultant to help you, your staff, and any of the other parties work through a process that ultimately allows you all to participate in a resolution? If so, you are looking for a neutral mediator-facilitator.

1. The definitions of these roles and others were originally developed in James H. Laue and Gerald Cormick, "The Ethics of Intervention in Community Disputes," in Gordon Bermant, Herbert C. Kelman, and Donald P. Warwick, eds., *The Ethics of Social Intervention* (New York: Hemisphere, 1978), 205–232.

munication work, the participants begin to feel that what they read—memos, reports—is tainted by the government's perspective.)

Early on in the process, someone will need to *assess the conflict*. The history of a dispute; patterns of disputing; various agendas (hidden or explicit); the special characteristics of the dispute; composition and organization of various parties; institutional, political, and policy factors; and available resources will all be important in designing a resolution process. If the conflict is fairly complex, some assessment work can be retained by the local government; some can be delegated to an outside researcher; and some can be delegated to a convener. Just be aware that many conveners will legitimately ask to complete some level of assessment personally to assure themselves of information about a dispute. (On the other hand, in less complex interpersonal disputes, many mediators will ensure their neutrality in a hearing by refusing to read any assessment of a case. In this type of dispute, mediators typically assess the case from the opening statements of the parties.)

Process or systems design involves conceptualizing and articulating the flow and structure governing a problem-solving process. A process design specifies the types of meetings to be held, their timing and order, the possible length of time for the intervention, and even information or policies to be discussed. If the issue concerns a recurrent conflict, the design of a conflict resolution system may be a natural extension of the process design role. It would be hard for a consultant to delegate this responsibility to a government office or agency, but the local government's collaboration on process and systems design is appropriate and important.

Once a conflict is assessed and an intervention designed, there may be a need for a *trainer or coach*. In complex multiparty disputes it is not unusual for whole teams to be inexperienced in collaborative problem solving and in basic nonpositional negotiation. It is well worth the cost to have an expert provide some training or coaching before formal negotiations begin.

At a minimum, the *administration or management* of a problem-solving process requires scheduling and arranging meetings, giving timely notification of meetings, preparing and disseminating written products, and disseminating materials produced by group members or technical consultants between meetings. Administrative responsibilities are not especially burdensome when a dispute is primarily interpersonal and not technically complex but can be a major drain on resources in technically complex multiparty disputes. Administration is easily retained by the local government when a dispute is less complex, but consider delegating it to the convener when a dispute involves many parties and technically complex issues.

A *chair or facilitator* conducts the problem-solving process, including all large group gatherings and many small group sessions. This responsibility includes working with all original parties, including agency staff, to explore involving additional people or groups whose participation is important to a good outcome; developing a consensus on ground rules and decision processes; developing an overall process agenda and time frame as well as agendas for individual meetings; supplying or suggesting technical aids (such as computer-assisted decision making); and shepherding each meeting, including most joint meetings and selected caucuses. Some facilitators want responsibility for preparing drafts of agreements or final agreements. Since one of the facilitator's primary roles is to protect the integrity of the overall process, it would be extremely difficult for a convener to let go of a significant portion of this responsibility.

Roles and skills.   Above all, the convener is a *communicator*: a buffer, educator, and translator. Active listening skills are critical, as is skillfulness as a speaker. A convener must hear what is being said, especially if it is negative, and be able to reframe statements as requests that will be more easily assimilated by opposing sides. A touch of the *clown* also comes in handy. Especially when exchanges are tense or everybody is tired, gentle clowning can be an invaluable energizer.

When two or three sides have articulated deeply held positions, it is common for everybody to miss important solutions or to get bogged down in details. This is where a convener becomes a *resource expander and visionary*. Group processes (visioning exercises, brainstorming, idea writing, proposal-generating caucuses) can be used to break mental logjams. Experienced conveners who have worked with the substantive area in dispute might even share knowledge from past interventions.

As a process slides toward an impasse (and impasses are an expected part of any process, not a sign of failure) the convener will become an *agent of reality*, reminding disputants of the time and money costs of litigation, of possible political costs of failure, and possibly of one side's power to impose an unwanted solution. The convener might delicately touch on the possible consequences of severing a work relationship or alienating an agency or constituent group. In a caucus setting, the convener will test the feasibility or workability of proposed solutions.

Once proposals are on the table, a convener's key responsibility is to *protect an emerging settlement*. Protection takes a number of forms: writing memos that rephrase proposals in acceptable language; reminding participants of proposals that have been temporarily forgotten; pressuring for specificity in the wording of agreements (when, where, how, who, how much, etc.) to ensure "do-able" steps and actual implementation.

The need for a *scapegoat* usually emerges during caucuses, less often during joint meetings. Being a scapegoat allows a convener to absorb group anger or to float risky proposals. Parties often propose solutions in the protected atmosphere of a caucus that they are reluctant to present to the other side. With permission and some rehearsing, the convener can forward the proposal as part of a collection of "dumb" questions. You can spot the strategy in leading statements like "I wonder what would happen if . . . " "This may sound crazy, but . . . " If the proposal is rejected with peals of laughter or anger, the convener, not the party, takes the fall.

Finally, the convener is the ultimate *process protector*. Violations of process ground rules—including suspicions that other parties are not negotiating in good faith, failures to perform as promised, uncontrollable outbursts, and lies—are just a few of the ways in which a collaborative process can be compromised. While flexibility is a hallmark of a good convener, so is a healthy dose of skepticism. When the process is violated, a good convener will check the intent and the likelihood of repetition. If violations continue and the integrity of the participants or the process is jeopardized, a good convener will call a halt to the intervention.

Personal qualities.   Years ago I ran across a list of qualities of a good neutral: According to William E. Simkin, an ideal mediator should possess patience, sincerity, tenacity, wit, physical endurance, dodging abilities, guile, the ability to keep a secret, a tough hide, wisdom, and investigative skills.[6]

Stulberg and Zack help me to add to Simkin's list.[7] Humility is important: As we encourage parties to struggle for solutions, good conveners maintain a balance between an expert's knowledge of the process and the mask of a bystander. We know *how* to resolve a problem, but we refrain from telling *what* a resolution might be.

The best conveners also develop a capacity for objectivity. Roger Fisher once described objectivity as an ability to pull your chair back from the table. Without objectivity, it is close to impossible to analyze rhetoric and proposed solutions or to strategize future transactions. But being objective does not mean being cold and calculating; good conveners are anything but cold. Instead, they are extremely sensitive to the needs of disputants and tolerant of the abuses they will undoubtedly receive. Creativity, intelligence, and resourcefulness are characteristics that begin to round out the picture of an ideal convener.

Finally, I would add optimism. Conveners must have a deeply held belief that a resolution can be found and that the parties themselves possess the capacity to uncover the resolution.

Screening conveners

By now you are muttering that these paragons of virtue simply do not exist. Well, they exist, and they come in all shapes and sizes, ethnic origins, genders, and ages.[8] Your final task is to uncover the various talents and perspectives in the folks who have asked to convene for you.

Having been interviewed for prospective jobs as a convener, I have often wanted to prime my potential employer to ask pithy questions that would really help differentiate me from the other candidates for the job. The list that follows is a combination of my pet questions and those of a number of colleagues.[9]

Be aware that screening interveners is a skill that develops with time. In the worst case, you may conduct a few rather vague interviews, but your strategy will improve as each interview informs the next and your goals and needs become clearer. You can always call consultants back in for further talks. Remember, too, that in a good interview, you will learn not only about possible interventions but about the conflict itself: it is in the consultants' interest to find out what they might be getting into, and their questions may give you a more complete view of the problem.

To expedite screening, some officials have developed a questionnaire that they send to prospective consultants before doing interviews. If your agency or program contemplates using neutrals on a regular basis—for personnel grievances or repetitive public policy confrontations for example—building a general file on neutrals gives you valuable information. Even if you are looking for a consultant for a single, fairly substantial project, using a questionnaire will provide an effective first screen.

The questions generally follow a time sequence, but mixing the order is fine. You will probably pick and choose among the questions, so I offer several examples in each category to expand your options.

Experience

1. What experience have you had with this level of conflict (e.g., an interpersonal issue, an internal group issue, a multiagency problem, a community problem, or a regional problem)?
2. Are you more comfortable with certain types of disputes (e.g., conflicts involving data, relationships, legal issues, values, how things are structured, policies, conflicting interests)?
3. What is your history with this technical area? (You are not

looking for an expert, but the consultant needs to be literate in the technical area, including appropriate jargon, key agencies or programs, and laws or regulations that might shape the negotiations and resolutions.)[10]

Training, process knowledge, and orientation

1. Tell me about your training as a convener. What is your academic or disciplinary background? (Knowing this will give some clues as to approach.) How long have you been doing this type of work? Have you worked with other conveners in the past? Whom? Would you mind if we used them as references? Are you a member of professional associations or societies? If so, which ones? (May indicate professional commitment, exposure to new ideas, etc.)

2. What kinds of practices, techniques, or approaches have you used in the past? What past experiences will help you with my situation? Are you especially comfortable with certain techniques? Do you prefer simple mediations or complex facilitations? (Here you might look for a fit between the technical sophistication of the intervention and the technical literacy of the people involved in the conflict.)

3. As you think about our situation, you probably can think of several ways of approaching the problem. For each of the possible ways, what do you see as advantages and disadvantages? (This is an important question in itself, but it also gives you some insight into the consultant's personality. The more you discuss pros and cons, the more you will learn about the consultant's flexibility, philosophy, and tolerance for engaging in dialogue.) How would you approach this situation: as a straight mediation, a complex facilitation, as a computer-assisted decision process, as a visioning process, etc.? What do you think makes this situation especially challenging? How will you address the challenge?

Personality

1. Tell me about your personal style: How do you prefer to conduct meetings? (Here you are looking for adaptability or flexibility. Can the consultant shift personal style to fit the culture, language, dress code of the various parties?) You might propose a scenario or role play and ask the consultant to work through the hypothetical scene.

2. What is your approach to conflict? (Here you are looking for a fit between the consultant and the kind of case that has prompted you to call. Will the convener try to settle the negotiation or resolve a relationship? Do you want someone to

spend time resolving a relationship that is not worth saving?) How easy is it for people or an organization to change? (This is not a trick question: change is usually at the heart of any dispute. Here you are looking for values, optimism, and a realistic assessment of the difficulty of change.)

Process parameters

1. How long do you see this process taking? About how many steps or meetings might it take? What would be your time frame for getting started, involving participants, working on the problem, completing the process? How available will you be? How often can you meet?
2. About how many participants would you involve?
3. What aspects of the process do you see doing yourself? Would anyone help you? Do you chair/facilitate meetings yourself? Will you ask someone else to do that?
4. What resources will you need to conduct an effective resolution process? What can we do to help? How have you worked in the past with the staff of sponsoring agencies? What strategy would you use to develop a relationship with agency staff in this situation? How much staff input would you want? How do you handle group memory, reports, and settlements? What would be your strategy for developing final agreements and for allowing the group to draft/critique agreements? How visible, active, or directive do you need to be to make your intervention a success?
5. How will you or your organization staff the project?
6. What might be an estimated cost? When and by whom would you expect to be paid? (In complex cases and even small, two-person cases, dividing the fees can be a sticky—but vitally important—issue that relates directly to credibility.) What happens to the cost if the process runs longer or involves more work than you anticipated? Any ideas about putting the needed resources together? (One idea would be to build a consortium of resources for complex cases. Resources are less of a problem for internal agency conflicts).
7. How would you engage the parties in a resolution process? How would you persuade reluctant players that they need to participate? How would you propose to keep participants involved throughout the entire process? Is the process a failure if participants drop out?
8. How would you propose to develop ground rules or guiding principles? What types of ground rules are important? How would you approach violations of principles? (An important aspect in complex disputes is the working relationship with the

press. How does the convener work with the press and with sunshine laws?)

9. What are your views on caucuses and private sessions?
10. Have you ever had to switch gears in the middle of a meeting, in the middle of a process? Tell me how you knew you needed to make a switch. In general, what tells you that you need to shift gears? How will you let staff know that a shift needs to happen?
11. To what extent do you think it is appropriate for conveners to provide substantive solutions? If you were to offer a solution, give me an example of how you might approach such a task.
12. To what extent would you work behind the scenes to develop a negotiating team? Do you see this as appropriate? What strategies have you found effective in dealing with conflict between parties on the same negotiating team?
13. To what extent would you work behind the scenes with parties to develop solutions?

Outcomes

1. What is your vision of a successful outcome? What would be the conditions of a successful conclusion? What might we do to be successful? (A successful outcome is as important to the consultant as it is to you, but you may not share the same definition of success. The consultant may envision a totally changed workforce, empowered to really handle their own disputes as early and as effectively as possible; the development of new policies and procedures for channeling future disputes; new personnel positions. You may see none of the above.)
2. What would prevent you from taking on this project? How would you know when to leave?

References

1. *Ask for references!* Ask references about the consultant's strengths and weaknesses (writes great reports; timely; good on his or her feet in meetings; good when things get hot; "reads" meetings well; good getting group memory back to participants; a great cheerleader; politically savvy; good with the press; not defensive or thin skinned; empathetic; optimistic, etc.).
2. Look for possible conflicts of interest. This is not a legal issue but an issue of neutrality. As more communities build a substantial consultant base, conflict of interest questions will arise (e.g., is the mayor's wife your prospective consultant; has the law firm represented one of the parties in the past).

Conclusion

There is a great deal of uncertainty surrounding a decision to search for a third-party intervener. On the one hand, you need to stop the disruption surrounding a conflict. On the other hand, you may be uncertain about what a consultant will do or how much it will cost; you may be uncomfortable about giving an outsider so much control; and you may be reluctant to consume time with a thorough screening process just when others want a quick and dirty solution.

A good screening process *will take time*—less time if you are simply looking for a mediator for a personnel dispute, and more time for more complex interventions. But the time is the best investment you will make.

1. James Laue, "The Emergence and Institutionalization of Third Party Roles in Conflict," in Dennis J.D. Sandole and Ingrid Sandole-Staroste, eds., *Conflict Management and Problem Solving* (New York: University Press, 1987), 17–29.
2. I am generally using the words *intervener* and *convener* as synonyms.
3. David W. Augsburger, *Conflict Mediation across Cultures: Pathways and Patterns* (Louisville, KY: Westminster/John Know Press, 1992). See Kurt H. Wolff, ed., *The Sociology of George Simmel* (New York: Free Press, 1950). Simmel was probably the first social scientist to point out this difficulty.
4. The list of questions is based in part on Margaret S. Herrman, *Mediation in a Regional Setting: Facilitating Dispute Resolution and Decision Making* (Washington, D.C.: National Association of Regional Councils, 1987); and Daniel Dana, "Mediating Interpersonal Conflict in Organizations," in Donald Cole, ed., *Conflict Resolution Technology* (Cleveland, OH: The Organization Development Institute, 1983), 29–39. The proverbs were provided by Augsburger.
5. There are many good listings of qualifications of neutrals. The materials presented are taken in part from Joseph B. Stulberg, *Taking Charge/Managing Conflict* (Lexington, MA: Lexington Books, 1987), 31–41; Arnold M. Zack, *Public Sector Media-*

tion (Washington, D.C.: Bureau of National Affairs, 1985), 22–31; and Christopher Honeyman, "On Evaluating Mediators," *Negotiation Journal* January 1990: 23–36.
6. William E. Simkin, *Mediation and the Dynamics of Collective Bargaining.* (Washington, D.C.: BNA Books, 1971), 53.
7. Stulberg, 31–41; Zack, 22–31.
8. We recently completed a certification process for mediators who are now serving a local juvenile court in Georgia. Participants ranged from a young woman in her early teens to a man in his late sixties and included several racial and ethnic groups. The ideal characteristics I described emerged throughout the group.
9. The colleagues included Catherine McKinney, a veteran mediator and consultant at the Vinson Institute; Geoff Ball, a master facilitator and management consultant in the Bay area; Dee Kelsey, a veteran facilitator and management consultant and one of the architects of the certificate programs in conflict resolution and facilitation at the University of Southern Maine; Robert Barrett, an ADR systems consultant in the Bay area and the former program officer in dispute resolution for the Hewlett Foundation; Juliana E. Birkhoff, a professor at the Institute for Conflict Analysis and Resolution at George Mason University and an expert in regulatory and technically complex

disputes; Michael Elliott, a professor at the Georgia Institute of Technology and the codirector of Southeast Negotiation Network; and the Ohio Commission on Dispute Resolution and Conflict Management, which publishes a pamphlet on how to be an informed consumer.

10. Some disputes are framed by existing laws, legislation, or administrative guidelines (e.g., disputes involving environmental or noise abatement regulations; ADA disputes, EEOC disputes; disputes involving welfare and disability claims; sunshine law disputes). Effective conveners avoid providing technical solutions drawn from their expertise in the area of the dispute. But a lack of grounding in a relevant technical area may also mean that the consultant will fail to ask important substantive questions, or that he or she will be perceived by substantively knowledgeable parties as off the mark or unfocused.

Managing Conflict in Law Enforcement Agencies

John M. Stafford

Local government managers are continually faced with the need to resolve conflicts within their own organizations. Conflict management in the workplace is especially difficult because the parties are involved in ongoing relationships: Neither is likely to leave the organization, and their work will keep them in contact with each other. If only to make their own jobs easier, managers must develop conflict management skills.

Managers have a variety of options for handling internal conflict. They can ignore the problem. They can acknowledge the problem and let the parties try to resolve the conflict themselves, stepping in only if it becomes clear that the parties' efforts will fail. They can try to mediate or facilitate a resolution, or they can step in and mandate a solution.[1]

Because of the nature of the work and the personalities of those who do it, police departments consistently provide extreme examples of the difficulty of resolving organizational conflict. Officers are hired, in part, for their assertiveness, independence, and willingness to confront conflict—attributes that make them less likely to avoid conflict within their organizations.

In police agencies, managers have traditionally solved problems by *ordering* a change in behavior or by punishing the parties involved, then documenting their efforts in case there is future disciplinary action. Unfortunately, the traditional approach doesn't solve problems: it makes them worse.

This article has three parts. In the first, I offer case examples to illustrate common myths about conflict management. In the second, I offer a framework to assist managers in managing conflict; the framework is in the form of questions to help you prepare to intervene in a conflict. In the third part, I describe a few basic techniques of conflict management. Although the examples come from a variety of law enforcement agencies, the term *police department* has been used for consistency, and the methods outlined will work in all organizations.

Four myths of conflict management

Myth #1: The manager as mediator

I was brought in to resolve a conflict in a midsized police agency. The conflict was between a civilian employee, an African-American woman, and her immediate supervisor, a white male. The employee felt that she was the victim of harassment and discrimination, and she and others had compiled a list of the manager's discriminatory comments.

The problem was about two years old and was affecting the operation of the unit. There was a prima facie case for discrimination, as two of the unit's four minority employees—an African-American male and a gay male—had resigned during the preceding year, citing the manager's discriminatory behavior as their reason for leaving. The only other minority member in the unit reported no discriminatory behavior.

The employee had chosen not to file an EEOC complaint, explaining that she had young children and could not afford to risk retaliation or termination. But each time the manager took any action that she felt was discriminatory, she took her complaint directly to elected officials, who then sent directives back down the chain of command ordering that the problem be resolved.

Accordingly, management tried a variety of methods to resolve the conflict. Senior management ordered a change in the manager's behavior. Structured interaction and mediation, using the manager's supervisor as mediator, were also tried. The parties' shifts were changed. Nothing worked: the dispute not only continued but was escalating, spreading tension throughout the unit.

As both parties had very good records, top management wanted to keep both employees. When nothing else worked, I was finally brought in, mediated several sessions and got agreements, but something about the interaction didn't feel right. I finally confronted each party in a private caucus, asking, "Why are you here? Why are you trying to mediate this?"

The woman's answer was, "Because if I don't, I know they're going to try to fire me." Whether or not she would have actually been fired didn't matter; she believed the threat was real and acted accordingly. After some pushing from me, the manager answered, "So I can fire her!" Neither party was trying to resolve the problem: She was trying to avoid being fired, and he was doing what he could to fire her. The question was, Why didn't their supervisor get this information during his efforts at mediation?

There are three principal reasons for the employee's and the manager's reluctance to "come clean" to their manager:

1. They did not perceive their manager as neutral. The mediator's neutrality is one of the most basic principles of mediation: he or she must have no vested interest in the dispute or its outcome. But a manager's position in the organization makes neutrality virtually impossible to achieve or maintain.
2. Because the employees knew that the manager's first loyalty was not to them or to their needs, but to the organization, they did not feel protected. They were particularly concerned that anything they said might be used against them; thus, they withheld essential information.
3. The employees mistrusted the manager because he had greater relative power than either of them. Managers tend to intervene in a more controlling manner with subordinates than with colleagues or superiors, and both the employee and her supervisor were aware of the manager's power to impose a solution if he chose.

The lesson here is that managers should not try to act as mediators in the classic sense. The most effective role for the manager is that of conflict resolution facilitator: one who tries to help parties resolve their own problems but maintains his or her position as the person with whom the ultimate responsibility for resolving the problem lies. Thus, the manager has an *openly acknowledged* vested interest in seeing to it that the dispute is resolved and does not have to "pretend" neutrality. At the same time, the manager can make it clear that he or she will not *dictate* a resolution, and will obtain outside assistance if necessary to enable the parties to settle the dispute themselves.

Myth #2: Communication can solve all problems

A conflict between a police chief and the president of the local police union came to a head after three weeks of talking. The chief wanted to change the current vacation policy, and under the "meet and confer" requirements of the contract, he needed to reach agreement with the union before implementing any "change in wages, hours, or terms of employment."

The conflict centered on how far in advance officers should be required to sign up for vacations. In a series of meetings, the union president and vice president requested that the chief give them a written draft of his proposal. The chief replied that he would deliver a draft when the union told him what it wanted. Both sides kept talking, but the talking only heightened the level of the dispute.

Finally the exasperated vice president exclaimed, "Would you just give us a copy of the policy so we can sue you?" The chief responded with, "I'm the chief, and as long as I'm the chief you're going to do it the way I tell you." Both sides immediately brought in their attorneys, an action that solidified the conflict. Eventually the city manager and the city council had to get involved to resolve the conflict.

This conflict boiled down to a lack of trust and the resulting unwillingness of either party to discuss options until the other party had. "Communication" could not have resolved this dispute, and continued talking only made the problem worse. Before trying to resolve a conflict by *talking*, ask yourself whether it is really a communication problem.[2]

Myth #3: All conflicts can be resolved by fair and equitable enforcement of rules and regulations

A conflict within a patrol team was threatening to spread beyond that team. Putting the story together, we found that it had started simply enough: One officer was known as a prankster. The other officer was known as a meticulous, by-the-book sort and was constantly being teased about his immaculate appearance.

One day, the prankster noticed the other officer's duty leather hanging outside his locker and said, "Once—just once—I'd like to see him work the street with messy equipment." Goaded on by his co-workers, he got some mud and covered the leather with it.

When the victim returned the next day and saw what had happened, he turned on the other officers—all of whom were waiting for his reaction—and demanded to know who had damaged his leather. He was greeted by "cat-that-ate-the-canary" smiles and a few giggles. The prankster finally admitted that he had done the damage and offered to pay to repair or replace the equipment. But because of all the teasing that had preceded this incident, the injured officer was not satisfied with the offer and took his complaint to the watch commander. Within minutes, the traditional pattern of discipline began.

When the watch commander formally interviewed him about the incident, the prankster confirmed the first officer's story and reaffirmed his offer to make good on any damages. He went back on patrol and, as all employees will, he told the story to the other officers on his shift. By the end of the next day, the story had spread throughout the rest of the department.

The other officers were waiting to see what management would do. They were upset with the injured officer for taking the complaint to management in spite of the prankster's offer and felt that the matter should have been settled by the two parties themselves.

Five days later, a letter of reprimand was placed in the prankster's personnel file. *Now* the officers were angry with the injured officer *and* management: Given the prankster's offer, they felt that *any* punishment was inappropriate.

The situation deteriorated the next day, when every employee received a memo from the chief restating department policy on damaging or destroying property belonging to the agency or its employees. The officers, who felt that they, too, were being disciplined, distanced themselves from the injured officer as well as from management.

The chief took what he deemed to be the necessary and appropriate action: He acknowledged the existence of a conflict between two employees. He took formal steps to investigate the validity of the accusation. He took proportional action to discipline the offender. And finally, he resolved any possible liability problems by reaffirming the department's policy regarding this type of infraction.

By fairly and equitably enforcing agency rules, management greatly worsened the conflict and alienated itself from its employees.

Remember that when conflict is involved, perceptions can be as important as facts—or policies. The chief went "by the book," which in this case ignored the feelings surrounding the conflict. The incident itself was the outward sign of a deeper problem, and when the chief used traditional disciplinary methods to deal with it, he ensured not only that the underlying conflict would continue to brew, but that it would spread and foster resentment against management.

Myth #4: Conflict management techniques can solve all problems. Most managers wouldn't dream of trying to use conflict management techniques to resolve certain kinds of disputes—those that involve illegal or dangerous activity, for example. In such cases, managers would take immediate action to stop the activity.

But some problems that involve neither illegal nor dangerous actions *are simply not resolvable through intervention.* The EEOC case cited at the beginning of this article is an example: Neither party trusted the other; they had opposing motivations; and one of the parties did not *want* to resolve the conflict except by his own method—namely, firing the employee.

According to Fisher and Ury, a party entering a negotiation should determine its BATNA—Best Alternative to a Negotiated Agreement.[3] As a manager faced with a conflict in your organization, you should follow Fisher and Ury's example and determine your BATIIC—*Best Alternative to Intervening in Conflict.* In other words, if you don't intervene, how might the conflict be solved? In certain situations, resolving the conflict through intervention is the least advisable option.

Preparing to intervene

Bazerman and Neale refer to five "prescriptions" for successful negotiations.[4] Altered here to fit conflict management, they are:

1. Assess what you will do if you can't resolve the dispute (BATIIC).
2. Assess what the parties to the conflict will do if you can't resolve the conflict.
3. Assess the *true* issues in the conflict.

4. Assess how important each issue is to each of the parties.
5. Assess how important each of the issues is to *you!*

The key to these five steps is to realistically determine the risks involved in failing to resolve the dispute and to identify the underlying issues for all the parties.

A manager who has decided to intervene in a dispute should consider in addition to Bazerman and Neale's prescriptions the following five questions:

1. Have you identified all the parties?
2. Does everyone agree on the existence, nature, and cause of the conflict?
3. After hearing the conflict outlined by the parties, do you agree with—or at least understand—the parties' views on the nature and cause of the conflict?
4. Have you made efforts to identify all of the parties' issues?
5. Have you done your homework: i.e., learned as much as you can about the people involved and their needs?

The five sections that follow examine these questions in detail.

Have you identified all the parties? This doesn't mean that you need to involve in the process anyone who has ever had anything to do with the conflict. What it does mean is that you should involve every individual whose participation will be *necessary* to resolve the conflict.

A city manager met over lunch with the attorney representing a local police union. Both parties engaged in a "feeling-out" process to gauge the difficulty of forthcoming negotiations. Taking his cue from things the attorney had said, the city manager assumed that the sessions would be easy that year and structured his negotiation accordingly.

Midway through the negotiations, things went bad when the union bargaining committee emphatically refused to consider one of his proposals. Shocked by the rebuff, the city manager turned to the union attorney and said, "I thought you said that they were going to be reasonable about this."

When the union president turned and asked what he was talking about, the city manager was so flustered that he told the bargaining committee about his lunch with the attorney. The union cancelled the rest of the bargaining session and fired the attorney.

Unknown to the city manager and the attorney, the bargaining committee had decided to take the lead in the negotiations: they felt it was going to be an easy year and wanted to get personal experience leading negotiations.

The city manager was on the right track in trying to build bridges and gather information about the other party's needs, but he didn't talk to the right people; in other words, he failed to *iden-*

tify all the parties whose participation was necessary to a resolution. In this case, a combination of poor communication and poor negotiation strategy created a high degree of conflict: the attorney and the manager failed to openly and explicitly discuss whether and how to inform the union about their informal prenegotiation talks; the union failed to inform the attorney of its plans to take the lead in the negotiations; and once talks went bad, the manager failed to "keep his cool" and blurted out information that could only damage his position. By failing to identify all the parties, the city manager was ultimately faced with a hard-line stance, as the union president tried to get even for what he perceived as collusion.

Do the parties agree about the existence, nature, and cause of the conflict?   Unless all parties agree about the principal aspects of a conflict, you will be trying to resolve a dispute while talking about apples and oranges.

Officers were complaining about the light bars on their patrol vehicles, claiming that the equipment "drew too much power" and wasn't safe.

The chief, preoccupied with other problems, put off talking to the officers about the issue in detail. When the complaints persisted, the chief decided abruptly to simply replace the light bars. Only afterward did he discover that the real problem was not the light bars themselves, but the *wiring* for the "alley light" portion of the bars: several of the units had overheated, causing the on-off switch to begin to smoke.

Failure to identify the real source of the problem led the chief to solve the wrong problem. If he had followed up on the complaints, he would have been able to focus on the real issue—the safety issue—and to ask, "How can we make this situation safe?" Ultimately the chief could have saved time and money for his department and himself.

After hearing the conflict outlined by the parties, do you agree with—or at least understand—the parties' views on the nature and cause of the conflict?   Because conflicts often arise from differences in perception, one of the most effective ways to resolve a dispute is to "get into the shoes" of the other party.

In the conflict between the city manager and the union president described earlier, the conflict intensified because of different perceptions: The city manager and the attorney perceived their talk over lunch as a *beneficial attempt to foster cooperative negotiations;* the union saw the meeting as *an attempt to circumvent the union.*

Negotiations between management and unions are, almost by definition, an effort to resolve a conflict, generally one arising from differing demands. Events in this case developed in such a way that a powerful additional element—lack of trust—was added, intensifying and personalizing the original conflict.

If the city manager had begun by "trying to get into the union's shoes," he would have asked himself how his action might be perceived by the union. The attorney, too, bears significant responsibility for not raising this issue. Even after negotiations had faltered, a skilled negotiator might have been able to salvage the situation by acknowledging the union president's views.

Remember: You don't need to agree with a party's position, merely to acknowledge that it is legitimate.[5]

Have you made efforts to identify all of the parties' issues?   If you don't know the issues behind a dispute, you can't help solve it. Even the parties themselves don't always know what all their issues are.

I was called in to mediate the division of property for an unmarried couple—police officers working for neighboring agencies—whose breakup had become violent and was threatening to spill over into the agencies that employed them.

I suspected that a simple division of property was not the real source of the problem. Neither party would budge, and their unwillingness to compromise was a warning that not all the issues had been identified.

The real issue came out during private caucuses: Just before moving apart, each member of the couple had talked to officers in the other person's department, dishing out all the dirt they could. Both felt that their reputations had been hurt.

Needless to say, the solution was vastly different once the real issue had been identified. But until we could find a way to address the couple's concern for their professional reputations, nothing else was going to be solved.

To resolve a conflict, you need to identify the issues. The more stubborn the parties are, the greater the chance of hidden issues.

Have you done your homework: i.e., learned as much as you can about the people involved and their needs?   In the EEOC conflict described earlier, one hidden need blocked any chance of resolution: the manager's need to see himself as a champion of civil rights. During an interview with the manager, I was struck by the strength of this view of himself. It turned out that in the mid-sixties, he had become his agency's minority recruiting officer, establishing the program in the face of resistance from both co-workers and superiors. The manager didn't see himself as bigoted or racist and viewed the problems in his department as stemming from incompetence and rebelliousness on the part of employees, not as a matter of race or sexual orientation. The manager's need to protect his self-image prevented him from seeing his part in the conflict.

Until we learned about the manager *as a person*, it appeared that he was simply being uncooperative. Although the effort was still only partially successful, that information changed how the conflict management process was structured.

Always learn about the parties and their needs. The more you know about the parties *as people*, the more easily you will be able to meet their needs and resolve the conflict.

Conflict management techniques

This section of the article describes practical methods used by successful conflict managers: all of the methods take practice, but with effort—and a reliance on *process*—these techniques work.

Establish ground rules.   Get agreement on the ground rules before beginning any conflict management session: This gives you one success to fall back on. Common rules include place, time, and length of meeting; no verbal assaults or name calling; no interrupting. The beauty of these agreements becomes apparent when things start to go bad. In the event that anyone, including yourself, violates these procedural agreements, negotiations can be stopped while the parties are reminded of their prior agreement, giving everyone a chance to calm down and refocus on the issues.

Expect emotions and acknowledge them.   Attacks and hardball tactics often mask anger and fear. Until you defuse the emotions, the process will go nowhere: angry or fearful participants will not be able to hear reasonable arguments.[6] Expect the emotional level to rise and fall in the course of the resolution process. Listen for the changes: they indicate the relative importance of the issues. Again, you do not need to agree that emotions are appropriate or justified; simply acknowledge them.

Let each party take the time to tell their story.   People trying to tell you everything of importance to them go through "the spiral": They will go around the loop once, then come back to the starting point and tell the story again, in a slightly different form.

If you cut off a speaker who has not completed the first loop of the spiral, he or she will go back to the start of the story and start again. If you continue to cut the speaker off, he or she will eventually stop talking—and will resent you. Not only has potentially vital information been lost, but the resentment is an unnecessary impediment to resolution.

To stop the spiral from going into a second "loop," use a simple question: "Let me see if I understand you correctly. Do you mean that . . . " Then restate the speaker's position. Finish by saying, "Is there anything I've misunderstood or left out?" Once the speaker says no, you can move the process to the next level by asking what that person thinks will solve the problem. The speaker will offer a solution—maybe an unacceptable one, but a solution just the same. Any proposed solution gives you something to work with. If participants try to rehash their stories, just keep focusing them on solutions.

In really difficult conflicts, where the parties were so entrenched that it seemed nothing could come out of the conflict management effort, I've had success with the following question: "If I were to make everything perfect here, what would that look like?" This question gives people permission to "dream," to step out of their reality and give you a possible solution.[7]

Look at yourself: How are you reacting to the conflict?   Accept that you can be one of the biggest obstacles to resolution—and the easiest obstacle to remove. And as conflict manager, one of your primary tasks is to remove obstacles to an agreement.

I heard a comment several years ago and have used it ever since to guide my own actions: "Whenever the person I am arguing with seems at their most stubborn, unreasonable, and angry, I hold a mirror up to myself and never fail to find that the face in the mirror is just as stubborn, unreasonable, and angry."

I have found that by the time the other person is so angry or unreasonable that I am *reacting* to his or her behavior, I am just as angry or unreasonable. It's then time to back up and reassess my role in perpetuating or worsening the conflict.

Determine whether the party is responding to something in particular or is simply a difficult person.   In a dispute in which someone seems to be particularly difficult (e.g., recalcitrant, obstructive, uncompromising) one of the first things to establish is whether the behavior is typical or has changed. A change in behavior usually indicates that something specific has happened, in which case your task is to locate the cause of the change. If, on the other hand, the party is *always* difficult, you need to develop a strategy for coping with that person as part of the conflict management process. Four questions can help you assess the situation:

1. Has the person behaved *differently* in *three* similar situations?
2. Was there a particular incident that may have triggered the troublesome behavior?
3. Are *you* reacting in a way that's out of proportion to the situation?
4. Will direct, open discussion improve the situation?

If your answer to all four questions is yes, chances are that you are *not* dealing with a difficult person. If the answers are no, the following guidelines will help you develop a coping strategy:

1. Stop wishing the other person were different.
2. Get some distance between yourself and the situation.
3. Formulate a plan to change the pattern of interaction. Remember that you have power through your ability to control your part of the interaction. Watch for behavior that elicits a positive reaction from the difficult person, then model your behavior to match it. Make it *easy* for the difficult person to interact with you—perhaps even to agree with you.
4. Implement your plan.
5. Monitor the effectiveness of your strategy, modifying it when necessary.[8]

Focus on resolving one problem at a time.[9]   It is entirely too easy to get sidetracked by trying to resolve a multitude of issues simultaneously.

Try to solve a smaller issue first. This builds a feeling of success to structure the rest of the conflict management effort. Reward the parties for trying to resolve the conflict with a small, quick agreement that will encourage further participation.

Conclusion

Conflicts occur for a variety of reasons—but whatever the cause, conflict is normal and to be expected.

To effectively manage conflict, managers need to look at the issues, emotions, and needs of the parties to the dispute—as well as at their own issues, emotions, and needs. And they must remember that most people are made quite uncomfortable by conflict management methods, even when they are effective. Moreover, no matter how effective the process, hurt feelings and resentment often remain. Only in the rarest cases will the parties leave "loving their neighbor."

Given these difficulties, why bother? A manager who successfully helps resolve an internal conflict has accomplished two things: first, he or she has enabled the parties to deal with the current conflict; second, channels of communication have been established that may forestall future conflict. And in time, it is possible to create within the organization an environment in which conflict management is seen as a viable, desirable alternative to continued disputes.

1. M. Bazerman and M. Neale, *Negotiating Rationally* (New York: Free Press, 1992), 148–151.
2 D. Stiebel, *Resolving Municipal Disputes*, 2d ed. (Oakland, CA: Association of Bay Area Governments, 1992), 12–23.
3. R. Fisher and W. Ury, *Getting To Yes* (Boston: Houghton-Mifflin, 1981).
4. Bazerman and Neale, 69–72.

5. W. Ury, *Getting Past No* (New York: Bantam, 1991), 40–44.
6. Ibid., 40–85.
7. Bazerman and Neale, 16–22.
8. R. Bramson, *Coping with Difficult People* (New York: Ballantine, 1981), 130.
9. D. Stiebel, *Resolving Municipal Disputes*, 2d ed. (Oakland, CA: Association of Bay Area Governments, 1992), 28–31.

Want to Resolve a Dispute? Don't Ask!

Dr. David Stiebel

The conventional problem-solving approaches of facilitation, team building, and consensus building can succeed when people are cooperative, but they often fail in stubborn in municipal disputes with recalcitrant players. Conventional problem solving won't work unless all the parties

- Want to resolve the problem
- Want to work together
- Can agree on a process for problem solving
- Can agree on a facilitator *and*
- Are willing to make an explicit commitment to participate.

Unfortunately, parties to a stubborn dispute are rarely that agreeable. It's *normal* for them to refuse to negotiate. That doesn't mean that agreement is hopeless. In fact, it's often better to begin resolving a dispute *without* asking the other person's permission in advance.[1]

Don't invite rejection

It's tempting to want the other person to commit to negotiate before you invest your time and energy in a thorny problem. But surprising as it may seem, the simple request "Do you want to negotiate?" can lead someone to take a stance that directly obstructs your objectives. You may succeed only in limiting your options and in having less power to resolve the dispute *after* asking the question than you did *before*.

This is an expanded version of an article that appeared in *Public Management* 72, no. 1 (August 1990). Copyright by the author.

In your view, "Do you want to negotiate?" means "Would you like to resolve this dispute and mend relations?" You expect the other person to say yes, if he or she wants to cooperate. But in an atmosphere of hostility, the other side rarely hears the question as intended, even if you use all the right words.

No matter how clearly you *say* "Do you want to negotiate?" the other person may think you *mean* "Will you commit now to changing your position?" The request to negotiate may come across as an invitation to offer concessions.

The other party's rejection of your invitation to negotiate may not be due to stubbornness but to self-interest:

- Agreeing to negotiate may signal a willingness to grant concessions.
- The number of potential concessions is unlimited.
- The person is afraid to appear weak.
- The person want to look tough, so you'll expect fewer concessions.
- The person wants to receive something before giving anything.
- The person sees no reason to act now.
- The person dislikes you or thinks that you won't change.

Inviting someone to negotiate is like leading that person into a dark room and asking "Do you like what you see?" It's like asking "Will you buy this car?" without disclosing the price. You're asking the other person to make an ambiguous commitment that might jeopardize his or her interests.

No wonder the other person says no. And if the person is going to say no, why ask? If you want to start resolving the dispute, just do it! Don't ask the person's permission. Don't give the other person the power to block your objective.

Once the other person says no, you may lose any hope of starting negotiation. At best, it will be much harder to begin resolving the dispute.

The wrong assumption

Consider the case of the city manager who was trying to improve labor relations in advance of contract talks with the municipal employees' union. The previous year, talks had deadlocked and produced a strike. The manager wanted to avoid the traditional bargaining pattern of exchanging extreme unilateral demands, so he told the personnel director to hire a consultant to develop a workshop in collaborative negotiation, to help labor and management learn methods of solving problems jointly.

When the workshop design was completed, the manager called the union president personally to invite her to negotiate collaboratively and to attend the workshop. She refused.

The manager was shocked. He had assumed that the union president would respond to his offer by thinking

- "My union should agree to negotiate collaboratively, since the city is showing good faith by suggesting it."
- "If I negotiate collaboratively, my union's long-term relationship with the city will improve."
- "Negotiations will be less stressful."
- "We may avert another strike."
- "We'll resolve other problems more satisfactorily."
- "Union members will praise me for this innovative move."

Predicting the response

After the union president rejected the city manager's overture, there seemed to be nothing he could do to improve labor relations to ensure smooth contract talks. He was at a stalemate before negotiations had even begun. Whenever he repeated his request to the union president, she would protest, "We already rejected that! We're not interested!" For her, defending that position had become a matter of honor.

That's the pitfall of asking the other person's permission to negotiate. When the person says no, he or she commits to a negative stance with regard to your request. Then you must somehow convince the person to *reverse* that negative commitment. And that was precisely the dilemma facing the city manager.

His predicament underscores a vital rule of municipal dispute resolution: *Don't ask a question unless you can bear to hear the answer.* Every time you ask for something, the other person has the option of saying no. Don't present an idea unless you can take the risk of a negative response. In this case, the manager gave the union president the option of refusing to collaborate, even though a refusal would not meet his needs. The manager would have benefited by anticipating the union president's response before suggesting collaboration.

In general, you can evaluate a planned negotiation move by asking yourself the following four questions:

1. From your perspective, what is the *best* response that the other person could make to your move?
2. What is the *worst* response that the other person might make? If the person takes this action, will it then be harder to resolve the dispute?
3. What response do you *expect* from the other person, on the basis of his or her self-interest?
4. Is the potential gain from your move worth the risk?

Uncovering motivations

At this point the manager enlisted my assistance in determining what to do next to improve labor relations. First, we needed to determine *why* the union president had responded negatively. So we asked ourselves some questions:

- What perceptions could have caused her to say no?
- How would her constituents have responded if she had said yes?
- What personal motivations might have prevented her from saying yes?

The manager viewed the union president as inflexible; the question was, *Why* was she being inflexible? What was she afraid of losing?

We reviewed a checklist of possible motivations, trying to determine which of the following factors might be important: *ego, control, security, key constituents, public image, perceptions, principles, precedent, finances, commitments, other options*, and *reflexive reaction.*

We examined both logical and emotional factors. We talked to union presidents elsewhere to try to understand the thinking of *this* union president. (It often helps to consult people in roles similar to that of the person you are trying to understand.) We finally came up with a number of likely reasons for rejection of the manager's invitation:

1. "If I negotiate the city's way, I may lose." (*Motives: ego, security, precedent, finances.*)
2. "The city will be in control, since I will have to learn the rules of this new game." (*Motive: control.*)
3. "This may be a way to exploit the union." (*Motives: security, finances.*)
4. "Some union members will think I have sold out by collaborating with management." (*Motives: key constituents, public image.*)
5. "My members may lose confidence in me and elect someone else." (*Motives: control, security, key constituents.*)
6. "The old way worked." (*Motives: precedent, other options.*)

In other words, the union president didn't trust the city, but the manager's proposal—collaborative negotiation—was an invitation that required trust to accept. The manager's expectations of the union leader turned out to be unrealistic.

A better strategy

The manager and I asked ourselves what constructive response we could realistically elicit from the union president. We figured she'd like to talk about how management needed to change.

In my role as city training consultant, I called the union president and sought her help. "I will be teaching the city's negotiators better ways to resolve disputes," I said, "So I would like to learn what mistakes this city routinely makes in dealing with the union."

Sure enough, the union president began reciting a litany of the city's errors. This action was constructive for both of us: it allowed the union president to identify management practices that were resented and that might be changed, and it enabled me to design better training.

After a few minutes on the phone, I said, "There are too many problems here to discuss in one phone call. But I can meet at a time convenient for you." The union president agreed to meet—because she wanted to continue criticizing the city to someone who shared her desire to help management improve.

If I had proposed a face-to-face meeting initially, she might have refused. After all, why should she spend time with a stranger working for the city (who would therefore not be trustworthy)? By waiting to suggest a meeting until I had earned credibility, I was making it easier for the president to agree to meet.

After several meetings, my working relationship with the union president had progressed to a point where she was critiquing the training outline. I suggested: "You've helped me so much in designing this training; it would be nice if you could be there."

By inviting the union president to the training after she had helped create it, I was making it easier for her to attend despite her initial refusal. Now her choice was whether to *continue* cooperating with the city, rather than whether to commit to the vaguely threatening idea of "collaborative negotiation."

Not only did the union president say yes, she invited other union representatives, too. People often want to participate in a program in which they've invested time and energy, especially if they're proud of the results.

Why it worked

The city effected cooperation even when the other side refused. Conventional methods such as team building, consensus building, or facilitation would not have worked, because the union president would not have cooperated.

You might think that we succeeded because we set an ultimate goal ("The union president should attend the training") and then designed a series of moves to manipulate the union president, brilliantly anticipating her responses several steps ahead.

In fact, we did the opposite. We didn't begin with an ultimate goal. That approach had already failed the manager. His invitation to negotiate collaboratively didn't produce the desired result because he was asking the union president to take an unrealistically large step.

As the manager discovered, an ultimate goal doesn't help if you can't get there from here. The union leader refused to accept the city's predetermined solution to its labor-relations problem. She felt manipulated and shut out of the city's decision-making process.

We couldn't invent the entire negotiation strategy in advance because, like most parties, the union president wasn't sufficiently pliable or predictable. Our strategy developed incrementally, as we followed these principles of municipal dispute resolution:

1. *Look behind the other person's actions.* We used the questions and checklist and talked to other union presidents to understand *this* union president's perceptions, fears, and motivations.
2. *Think of a realistic response to elicit from the other person.* We wanted the union leader to criticize management, to meet, to critique the training outline, and eventually to attend the session. These desired actions were realistic for us to seek, since each step enabled the president to further her objective of helping the city to change.
3. *Decide how to elicit the desired response.* By soliciting and responding to the union president's critiques, I made it easy for her to take one desired action after another. By contrast, the manager was making it hard for the union president to negotiate. He was seeking a commitment to bargain, which would have required the union to review its policy and consult constituents. But the union president felt no constraints when it came to criticizing the city.

Thus, we proceeded incrementally, making it easy for the union president to make one constructive response after another. She didn't take one single step that in itself achieved the city manager's objective: each step built on the preceding one, culminating in a satisfactory outcome.

We couldn't forecast the precise result—that the union president would participate in collaborative training when she had initially refused. But we knew that the final outcome would be positive, because each step along the way was benefiting the city.

The union president was fully aware of what she was doing. She was working with us because the city was showing a new openness to labor's perspective, and she attended the training because she had helped design it.

When proceeding incrementally, how can you verify that you're really moving toward resolution? You can ask yourself these two questions:

1. What is the person's present response to the situation?

2.   Does that response help meet your needs?

If so, you're making progress. If not, think of a better response to elicit.

Don't feel compelled to get the other person's commitment to negotiate. We engaged the union president informally, in a low-risk, nonthreatening way—without calling it negotiation. As this example demonstrates, negotiation does require the other person's participation—but not explicit consent. You can engage the other person informally, and he or she will participate—if your approach is appealing.

Finally, do not propose cooperative problem solving unless you will be satisfied with a negative reply. You don't need permission to negotiate. Just do it!

1. For additional information on this topic, see David Stiebel, *Resolving Municipal Disputes: When Talking Makes Things Worse, Someone* *Won't Negotiate, There's No Trust* (Oakland, CA: Association of Bay Area Governments, 1992).

The Seven Deadly Syndromes of Dispute Resolution

Mediators and other dispute resolution professionals occupy some of the choicest seats in the theater of human experience. When it comes to responses to conflict and styles of dealing with it, they've seen it all—from behaviors that help people satisfy their real needs to those that get in the way of reasonable settlements.

Since personal foibles seem to draw more interest than personal strengths (as evidenced by the universal fascination with gossip), this article will call attention to and classify some of the common frailties exhibited when people try to deal with conflict. These syndromes, as I'll call them, are attitudes and behaviors that disputants get stuck in—and that mire them more deeply in a dispute and keep them from reaching for solutions.

My purpose is twofold: first, to heighten sensitivity to counterproductive attitudes and behaviors; second, to suggest some remedies for these maladies.

Many of the syndromes can be traced to some kind of illusion or another: illusions about the nature of conflict; illusions about power, knowledge, or independence; optimistic illusions; illusions about the rationality of human behavior or the outcome of complex processes. (See Figure 1.) In the second part of the article, I'll discuss some means of combatting such illusions.

The Scarlett O'Hara Syndrome

One of the most memorable scenes in the movie *Gone with the Wind* is the one in which Scarlett reclines on a stairway, bemoaning her fate but deciding to "think about it tomorrow." The Scarlett O'Hara Syndrome—also known as avoidance—is probably the most per-

---

Ozzie Bermant is Director of the Concordia Systems Group, Potomac, MD.

vasive of all and comes in two different versions: the benign and the malign.

Sandra Smith, a lawyer hired by Center City as an administrator for economic development, was expected to use her vaunted connections to help attract large corporations or enlarge their activities in the city. During her six-month probationary period, she failed to produce either plans or results. Her supervisor, the assistant city manager, was dissatisfied but never confronted Smith because of his extreme discomfort with controversy. Instead, he gave her a satisfactory appraisal and shifted her to another position, where she was overpaid and performed in a middling way. After three years, Smith, dissatisfied with being passed over for promotion, sued the city, claiming gender discrimination.

The lesson here is that although it may be harmless in intent and is often the action of a gentle soul, even benign avoidance can be dangerous. Some problems simply won't go away.

Malign avoidance, on the other hand, is often characteristic of a schemer who wants to be able to say "Gotcha!" during an anticipated future conflict. An example is the public works manager who notes some deficiencies in a building project; but rather than deal

Syndrome	Symptom	Illusion
Scarlett O'Hara	Avoidance	If I ignore it, it will just go away.
Mr. Potato	Rigidity	I can't be any different than I yam.
Jack Webb	Only facts, no feelings	Ours is a totally rational world.
Torquemada	Righteousness	The world is doomed, unless you do as I say.
John Osborne	Staying angry	Revenge is not only sweet; it's cheap.
Frank Sinatra	Controlling; being a Lone Ranger	What's good for me is good for you, but who cares what's good for you, anyway?
Shah of Iran	Positional bargaining	I can win if I just stick to my guns; after all, I have so many guns.
Tunney-Dempsey	Repeated miscalculation	Don't bother me with details.

Figure 1. Syndromes, symptoms, and the illusions they spring from.

with them when they occur, he stores the information away. Then, when the project is at an end and the contractor bills for extra work, the manager brings out all the "dirty laundry" he has saved up. The negotiations that were avoided initially have now escalated to battles, lawsuits, and expensive and dramatic trauma. And the pattern continues to repeat itself: both the manager and the contractor expect claims and counterclaims as a way of life.

Avoiding confrontation isn't always wrong. Choosing not to confront conflict can be appropriate when the issue is trivial or when future conditions may make for a more successful negotiation. Although strategic avoidance often makes sense, it is sometimes difficult—even in hindsignt—to distinguish between benign or malign avoidance and an authentically strategic approach.

The Mr. Potato Syndrome

Bill Grubb is an earthy, no-nonsense foreman in the school district's maintenance department. His salty language and gruff manner irritate some and endear him to others. In the last few years, with changes in the nature of the work and the increasing importance of computer technology, there are now more women under Grubb's supervision and fewer "good old boys." At a team-building session last fall, he was surprised to find that several employees—both men and women—found his behavior intimidating, sexist, and abrasive enough to affect the quality of their work. His reaction was, "That's the way I am. Take it or leave it; I'm not changing my style to accommodate a few oversensitive ninnies." This drew a laugh from some and smirks from others. Meanwhile, three highly qualified technicians have resigned in the last six months.

The Mr. Potato Syndrome, or, "I yam what I yam and that's all I yam," is perhaps understandable: when we find that a particular way of responding works well for us, we may have very little idea of the effect of such behavior—such as loss of support or attention from some co-workers or subordinates. But as the psychologist Milton Erickson has said, "The person who is most flexible is the most powerful." Flexibility in approaching conflict need not compromise quality or the values of an organization.

The Jack Webb Syndrome

Mary Means is head of the management and budget department for Copake County. Since taking over the job two years ago, she has transformed what was once a poorly regarded unit into one that has a reputation for responsiveness and efficiency. About six months ago, she told her staff that their performance appraisals would be based partly on the amount of her time that they "wasted" in rambling discussions with her. She said there were too many issues and too many people to deal with for her to engage in small talk; the staff's presentations were required to follow a strict, facts-oriented outline that she provided.

Last month, three members of the county council raked Means over the coals because of her failure to consider how reductions she had proposed would affect a community improvement project that had a long and touchy history in the county.

Jack Webb used Officer Friday's famous line—"Just the facts, ma'am"—with dramatic and comic success, but the approach has its limitations. When people are involved, it's important to get the "story" as well as the facts.[1] Even though the story may be clouded by emotion or subtleties and require patience to uncover, knowing the story as well as the facts improves the decision-making process and can reveal options that would not otherwise have surfaced.

The Torquemada Syndrome

Jasper Blake is a senior planner in the state transportation department. He has a Ph.D. in community planning and very definite ideas about the ideal mix of highway and public transit facilities. Last year he worked with a citizens' advisory committee to develop plans for a major transportation corridor in Montford, the state's most affluent county. After nine months of arduous work and compromise, the committee agreed on an approach; but because Blake felt that it was not in keeping with his own ideas, he managed to convince state officials to turn down the citizens' proposal. The members of the committee felt angry and betrayed. Last month, after a disastrous meeting in the county in which Blake tried to sell his own plan, the chairman of the county council wrote the governor asking him to prohibit Blake from ever showing his face in the county again. Meanwhile, the transportation problems in Montford worsen by the day.

Torquemada, the notorious agent of the Spanish Inquisition, is now reviled—but at the time, he and his king thought they were the agents of righteousness. Although their actions are less bloody than Torquemada's, some government officials today take a similar approach, leaving in their wake citizens who feel victimized by very smart people armed with computer printouts. Learning how to build consensus in matters of public policy takes skill, patience . . . and humility. When a leader loses the public's trust, as Blake did, knowledge and vision can be casualties of the conflict.

The Frank Sinatra Syndrome

The county comptroller, Ted Dow, delegated his deputy, Teresa Richman, to represent the finance department at committee meetings that were to decide critical issues of fiscal policy. She was briefed on her boss's goals and told to represent his position, but she was not given authority to make decisions. Richman communicated the gist of the discussions to her boss, but since Dow was not present at the meetings, it was hard for him to appreciate the differing points of view that were presented. As Dow refused to modify his original position or give Richman any leeway to make decisions, the committee members became increasingly annoyed with Richman. She kept playing for time, but Dow would not move or even take sufficient time to discuss the issues with her. Eventually the committee disbanded, and the necessary decisions were made by the county executive. Richman's reputation and that of the comptroller were both tarnished, and they were not asked to participate in the next round of talks.

Frank Sinatra's paean to independence—*My Way*—may work in song, but government decision makers are Lone Rangers only at their peril. Surrendering control may be a terrifying experience, but many negotiations fail because those who have been sent to the table don't have the authority needed to close the deal. A leader who chooses not to be directly involved is deprived of the opportunity to hear all the information necessary to make a wise decision. (Sometimes an incomplete transfer of ownership is a kind of malign avoidance—an attempt to get one's way through an intermediary, then to disown the result if it doesn't turn out right.)

The John Osborne Syndrome

After days of negotiation and after reaching agreement on several points, Jim Mather was considering the offer from Prudence Winship, the president of Acme Supply. Mather, head of purchasing for Central City, had sued Acme for overcharging and failure to deliver quality goods. Because of what he perceived as years of unethical dealing, Mather flat-out hated Winship. Their negotiations had been sparked by many angry exchanges, but they finally seemed to be closing in on the numbers. After a pause, Mather flushed, leaned forward, and put his face close up to Winship's. Then he burst out with "You so-and-so, I want to see you pay for your slimy tactics and then be barred from ever doing business anywhere!"

Two years later, a court awarded the city the same amount that Acme had offered, but the city had spent 60% of that sum on legal fees. Winship was off to another job, Acme had merged with another supplier, and Mather was still angry.

John Osborne wrote the play *Look Back in Anger*. The inability to let go of past hurts—real or imagined—can lead to a perpetuation of the pain. Revenge is an expensive indulgence. Sometimes the anger between parties hangs on so long that they don't even realize that conditions have changed and that they, too, may have been tempered by experience and time. Successful mediation or negotiation often involves reducing the anger so that the logic can begin to flow and people can assess what is best for them and move on.

The Shah of Iran Syndrome (or, "Position Is Everything")

The Shah learned the hard way that position isn't always what it's cracked up to be. Neither is "position" very powerful when it defines a fixed stance in a negotiation, leading a party to cling to a "want" that may not reflect or satisfy a real "need."

The systems analyst is explaining why he wants $10,000 compensation for racial discrimination: others have received promotions and rewards that were due to him. He cites one instance in which he was transferred to another division, not of his choosing, while a less experienced white employee is still working at his old location.

His former boss is baffled by the charges; he explains that the employee who is working in the analyst's old office is a temporary taking care of minor details until the operation shuts down. The boss asks for more proof of discrimination; the analyst keeps insisting that he wants money and justice.

The mediator notices a slight break in the analyst's voice when he describes the offhand, casual way he was told about his transfer. A bit later on, in a private session, the mediator asks, "Tell me—if you had been told in a different way, would you be here making these charges now?" The man snaps back: "Of course not." The mediator uses that information to focus on the real needs behind the claim.

One-half hour later, the boss apologizes for the casual way he treated the employee and agrees to recommend a monetary award for distinguished service and an official commendation. The analyst drops the charges.

Someone once said that hell is a place where no one knows what their real needs are. In this case, the analyst wanted a safe place to vent his anger but could not articulate his real need: to feel appreciated and valued for his work. The manager learned a bit about himself and the importance of paying attention to the needs of others, especially in times of organizational stress. In a dispute, "positioning" sometimes masks uncertainty about a need with a veneer of assurance and insistence. Mediators, managers, counselors, and friends can try to see beneath that veneer.

The Tunney-Dempsey (Math Anxiety) Syndrome

Beyond the memory of most people is the story of the first Tunney-Dempsey fight, where a "long count" enabled Tunney to recover and upset Dempsey for the world's heavyweight championship.

The negotiating teams had been working for months on talks with the sanitation department and its union. The sticking points were the cost-of-living increase and the increasing cost of the health plan. After a costly one-month strike, these items are finally agreed upon; all the parties were weary and anxious to end the negotiations.

When work resumed the following week, disturbances broke out at the incinerator and dump sites because union and management had different views about when the work shift started under the new agreement. It seems that although new working hours were agreed upon, the exact time that the shift began had not been defined or calculated. Management felt that there should be no overlap in pay as one shift dressed and was transported to the yards to relieve the previous shift. The workers felt otherwise. There were two more weeks of sporadic wildcatting before the details were worked out.

The most masterfully run mediation or negotiation in the world still requires somebody who can count. Yet it is surprising how often the Tunney-Dempsey Syndrome causes people to transfer responsibility for "counting" or to give it less attention than it deserves.

(By the way, this is the *eighth* syndrome—a testament to the author's dislike of detailed counting.)

Remedies

There is no single "cure" for these syndromes, but there are ways of combatting them. When you observe that a party to a conflict is exhibiting symptoms of one or more syndromes, the first step is to recognize that he or she is "stuck" and needs some assistance; the second step is to try to remedy the situation through "counterillusionary" devices, through training, or through administrative remedies.

Counterillusionary devices

1. Confront the illusion, without naming it as such. Encourage some reality testing by describing examples that reflect an opposite point of view. Demonstrate that other approaches have been used successfully to deal with similar problems.
2. Use indirect questions, such as "Tell me more about why you think this claim is worth 10 million dollars."
3. Work to create the widest range of possible options for settlement and carefully evaluate the social, psychological, administrative, and monetary costs of each. Discuss the illusory notions of absolute power on the one hand and utter powerlessness on the other.
4. Discuss the importance of maintaining and improving future relationships among the disputants and others affected by the controversy.
5. Validate the legitimacy of feelings that may be keeping people tied to a syndrome, and move on from there.
6. Keep bringing the future back into the discussions.
7. As Ury and Brett suggest in *Getting Past No*, invite yourself or the other party "to the balcony" for a more objective look at the situation and a moderation of the emotional factor.
8. Use experts that are acceptable to both parties.
9. If you get "stuck" on anything, let it be optimism.

Training remedies

1. Make "every manager a mediator" your goal. Though they may not be officially anointed as such, ensuring that managers develop the skills that mediators possess would prevent many minor disputes from escalating into major ones.
2. Improve communication skills. Though it's a standard part of mediators' training, this can stand by itself as a remedy for some syndromes. An important part of the training is an increased awareness of patterns and styles in the way that individuals deal with conflict. Listening skills, the clear expression of facts and feelings, and the development of various questioning approaches should also be included. Finally, encourage the use of language that is healing rather than abrasive, empathetic rather than judgmental, and efficient rather than rambling.
3. Develop problem-solving skills through structured, analytic approaches as well as nonstructured (creative) approaches.
4. Build facilitation skills in your organization so that more people feel comfortable taking responsibility for an efficient, effective, and nonthreatening way of managing meetings and small group processes.
5. Train to increase awareness of the value of diversity. Take care, however, to avoid trainers who are judgmental and try to impose values.

Administrative remedies

1. Establish ground rules for the way a particular negotiation (or meeting, mediation, hearing, arbitration) will be run. Get agreement on them and use them to reduce disruptions and dysfunctional behaviors. Include in the rules an understanding of the decision-making authority of participants.
2. Establish a scheduled, regular self-examination for individuals and the organization to examine the quality of relationships, e.g., to consider "ticking bombs" and attend to decaying alliances. This could be part of an annual strategic or tactical planning process.
3. Establish a thorough recordkeeping and analysis process for personnel issues. Turnover and absentee information, gender and racial statistics, employee satisfaction surveys, managerial performance, and comparisons with other government bodies are all important factors to consider in unraveling a problematic pattern of employee relations.
4. To achieve the most comprehensive view of possible solutions and their effects, form problem-solving teams with as diverse a population as possible. Diversity of skills, experience, race,

gender, position, economic status, and values should be weighed prior to the formation of committee and groups.

Conclusion

The syndromes discussed here do not serve us well. They inhibit the progress of rational solutions, the legitimization of emotions, and the ability to deal with conflicts arising from the rapid pace of change in today's workplace. But they need not become lingering diseases if they are anticipated, prepared for, recognized, and dealt with.

1. This concept is borrowed from Charles Bethel of the Multi-Door Program in the D.C. Superior Court, Washington, D.C.

PART 3

Making the Most of Meetings

Ground Rules for Effective Groups

Roger M. Schwarz

Why is it that some groups are able to tackle difficult tasks, pull together, and solve problems in a way that makes their groups effective, while other groups are overcome by their tasks even though their members have the necessary technical skills and are highly motivated? One reason is that some groups have an effective set of ground rules—implicit or explicit—that guides their behavior. When members follow these ground rules, they are better able to communicate, handle conflict, solve problems, and make decisions.

In this article, I describe a set of sixteen ground rules that groups can use to work more effectively. I explain why they work and, using specific examples, illustrate how to use them. A group can benefit from these ground rules to the extent that (1) it is responsible for solving problems, (2) it deals with complex or nonroutine problems, (3) each member is treated as making an important contribution, (4) group decisions require the commitment of every member to be effectively implemented, (5) the group meets regularly, and (6) the group has sufficient time to solve problems. Groups for which the ground rules are appropriate include management teams, participants in regular staff meetings, and task forces. With some modifications, they also are appropriate for elected or appointed boards.

Although these ground rules can help a group become more effective, they are not a panacea. The ground rules neither replace the struggles of group development, reduce the risks of openness,

Reprinted from *Popular Government* 54, no. 4 (1989): 25–30. Reprinted by permission of the Institute of Government, The University of North Carolina at Chapel Hill.

nor overcome the lack of trust that often prevents groups from using them in the first place. Using the ground rules will not ensure that members will agree with each other, but it will increase the likelihood that conflicts between members will be constructive. Finally, the ground rules are not a quick solution. Although they are easy to understand, they are difficult to implement. To use them effectively, a group must practice them regularly over time.

The ground rules are based on three values: valid information, free and informed choice, and internal commitment.[1] To solve problems effectively a group must have *valid information*. Maximizing valid information means that members share all information relevant to an issue. In addition, they share the information in a way that enables other members to determine for themselves whether the information is valid. The second value, *free and informed choice*, requires that members make choices based on valid information and that they can define their own objectives and the methods for achieving those objectives. And the third value, *internal commitment* to the decisions, means that members feel personally responsible for the decisions the group makes. Each member is committed to the decision because it is intrinsically satisfying, not because there are rewards or penalties leading him or her to be committed, as in the case of "external" commitment.

The three values reinforce one another. Members require valid information to make an informed choice. When members make free choices, they are more likely to be internally committed to those choices. When members are internally committed to decisions, they are more likely to monitor the decisions to see that they are implemented effectively. This, in combination with the ability to make free choices, leads members to seek more valid information.[2]

The ground rules

Just as the ground rules are based on three reinforcing values, they also are supported by each other and work together. To fully appreciate this, think about how each ground rule reinforces the others.[3]

Share all relevant information.   This ground rule means that each member tells the group all the information he or she has that will affect how the group solves a problem or makes a decision. The sharing ensures that members have a common base of information, and it includes sharing information that does not support your position. For example, imagine that the group is deciding whether to institute flexible working hours in the department. You want very much to have flexible working hours but think that it may require more careful coordination of scheduling. You also know that if others knew of the increased difficulty, they might not be as supportive of the idea. Here, sharing all relevant information means telling the group about the possibility of increased scheduling difficulties, even though the information may reduce the chances that flexible hours will be established. One indicator of whether members are sharing all relevant information is if they are sharing information that does not support their positions.

Be specific: Use examples.   Specific examples use directly observable behaviors to describe people, places, things, or events. Unlike general statements, specific examples maximize valid information because they enable other members to determine whether the examples are valid. For example, if Bob makes the general statement to the group, "I think some of us are not doing their share of the work," other members cannot determine whether the statement is valid. Members cannot observe who "some of us" are; neither can they directly observe whether some are "not doing their share of the work." In contrast, if Bob states specifically, "Sam and Joe, you did not complete and distribute your section of the report," other members can determine whether the statement is valid by directly observing whether Sam's and Joe's section of the report is complete and whether they distributed it.

Explain the reasons behind your statements, questions, and actions.   This ground rule simply means telling others why you are doing what you are doing. It is part of sharing all relevant information. For example, if you ask the group for statistics on the number of days that people are late to work, you might say, "I am asking for this information because it will give me a better idea of how flexible working hours may have an effect on tardiness and absenteeism." Explaining your reasoning helps people interpret your behavior correctly and reduces the chances of people assuming or inferring things that may or may not be true. I will discuss this further in the section on testing assumptions and inferences.

Focus on interests, not positions.[4]   Focusing on interests enables members to share relevant information so that they can solve problems in a way that enables all members to be internally committed to the solutions. To make decisions to which all members are internally committed, members must find a solution that meets everyone's interests. The most effective way to do this is for members to start by identifying their own interests. Unfortunately, many groups start by talking about solutions or positions. For example, if the group is trying to solve the problem of when to meet, one member may start by saying, "I suggest we meet every other

Monday at 7:30 A.M." Another may respond, "My position is that we should meet the second day of each month."

A person takes a position because it meets his or her interests: a person's position is simply that person's interests combined in a way that can be implemented. For example, the person who suggested meeting every other Monday at 7:30 A.M. was interested in meeting early in the morning before work began to pile up on her desk. The person who wanted to meet the second day of each month was interested in meeting immediately after a relevant biweekly computer report became available.

The problem with starting with positions is that people's positions are often in conflict even when their interests are compatible. This occurs because people tend to offer their positions after they have provided for their own interests, but before they have included the other members' interests. In the meeting example, each member's solution was rejected by the other because it failed to meet the other's interests. However, had each member been aware of the other's interests, either one could have offered a solution that satisfied both.

To focus on interests rather than positions, start by asking each member to list the criteria that must be met in order for him or her to accept any solution. For example, if a group were to buy a car, one member might be interested in a car that can hold all six group members. Another might be interested in a car that uses fuel efficiently, while a third member might be interested in a car that has a good repair record. Notice that none of these interests specifies a particular car (position). If a member states a position (such as "I want to buy a Chevy"), point that out and then say something like, "What interests do you have that lead you to favor that position?"

Eventually, when every member has stated his or her interests and the group has agreed to use them, members can begin to generate solutions or positions. In the car example, solutions would be the names of specific cars. When a member offers a solution, it helps to point out how that solution meets the interests on which the group agreed. In this way, the group is assured that there will be consensus about the solution.

Keep the discussion focused.   Focusing the discussion means ensuring that members are discussing relevant issues, everyone is focused on the same issue, and everyone fully understands the issue. Sometimes a group spends time discussing issues that are irrelevant to its task. To get a group refocused on relevant issues, it helps to identify how the group got off the track: "We began this discussion talking about workloads, and now we are talking about

NORTH CHICAGO
PUBLIC LIBRARY

photocopiers. I think we have gotten off the track; do others agree?"

Other times group members are focused on different issues. To get everyone in the group focused on the same discussion, it helps to identify the various issues that people have raised: "I think we are talking about different things. It sounds like Leslie and Debra are talking about the problem of coordinating different schedules, but Nancy and Hank are talking about how it will affect the amount of work we can accomplish. Do other people agree that we are talking about different things?" If other members agree, ask which topic would be best to talk about first.

One particularly crucial time when members need to be focused on the same issue is when the group is defining the problem on which they will work. If various members believe they are solving different problems, the group will not accomplish its task.

Keeping the discussion focused also means discussing an issue until all members understand it. This ensures that every member will have the same information and will be able to make an informed choice. If even one person does not understand something, the group needs to discuss it until it is clear to everyone in the group.

Don't take cheap shots or otherwise distract the group.   At some time, almost everyone has been the target of a cheap shot— a witty or snide remark that insults someone. In addition to the fact that cheap shots make people feel bad and do not help the group, there is a very practical reason for not using them. After someone is the target of an insult, he or she usually spends some time thinking about the comment—wondering why the comment was made, being angry, or thinking about clever comebacks to use later in the meeting. In any event, the person usually is distracted from the group's conversation. When distracted, he or she cannot participate in identifying and solving the problem being discussed. As a result, the person may later withhold his or her consent.

When everyone's full participation is needed, members cannot afford to distract each other. In general, members should not engage in any behavior—such as sidebar conversations or private jokes—that distracts the group from its task.

It is all right to disagree openly with any member of the group.   Disagreeing openly increases the amount of valid information. Sometimes the group membership makes it difficult for some members to disagree with others. For example, a member whose supervisor (or whose supervisor's supervisor) is also a member of the group may find it difficult to disagree with him or her. Sometimes groups are made up of subgroups, and members of one subgroup are reluctant to disagree with each other in front of another subgroup. For example, managers may be reluctant to disagree with each other in front of employees.

It is all right to discuss undiscussable issues.   Every group has what are called undiscussable issues. These are issues that are relevant to the group's task but that members believe they cannot discuss openly in the group without some negative consequences. Some examples include members not performing adequately, mem-

---

Helping boards work

Many of us who are involved in conflict resolution work also serve on boards, task forces, or other working groups. These roles constantly challenge our ability to apply the techniques we teach and words we preach to our own peacemaking and conflict resolution organizations.The goal of this article is to provide a useful tool for improving the work of boards and other decision-making bodies.

Using consensus.   The word "consensus" comes from the Latin *consentire*, meaning to feel with or perceive with. It may also come from *concinere*, meaning to sing or make harmony together. Many nonprofit organizations choose consensus as their decision-making method, which they understand to mean that decisions are made when all agree to them, rather than by majority vote. What is often lacking, however, is a thorough discussion within the group about what to do if it does not reach consensus.

  In discussing the meaning of consensus, the group needs to decide whether it will use "pure" consensus, with no alternative method for decision making, or "modified" consensus, with a fallback method (such as voting or executive decision) in place. Both can work; what is critical is that the group be clear about which method it is using *before* it begins a decision-making process. It is also useful to define precisely the circumstances under which the fallback method will be used (e.g., the time limit is reached, for minor spending decisions). Where a hierarchical fallback process is in place it is important for the person in charge to convey clearly when the group has control of the decision making and when s/he has the final word.

Straw-poll consensus.   Consensus-based groups often "talk an issue to death" as they struggle for unity. The following "straw-poll" system is a method for keeping the consensus process streamlined. The process is this: After the board has had sufficient time for discussion about a particular topic, the chair asks each member to hold up fingers showing where s/he is on the levels of consensus scale shown below. If a quick scan of the room suggests all 1s or 2s, the group can quickly see that consensus has been reached. This process

---

bers not trusting one another, and members being reluctant to disagree with superiors who are also group members. Unfortunately, because these issues often raise feelings of mistrust, inadequacy, and defensiveness, members usually deal with the issues either by not talking about them at all or by talking about them outside the group with people they trust. However, such issues are usually critical for the group to resolve, and as long as they remain undiscussable the group's performance may suffer. In order for the group

---

shortcuts extra discussion or speech giving. If there are those indicating 3s, 4s, 5s, and 6s, further discussion will be needed to reach unity.

No matter what the straw poll shows, it is a good idea to ask if there is need for further comments or discussion. The caution with such a system is that when even one person is not in unity with the decision, the group needs to take the time to listen to and consider what the person has to say. Then the group needs to decide whether the decision making will be delayed to a later time to give more chance for reflection, research, etc., whether it will continue working right then to find a solution that will be mutually agreeable, or whether it will use its fallback decision-making method.

To reiterate, the purpose of this method is to shorten the time needed to reach consensus and to give everyone a voice, not to compromise the careful listening, reflection, respect, and trust that must accompany the use of consensus. One final note: Considerable time is often spent trying to bring everybody to a 1 or 2 level of consensus. Often, when the decision is a noncritical one, it is workable to have a few people at 3 and even 4. Probably one would want higher levels of consensus on decisions affecting the fundamental character of a program.

The levels of consensus

1. I can say an unqualified "yes" to the decision. I am satisfied that the decision is an expression of the wisdom of the group.
2. I find the decision perfectly acceptable.
3. I can live with the decision; I'm not especially enthusiastic about it.
4. I do not fully agree with the decision and need to register my view about it. However, I do not choose to block the decision. I am willing to support the decision because I trust the wisdom of the group.
5. I do not agree with the decision and feel the need to stand in the way of this decision being accepted.
6. I feel that we have no clear sense of unity in the group. We need to do more work before consensus can be reached.

Source: Dee Kelsey, "Helping Boards Work," *Conflict Resolution Notes* 8, no. 3 (1991): 43–44. Reprinted by permission.

to maximize valid information and allow members to make free and informed choices, members need to make undiscussable issues discussable within the group. One way to achieve this is to show that undiscussable issues can be discussed: "I realize what I'm about to say may be considered an undiscussable issue, but I think we can be a more effective group if we deal with this issue." Group members also can explore their concerns about discussing these issues without actually discussing the issues themselves. If members can be assured that their fears will not be realized, they will be more willing to talk openly about these matters. Finally, once the group successfully discusses one undiscussable issue, members may find it easier to deal with others.

Share appropriate information with nongroup members.   To be successful, a group must work well internally and must work well with people outside the group with whom they are interdependent. Working effectively with nongroup members includes continually sharing information with and seeking information from those whose work affects and is affected by the group. Consequently, the group must decide what information is appropriate to share with various nongroup members and how to share it.

Make statements; then invite comments about the statements.   Making statements and then inviting comments about them means expressing your point of view (making sure to explain your reasons) and then asking others whether they agree or disagree. For example, you might say, "I think it would help to give department heads their own budgets to work within, so that their accountability will be commensurate with their responsibility. But, some of you may feel differently. I'd like to hear what each of you thinks about my idea, even if you disagree."

Inviting others to comment on your statements encourages them to question and challenge your ideas and helps turn the discussion into a dialogue rather than a series of unrelated monologues. The discussion that results enables the group to determine the validity of the ideas and enables each member to make an informed choice. It may seem counterproductive to encourage disagreement, yet reaching a decision to which all members will be committed requires that members identify their disagreements and resolve them.

Test assumptions and inferences.   When you assume something, you consider it to be true without verifying it. When you infer something, you draw conclusions from things people say. Imagine, for example, that Bob, the group's chairperson, observes that Hank, although very productive, has considerably more work than any other group member. To lighten Hank's workload, Bob begins transferring some of Hank's work to other members. One day, when Bob tells Hank he will no longer have to prepare a certain report, Hank replies, "Is there anything else I'm doing that you don't like?"

Bob had assumed Hank would know why he was trying to lighten his workload, and Hank had incorrectly inferred that Bob was dissatisfied with his work. Furthermore, Hank did not test his inference with Bob and thus could not find out that it was incorrect. Consequently, Hank became angry at Bob unnecessarily.

Testing assumptions and inferences enables members to get valid information to make informed choices. If you are going to react to someone or make a decision based on something you inferred, make sure that you test whether your inference is correct. In this case Hank could have said, "When you started removing some of my duties, I inferred that you were dissatisfied with my performance. Am I correct?"

Agree on what important words mean.   This ground rule is an extension of "Be specific: Use examples." When members unintentionally agree or disagree with each other, it is often because the same word means different things to them. For example, imagine that a group decides to make decisions by consensus. However, to some members *consensus* means general agreement, while to others it means unanimous agreement. The first time the group makes a decision that has general but not unanimous support, it will discover that it had not agreed on the meaning of consensus.

One way to determine whether all group members are using a word to mean the same thing is to ask them the first time the word is used. You might say something like, "You used the word *consensus*. To me consensus means unanimous agreement and not general agreement; is that what consensus means to you?" Notice that in describing what a word means to you, it helps also to describe what it does not mean.

Jointly design ways of testing disagreements and solutions.   Imagine that the group is discussing whether the organization responds quickly enough to citizen complaints. Diane believes that citizens are getting timely responses, but Kate disagrees. Normally in disagreements like this, each person tries to convince the other that he or she is wrong. Diane will offer all her evidence to support her position, and Kate will do the same for her own position. Each may doubt the other's evidence, and neither will offer evidence to weaken her own position. Even when the disagreement is over and won, the "loser" is still likely to believe she is right.

If Diane and Kate jointly designed a way of testing their disagreement, it would work like this: Once the two realized that they disagreed, one would suggest that they work together to discover the "real facts." To do so, each would have to be willing to accept the possibility that her information may be inaccurate. Then they would jointly develop a method to test out which facts are real. The method would include jointly agreeing on whom to speak with, what questions to ask them, what statistical data to consider relevant, and how to collect the data. For example, they might agree to speak with several employees, to talk with a sample of callers from past weeks, and to review an agreed-upon number of written complaints. Diane and Kate might also agree to speak jointly to each of these people, so that both can hear the same conversation. Whatever method they use, it is critical that both agree to it and agree to use the information that comes from it. Once Diane and Kate have collected their information, they should discuss it together and reach a joint decision about the real facts.

One important question to ask when jointly testing disagreements is, "How is it possible that we are both correct?" Often members have different sets of facts because they are talking about different times, places, or people. In this example, both Diane and Kate could have been correct; calls from citizens could have been responded to in a timely way in some units but not in others.

By jointly resolving disagreements, members are more likely to be internally committed to the outcome because they freely agreed to the test.

All members are expected to participate in all phases of the process. This ground rule means simply that each member's participation is essential for the group to work effectively. Because each member has a different position in the organization, he or she will likely have different experiences and views about how to solve problems. In order for the group to benefit most from these different views, everyone must contribute to the extent that he or she has relevant information to share.

Make decisions by consensus. Making decisions by consensus is the heart of the ground rules. Consensus means that everyone in the group freely agrees with the decision and will support it. If even one person cannot agree with a proposed decision, then the group does not have consensus.

Consensus ensures that each member's choices will be free choices and that each will be internally committed to those choices. Consensus decision making equalizes the distribution of power in the group because every member's concerns must be addressed and his or her support is required in order to reach a decision. For example, if a member needs to understand more about an issue, the member can withhold consent until he or she understands the issue. Reaching consensus usually takes more time than voting because it is hard work to find a decision or solution that everyone fully supports. But because people are internally committed to them, in the long run decisions made by consensus usually take less time to implement successfully and encounter less resistance.

When the group thinks it is about to reach consensus, one member should state the decision under consideration, and then each member should say whether he or she consents. This avoids the mistake of assuming that silence means consent. Voting is not allowed in consensus decision making, but the group can take straw polls to see whether it is close to consensus and to see which members still have concerns about the proposed decision. To reach consensus, members must agree without feeling pressured by the group.

Consensus should be used throughout the time a group is solving a problem, not just at the end, when members are selecting the best alternative. Each time that the group is about to move to the next step of the problem-solving process, it should get consensus.

Individuals are often reluctant to use this ground rule because, in their experience, groups rarely are able to reach consensus and because they fear that key decisions will not be made. However, the reason many groups are unable to reach consensus is because they do not have an effective set of ground rules; following the other ground rules in this article will increase the chances that a group will reach consensus. It is important to remember that these ground rules are most appropriate when the full group must support the decision in order for it to be implemented effectively. Under this condition, the alternative to reaching consensus is to make a decision that will not be effectively implemented.

Do self-critiques.   For a group to become more effective over time, it must have some way to systematically incorporate its successes and learn from its mistakes. Self-critiques provide a way to do this. This is how they work: Before the end of each meeting, the group asks itself three questions:

1. What ground rules did we use well?
2. What ground rules do we need to improve on?
3. Exactly what will we do differently next time?

For the critique to be helpful, when answering each of the questions, members must be very specific and give examples (which itself is a ground rule). For example, John might say, "I think Debra helped the group focus on interests, not positions, when she asked Bob what interests led him to oppose flexible working hours. Do others agree?" A general comment like "I think we all could do a better job of staying focused" does not help the group identify exactly how the group lost its focus.

Giving someone negative feedback can be difficult, but it is easier if you give it in a way that is consistent with the ground rules, such as making your statement and then inviting people to disagree with you. If members keep in mind that the purpose of the self-critique is to improve the group's performance, that also makes it easier to give negative feedback.

One way to conduct effective self-critiques while reducing the amount of negative feedback that members give each other is for each member to identify ground rules that he or she has used well or poorly during the meeting. After each member has taken responsibility for assessing his or her own performance, members can then give each other feedback.

Because self-critiques can be uncomfortable and because groups are often pressed for time, sometimes groups do not conduct them. Ultimately, however, the only way a group can systematically improve its performance is to learn from its own experiences continually—by doing self-critiques.

Putting the ground rules to use

For these ground rules to be helpful, everyone in the group must understand them, agree on what they mean, and commit to using them. One way to achieve this is to ask members of the group to read this article, discuss it in the group, and then decide whether they want to use this set of ground rules. Because the ground rules are based on valid information and free and informed choice, group members should agree to use the ground rules only after they have considered them carefully.

Often I am asked whether it is possible to use only a subset of these ground rules.[5] Because each of the sixteen ground rules supports the others, removing one reduces the degree to which the group will be able to maximize valid information, free and informed choice, and internal commitment. Nevertheless, it is probably more effective to use some of the ground rules than to use none. Because valid information is necessary not only for internal commitment and free and informed choice but also for each of the ground rules, groups seeking to use a subset should, at a minimum, adopt those designed to maximize valid information.

Although these ground rules are relevant for a wide range of groups, they are not exhaustive. Some groups may find a need for additional ground rules to help them accomplish their particular tasks.

Once the group has agreed to use these (or other) ground rules, it must develop a way to ensure their use. This requires that the list of ground rules be visible to members when they are meeting as a group. A poster-sized list can be hung up in the group's meeting room or each member can receive a pocket-sized list. Whatever the method, members should agree to refer to the ground rules during the meeting when they are trying to use them. For example, one member might say, "Beth, I want to test out an inference I made from your statement," or "Tim, what is your interest behind that position?" By explicitly referring to the ground rules, members are better able to evaluate how well they are using them. Finally, toward the end of each meeting, the group should do a self-critique (described above). This will help the members identify how well they have used the ground rules and where they need to improve.

Getting members to use the sixteen ground rules consistently is a difficult task. It will take numerous meetings before members develop the skills required by the ground rules. Old groups that have worked together before without using these ground rules may already have an implicit set of ineffective ground rules that conflicts with the new ones. In this case, the group may have to identify its implicit, ineffective ground rules and agree to replace them with the new set. Ultimately, the more the group openly discusses how it is using the ground rules, the sooner its effectiveness can increase.

Using these ground rules may require taking risks, to the extent that members of the group distrust one another. Specifically, members will have to risk sharing information that they fear may be used against them. To reduce (but not eliminate) this risk, group members—especially superiors in the group—can agree not to do so. In addition, the group also can decide that if a member believes he or she has had information used against him or her, that issue can be discussed in the group. To build trust, ultimately members must be willing to take these risks.

1. Chris Argyris and D. A. Schön. *Theory in Practice: Increasing Professional Effectiveness* (San Francisco: Jossey-Bass, 1974).
2. Argyris and Schön, *Theory in Practice.*
3. Ground rules 1, 3, 8, 10, 11, and 13 are based on Chris Argyris, *Reasoning, Learning, and Action* (San Francisco: Jossey-Bass, 1982).
4. This ground rule is based on Roger Fisher and William Ury, *Getting to Yes* (New York: Penguin Books, 1982).

5. In some cases people want to omit one or more of these ground rules because they think that the rules and other rules the group follows are mutually exclusive. For example, some groups (such as elected bodies) have bylaws that require decisions to be made by voting, which the groups consider mutually exclusive with consensus. However, groups can attempt to reach consensus even if, ultimately, they must decide by a vote.

The Samoan Circle: A Group Process for Discussing Controversial Subjects

Lorenz Aggens

Public officials or agency staff often need to hear from concerned publics about their problems, needs, fears, and values before a decision is made on an issue of controversy in the community. People with opposing views will often fill a large meeting room, their mood charged with emotion. Many people in the room may hope to influence the decision by their cheers or booing. Because each person is likely to get only one chance to speak, statements may have been written out for reading, or some especially articulate person will have been chosen to speak for a group of citizens. That responsibility, and the size and temperament of the audience, promotes oration by speakers and the use of words more designed to stir emotions than to share personal opinions and feelings about the subject at issue.

The person responsible for conducting such a meeting usually feels great personal stress over the need to "control" the meeting and ensure that the discussion is equitable and moderate. In attempting to be "in charge" while being fair and neutral, the person presiding over the meeting will often use tactics that will be seen as capricious or arbitrary by those vying for special recognition and influence. It was after just such a meeting that the idea of the Samoan Circle was born.

Adapted from *Public Involvement Techniques: A Reader of Ten Years' Experience at the Institute for Water Resources*, prepared by James Creighton, Jerry Delli Priscoli, and C. Mark Denning (Fort Belvoir, VA: Institute for Water Resources, Army Corps of Engineers, 1983), 271–77. The article was originally entitled "The Samoan Circle: A Small Group Process for Discussing Controversial Subjects." Used by permission of INVOLVE: Lorenz Aggens and Associates, 1915 Highland Avenue, Wilmette, IL 60091.

The Samoan Circle meeting process is designed to facilitate the discussion of controversial issues when there is a large group of people interested in the topic.[1] Its principal value is in the opportunity it affords for an exploration and exchange of knowledge and opinion where the large size of the group, or an environment of controversy, might disable other kinds of meetings. This meeting process is also useful when the possibility exists that no one person could be accepted as a fair moderator by all who might seek to be involved in the discussion.

The process does not resolve conflict. It is intended for the fullest possible exchange of information about an issue in anticipation of other group processes better designed for decision making or conflict management. However, some users of the Samoan Circle have experienced the spontaneous resolution of conflicting views and agreement on actions required—apparently as a result of the contestants in a controversy having heard one another for the first time. It is not recommended, however, that users of this process anticipate this result.

Other types of meetings should be used when the organization that has called the meeting wants to present information to those in attendance, or when the sponsoring organization is likely to be required to answer a lot of questions or defend itself or its propositions to all others present at the meeting.

The most notable characteristic of the Samoan Circle is that there is no one who is the chairman, or moderator, or facilitator. It is a leaderless meeting. Responsibility for discipline in this kind of meeting is vested in everyone, rather than in meeting leaders. Everyone has, and will quickly see that he or she has, a clear stake and part in maintaining an orderly environment for discussion.

Room arrangements

As many chairs as seem needed for the meeting should be set up in concentric circles, with the inner circle big enough in diameter to allow for a round table with five chairs. (The 60″ round table commonly used in hotel banquets is ideal. Five chairs provide space for what many researchers feel is the optimum size group for discussions.) There should be enough space around the central table and five chairs for people to walk around them without having to climb over the legs of those sitting in the first circle of seats. Four or more aisles should be left open to permit people to move easily from seats in the concentric circles to seats at the center table. For large groups, a microphone should be placed on the center table to ensure that discussion across this table can be heard easily by everyone in the room—but it is destructive to the group dynamic intended if this microphone is handed around the table as each person takes a turn talking. People at the center table should be talking to one another, personally, at close range. They should not be coming to the center table only to gain access to the microphone in order to whip up enthusiasm among allies in the audience. An omnidirectional microphone (taped down, if necessary) in the center of the table should be used—but only when this is made absolutely necessary by the size of the group. (See Figure 1.)

Starting the meeting

After the group has been called to order by the person who will begin and end the meeting, it should be stated that the purpose of the meeting is to learn from one another as much as is possible about the topic that is at issue in the community—including facts, problems, obstacles, needs, values, solution ingredients, suggestions for improvement, and new ideas. Representatives of the two or three sides that may be contesting the issue could share in this

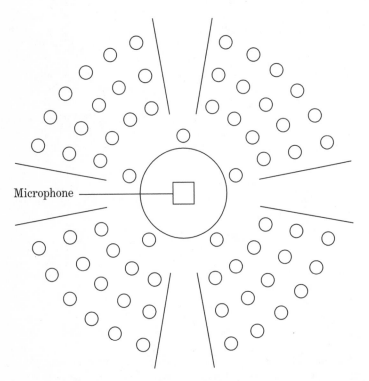

Figure 1. Room arrangement for the Samoan Circle.

introduction in an effort to strengthen the realization that the meeting process is not a contrivance or manipulation of one side by the other. Here is a sample of the words used on one occasion to launch this kind of meeting:

[After statement of purpose] We hope that we can learn from one another by sharing our views—freely, openly, and candidly. To make this possible in a short period of time, we would like to use a meeting process that overcomes a number of the problems you may have experienced in having a productive and orderly discussion in a large group. This meeting process may be new to you, but it is easy to understand. It is designed to run on the energy of your knowledge and opinions. It will be guided by your interests, and moderated or disciplined by your commitment to democratic principles. The success of this meeting will not depend upon the parliamentary skills or leadership of a chairman or moderator—it will depend upon your willingness to participate, to share, and to use differences of opinion as stepping stones to new ideas and solutions, rather than as stumbling blocks to progress. All meetings have rules. Here are the rules for this one:

1. Anyone may participate by making a statement, asking a question, answering a question, taking exception to or confirming another person's opinion, making a rebuttal, and so on. But to do any of these things, the person who wants to say something must come to this center table and take a seat. Once there, he or she may interrupt, or wait for an opening in any discussion that is going on. The person taking a seat can join in the discussion or try to change its direction, or raise a new topic.
2. The discussion at any one time is limited to the five people who can be seated at this table. If you come to the table, you may stay as long as you feel you have a contribution to make to the discussion. You may leave and return again as often as you wish. If there are no vacant seats at the table and you want to get in on the discussion, stand near the table until someone gives up a seat. The more people there are standing near the table waiting for seats, the more this should signal those sitting in the discussion to evaluate their own need to continue to participate. If you want to talk to one of the people at the table, stand directly behind that person's chair as a signal to the others at the table that you want one of their seats.
3. If you want to cheer, or groan, or make any other noises to represent your opinion, please come to the table, take a seat here, and then do it. Once I leave this table, I will be bound by these same rules. The discussion will go on until there is no one left at the table, or until the time for adjournment arrives.

If there are no other questions, we can begin the discussion.

It is helpful, after the instructions are given, to have one or two people who have previously agreed to "break the nice" come to the center table and begin the discussion. The first person at the table, or anyone who is left alone at the table, is in fact talking to everyone in the room, and this may be a bit awkward for some people. Once a second person comes to the table, the discussion becomes a more personal conversation, and the theater-in-the-round condition disappears.

People from the organization that called the meeting should not assume any privilege in communicating that is not afforded to other participants. If a question is asked that the organization should answer, a representative of the organization should move to the table and respond from there. When the answer has been delivered, the representative should move back to the audience seats. If the meeting needs some redirection or the process needs clarification, the person "in charge"—the one who made the opening comments—should seek a seat at the table to make this statement.

Meeting dynamics

Once there are two or more people involved in the discussion, the talk takes on the "you-and-I" character of communication at short range. The oratory and belligerence that are common when "discussion" is taking place across the width of a 30-foot room lessens when people of different persuasions close the physical distance between them. Discussion across the round table is usually (but not always) more relaxed, temperate, conversational, and instructive. If people feel the need to assault one another over their convictions, oceans of space will not prevent this.

When all the seats at the table are filled and a person comes to the center to wait for a vacancy to develop, it is not uncommon for everyone at the table to stand up and leave. The sense of self-discipline invoked by this unchaired meeting process is very strong in most groups. On the other hand, when no one comes to the center table to wait for a vacancy, those sitting at the table feel free to expand their discussion and register their opinions and feelings several times. Sponsors of this meeting process usually have to suppress the inclination to rush into such situations and shut off a talkative person, or suggest, in the name of equity, that others might want to be heard. If and when such actions are needed, plenty of time should be given for the group to make its own interruption of a monologue, or to show its need for more participant involvement by individual actions to accomplish this. Any guidance from meeting sponsors should be given by someone who takes a seat at the table to express that need as a personal opinion.

Meeting records and evaluations

A number of things can be added to the meeting process to make a record of transactions and to achieve some degree of "closure" that points to further action. Comments can be transcribed and the process used as a form of public hearing. (However, this meeting format seems inappropriate when formal written statements are being read into the record.) Minutes can be kept. Decision makers can be identified as auditors scattered throughout the audience. Comments can be written on newsprint on a wall. This can be done as a sequential list of opinions stated, or as a series of categorized lists—such as "advantages" and "disadvantages"; or "strengths of the proposal" and "suggestions for improvement in the proposal."

At the end of the meeting, time might be left for everyone in attendance to scan the newsprint listing of comments and to leave behind some kind of ballot that would give the sponsoring organization some indication of how people felt who did not participate in the discussion. Those present might be asked to turn in sheets of paper or file cards on which they indicated the points they strongly agreed with and those they strongly disagreed with. They might pick the five or ten items that they felt were the most important statements of the problem, need, objective, or other answer to the question that had been discussed—and even rank these in order of importance.

Ending the meeting

Discussion can be allowed to run its course if there is no time required for adjournment. The meeting room will gradually empty until there may be no more people left except for an intensely interested group at the center table. If time limits or the need to move on to another agenda topic requires the ending of the discussion before everyone has left the center table, a number of things can be done. Someone who is responsible for the time limits can take a seat at the table, call attention to the disappearing time, and remind the group of the agreed-upon time for ending the meeting. This often causes a flurry of activity by people who have been holding back but who are still intent upon getting their point of view heard. An announcement of the need to close the discussion should be made early enough to accommodate this last-minute rush.

When the time to end the meeting is about five to ten minutes away, the person who started the meeting can move to the table, wait for a seat to be vacated if none is already empty, and withdraw that chair. Continuing to stand near the table, the "meeting-ender" can withdraw each chair as it is vacated. This action is frequently acknowledged by the audience with understanding chuckles and, sometimes, by a last-minute rush. The message "I need to end this meeting" is clear and nonthreatening; but the person ending the meeting should avoid cutting off last-minute participants from at least some chance at expression unless this is absolutely necessary and the need is obvious to all concerned. If any concluding comments are needed, these can be made when the person ending the meeting takes possession of the last chair.

The Samoan Circle has been used successfully by a variety of public agencies and private organizations in meetings with as many as 400 persons in attendance and as few as a dozen. Satisfaction with the meeting process seems to be related to a recognition by meeting sponsors and participants that it provided an environment for discussion of a controversial subject where other, more conventional meeting processes had failed them in the past. In using this process, sponsors have modified it to fit peculiar circumstances, or to make it "feel" better to the personalities involved. Reports of these organizations on their use of the Samoan Circle have contributed to a better understanding of the process and to its description for others' use.

1. The group process described in this article may have originated in the Pacific islands, although not necessarily in Samoa. The process was dubbed "Samoan Circle" by staff of the Northeastern Illinois Planning Commission, and the name has continued to be associated with the process.

Designing and Conducting Public Meetings

James L. Creighton

Selecting a meeting format

There are numerous alternative formats for public meetings. Appropriate format depends on: (1) the purpose of the meeting, (2) the size of the audience expected, (3) the level of interaction needed between participants, (4) familiarity with meeting formats, and (5) credibility of your organization on this issue.

The purpose of the meeting. Selection of a format will depend upon what is to be accomplished during the meeting. Some of the reasons for public meetings are

- To provide information to the public
- To seek views, preferences, or ideas from the public
- To encourage interaction between groups
- To obtain agreements on ways of dealing with issues.

If the purpose of a meeting is to inform the public, then a large general meeting may be entirely appropriate. But if the purpose is to try to get agreement, a large public meeting is probably ineffective. A workshop, or some other form of meeting providing for substantial interaction, is much more likely to result in an agreement. The point is, the format of the meeting should reflect the purpose of the meeting.

The size of the audience. Another major factor in selecting a meeting format is the size of the audience. If an audience is very large, it becomes cumbersome to use small group processes. If the

Adapted from Chapter 20 of *Public Participation Manual* (Washington, D.C.: Program for Community Problem Solving). Reprinted with permission. Sponsored by six national organizations, including ICMA, the Program for Community Problem Solving seeks to help communities develop a civic culture that nurtures and supports inclusive and collaborative decision making processes. It serves as a clearinghouse for information on written resources, consultants, success stories, and technical assistance.

audience is broken up into small groups, for example, the logistics
of providing flip charts, meeting rooms, etc. for all the small groups
becomes very complex.

Level of interaction needed. The level of interaction required
depends both on the purpose of the meeting and the level of interest of the participants. Some tasks require discussion between people and groups, e.g., to get agreements. Meetings designed for these
purposes always require a high level of interaction. People who are
very interested in a topic will probably be willing to use a structured process or other meeting format that encourages participation. If people are only moderately interested in the topic, a more
passive format may be appropriate.

Familiarity with meeting formats. If people have participated
previously in meetings where small group processes were used successfully, they will be more comfortable in using this kind of format
again. Otherwise there may be discomfort with unorthodox meeting
formats.

Credibility. Whenever a meeting format is used that is new or
different, the willingness to accept that format may depend on the
motives the public attributes to the staff for selecting that format.
If people are suspicious that a new format is being proposed to
"control" them or "divide and conquer," they will resist that format.

Options for public meeting formats

Among the most common meeting formats are the following:

Public hearing. A public hearing is a large group meeting during
which people make prepared statements. Normally there is little
interaction among speakers, or between speakers and the people
conducting the meeting. Often there is a court reporter or some
other formal system of recording comments. Extensive experience
with hearings shows that they are not a particularly effective form
of public participation, so they should be used primarily to meet
legal requirements or to sum up following other forms of
participation.

Public meeting. The term *public meeting* is often used for large
meetings in which the procedures are more informal than in a public
hearing, permitting somewhat more interaction. The term is also
used as an umbrella for all types of meetings.

 A variant of the public meeting is the "town meeting." Originally the term was used for an annual decision-making meeting,
with issues resolved by majority vote. In current practice, the term

is used for a large meeting for discussion of any topic of concern—not just a single, pre-announced topic—but without the voting.

General guidelines for designing and conducting large public meetings are provided later in this article.

Briefing/question-and-answer. A briefing/question-and-answer meeting is primarily designed to get information out to the public, rather than to listen to public comment. The meeting usually starts with a quick "briefing" (a presentation by staff or experts), followed by questions from the audience. This could be followed by public comment, if desired.

Panel roundtable. One way of promoting interaction, while basically using a large-group format, is to select a panel of individuals representing differing points of view to discuss an issue. This could be followed by questions or comments from the audience, or small group discussions.

Preparation checklist

Here are some key tasks to accomplish in setting up a meeting:
- Define the purpose of the meeting—what needs to be communicated to the public, what information is needed from the public.
- Talk with leaders of key interests and other potential participants to get a good understanding of the level of interest in the issue and the attitude toward the meeting.
- Prepare a meeting format and agenda; if the topic is controversial, review it with leaders of the different interests.
- Select location, time, and date.
- Publicize the meeting (invitations, press releases, newspaper notices, advertising, feature stories in the press).
- Prepare a background statement for the media so they have accurate information prior to the meeting.
- Advertise the meeting at least two to three weeks before, on the day before, and on the day of the meeting.
- Ensure proper arrangements for seating, public address system, refreshments, access to the hall, projection screens, table for slide projector, displays, wall maps and charts, and the printing of agendas and other handouts.

If using visual aids, be sure they are big enough and clear enough for the room size. Remember, simplicity is the key in any graphics. You can always explain anything related to the graphics; however, it is easy to turn off an audience totally if they can't see or understand your graphic presentation.

Large group/small group.   Even if the number of participants is large, it is still possible to break the meeting down into small discussion or work groups to increase interaction. Often each group is given an assignment or task to complete, then reports are given to the large group by spokespersons selected in the small groups.

Samoan Circle.   The Samoan Circle is one form of large group/small group meeting. It is designed to permit the kind of interaction that only occurs in small groups, but witnessed by a larger group. The meeting room is set up with an inner circle of 5 to 6 chairs. The rest of the chairs are set up in surrounding outer circles. Initially everybody is seated in the outer circle. Anybody who wants to speak must move to the inner circle. Once people have had their say, they return to their original seat. If all the seats in the inner circle are full, people who want to speak stand behind the chairs in the inner circle and wait for a chair to empty.

Workshops.   Workshops are highly interactive meetings, usually designed for a group of 25 people or less. Frequently, workshops involve a specific task, such as developing or ranking alternatives. More information on workshop design is provided later in the article, as it is a particularly effective participation technique.

Open houses.   Open houses are held in a facility that can accommodate displays or models, as well as a large crowd of people. Participants are invited to come at any time during a set period of time. Participants can examine the displays or models, chat with staff, form discussion groups, or just interact informally. People come and go at will. The open house could also be followed by a more formal public meeting. Additional guidelines for conducting open houses are provided later in this article.

Coffee klatch.   A coffee klatch is a small meeting in a private home, usually with coffee and cookies served. Because these meetings are informal and in a private home, participants are likely to discuss issues in a personal manner, rather than as official representatives of interests.

Seating arrangements[1]

Seating arrangements are a direct reflection of the type of meeting to be held and the relationship among participants. For example, seating agency staff at the front of the room, with the audience in rows, establishes a relationship in which all participants talk to the meeting leaders at the front of the room, rather than to each other. This is appropriate for information giving, but not for interaction among participants. As is the case with the selection of a meeting format, the selection of a seating arrangement depends on the purpose of the meeting.

Information giving.   In this function the agency is communicating information to the public. Information could include the nature of the study, the issues which have been identified by the agency, the available alternatives or the plan selected by the agency. Since information must flow from the agency to all the various publics, it is appropriate to have a meeting format which primarily allows for presentations from the agency with questions or responses related to that information or requests for additional information. This means that the classic meeting with one person at the front of the room making a presentation to an audience in rows—which is a suitable and efficient method for communicating information—may be a suitable format for this function.

Information receiving.   In this case the public possesses the information, which could include public perceptions of needs, problems, values, impacts, or reactions to alternatives. When the agency needs to acquire information held by the public, opportunities must be provided for the maximum number of people to provide information to the agency. This criterion is not met when only one person can speak at a time addressing the entire audience. As a result there may be a need to consider breaking the audience into smaller groups so that comments may be collected on flip charts, or to utilize techniques in which each participant can provide information on 3 × 5 cards (as in the Nominal Group Process technique), or to employ any other method that allows for the maximum number of people to be providing information at the same time. To serve this function it is not absolutely necessary that opportunities be provided for discussion or interaction unless that discussion and interaction is necessary to generate new information.

Interaction.   While interaction clearly involves both information giving and information receiving, it serves the additional purpose of allowing people to test their ideas on the agency or other publics and possibly to come to modify their viewpoint as a result of the interaction. With this function it is not the initial information given or received which is critical as much as the process of testing, validating and changing one's ideas as a result of interaction with other people.

Interaction by its very nature requires that an audience be broken down into groups small enough so that there is time and opportunity for individuals to exchange information and ideas and discuss them all thoroughly. This usually means either that meetings are limited in size such as a coffee klatch or advisory committee meeting, or that any larger meeting is broken down into small groups during the period in which this function is being met. There is no way that a large public meeting will provide anything more than minimal opportunities for interaction.

Consensus forming/negotiation.   A step beyond interaction is to begin to move toward common agreements. Interaction alone may not ensure any form of agreement, but in consensus forming/negotiation the interaction is directed toward agreement on a single plan by all of the critical publics.

Like interaction, consensus forming/negotiation also requires intense interaction and therefore must be accomplished in some form of small group. In addition, the requirement for consensus formation usually means that some procedure is utilized which assists the group in working toward a single, agreed-upon plan rather than allowing for simply an open discussion with no specific product.

Summarizing.   This is the need at the end of a long process to publicly acknowledge the agreements that have been reached and reiterate the positions of the different groups toward these agreements. This function is required both to give visibility to the entire decision-making process which has taken place and to form a kind of closure now that the process is ending.

It may again be suitable to use large public meetings as a means to serve the summarizing function. In this way individuals and groups can be seen taking positions and describing their involvement in the planning process which has preceded this meeting. This does not, however, automatically mean that a public hearing is the appropriate form of meeting to serve this function, as there are many creative and less formal means by which a visible summary may occur without the legalistic procedures of a formal hearing.

Matching the function to the seating plan.   The seating arrangements shown in Figures 1 and 2 are both suitable arrangements for large audiences and are particularly suited for information giving. They may also be suitable for information receiving or the summarizing function.

The optimal seating arrangement for interaction and for consensus forming/negotiation is the circular arrangement shown in Figure 3. Since it is usually difficult to obtain individual tables and desks, the next most frequent seating arrangement that is still appropriate for interaction and consensus formation is the seating arrangement shown in Figure 4. The critical features of these two seating arrangements is that eye contact can be established and maintained by all participants with each other, and that the physical

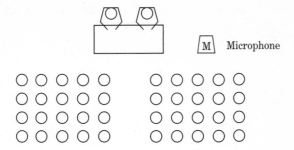

[M] Microphone

Figure 1. Seating arrangement for a large audience.

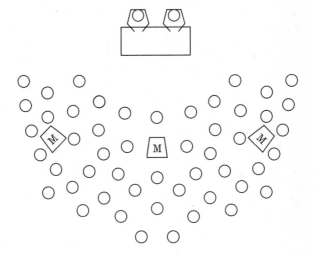

Figure 2. Alternative seating arrangement for a large audience.

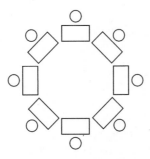

Figure 3. Seating arrangement for interaction and consensus forming/negotiation.

distance between the participants is not too great. Since it is not always possible to get the trapezoidal tables shown in Figure 4, an alternative seating arrangement which accomplishes the same purpose although leaving some gaps between participants is the configuration using rectangular tables shown in Figure 5.

Any of these configurations (which are essentially variations on a circle) have an upper limit of approximately 25 to 30 participants before the physical distance from one end of the circle to the other is so great that communication becomes constrained and unnatural. There are, however, seating arrangements which will allow for up to 100 participants in a seating configuration that still clearly communicates that the purpose of the meeting is interaction between

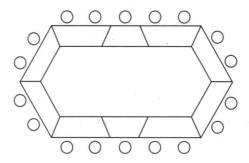

Figure 4. Alternative seating arrangement for consensus forming/negotiation.

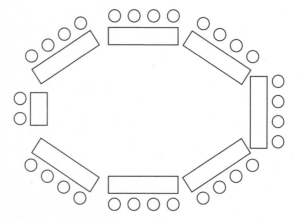

Figure 5. Seating arrangement for consensus forming/negotiation when trapezoidal tables are unavailable.

the participants. Figure 6 shows such a seating arrangement. While the number of participants is greatly increased by this room arrangement, it remains clear that the purpose of the arrangement is to encourage communication between the participants rather than simply between the participants and the agency leaders.

When an agency wishes to combine both an information-giving function and an interaction function, then the room arrangement shown in Figure 7 may be suitable. If the facility in which you are meeting does not permit for both functions in the same room, then it might be worthwhile to consider holding meetings in schools, where it is possible to hold the main session in the auditorium and break the participants into small discussion groups to be held in individual classrooms.

An alternative format, which can be used when participants will be working in small discussion groups, but there is still some need for the agency to supply information to all the participants, is the banquet format shown in Figure 8. A banquet seating arrangement is a natural arrangement for a large group/small group meeting. People can turn to hear the opening presentation, then turn back to the people at their tables as the group with whom they will communicate. This means that the assignment to tables must create a random mix of people at each table, so that groups have a mix of opinions.

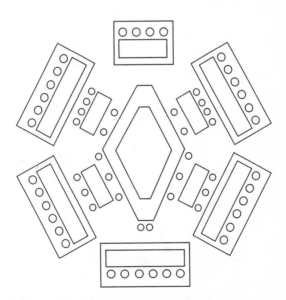

Figure 6. Seating arrangement for large-group interaction.

Time and place of meetings

Meetings should be held at a time and place convenient to the public, with the convenience of staff a secondary consideration. Usually this means that meetings will be held in the evenings, although meetings to be attended primarily by representatives of government entities or organized groups may be more convenient during the day.

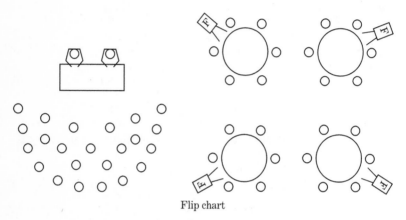

Flip chart

Figure 7. Seating arrangement combining information-giving and interaction functions.

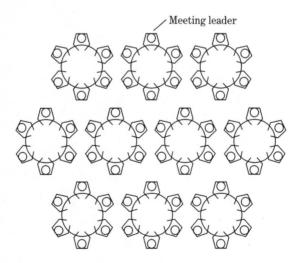

Meeting leader

Figure 8. Seating arrangement for information giving and small group discussions.

One of the first considerations in selecting a meeting place is whether the facility can accommodate the desired meeting format and seating arrangement. Depending on the circumstance there may be times when it is more appropriate to meet away from agency facilities, on "neutral" ground. Other factors to consider in selecting a meeting place include:

- Location of the facility (central or outlying)
- Public transportation access
- Space for parking
- Safety of the area
- Handicapped access.

Guidelines for leading meetings

The manner in which meetings are led is a major factor in their effectiveness. An ineffective leader can cause the public to believe that the meeting was poorly run and a waste of time, while an autocratic leader can create resentment and antagonism toward the agency or government.

Conducting a public meeting is an art. It requires a balance between openness to meeting the needs of participants and firmness in pursuing the agreed-upon agenda. If there is strong public concern over issues, the chairperson may be held in suspicion or openly challenged. An effective leader is one who is flexible enough to change formal meetings rules when appropriate, to accept comments from the audience even though they may be emotionally laden, and to convey enthusiasm, sincerity and commitment to the public participation process.

Here are some guidelines for preparing to chair a meeting:

- Check out the agenda with participants before starting (remain open to altering the agenda).
- Limit speakers only when necessary to give fair time to others.
- Never put down or ridicule a speaker who has annoyed or challenged you (courtesy is always necessary, especially when limiting a speaker or ruling a topic out of order).
- When soliciting comments, look around the room systematically and leave enough time for hesitant people to come forward before moving on.
- Treat all points of view as valid, and do not editorialize on what people present (you are a facilitator, not a judge).
- If people seem uncomfortable with the way things are going, ask for comments and deal with them directly. Sometimes a "straw vote" helps clarify how an audience feels about an issue. For example, you may ask, "How many people feel we will need some time limits?"

In many organizations, the tradition is that the highest-ranking official leads the meeting. The advantage of this is that the public likes to know that its comments are being heard by someone high up in government. In addition, many top executives have good presence in front of an audience. The disadvantage is that it is harder for a top official to appear neutral. He or she may instead—under pressure—make commitments that should not be made. Also, antagonistic groups are more likely to try to use an attack against a high-ranking official as a way of undermining the government's position. One alternative is to have the highest-ranking official open the meeting, say a few words of welcome, then turn the meeting over to a moderator or facilitator. This makes it very clear that management is at the meeting to hear the public's comments, but the chair's role is to establish and maintain a structure that works in everybody's interests, and is not just a role bestowed by virtue of rank. If a manager is particularly skilled at leading meetings, though, the skills may compensate for the risks of having the top manager up in front of the meeting. On the other hand, managers sometimes have a grandiose image of their meeting skills, since it may be hard for their subordinates to provide negative feedback.

Guidelines for designing and conducting large meetings

Normally—except where legally required—the formal procedures of a public hearing should be avoided. The more formal the procedures are, the more people either feel intimidated by the procedures and will not speak, or feel resentful at having to "play the game by the government's rules."

Just because a meeting begins with a large audience does not mean that it has to stay that way. Depending on the purpose of the meeting, it may be possible to break a large audience down into small work groups which either present brief verbal summaries at the end of the meeting, or hand in written reports. This approach can be effective if the purpose of the meeting is to collect information from the public, such as problem identification. If the topic of the meeting is very controversial, though, people may resist being broken up into small groups, viewing this as an effort to "divide and conquer." Under these circumstances, people may want to hear how everybody feels, and efforts to use sophisticated meeting designs may be seen as an effort to manipulate the public.

If working groups are used, these general rules apply:

- Each subgroup should have a prepared agenda or assigned task.
- Each subgroup should have a facilitator and recorder who know the task of the group, even if the facilitator and recorder are people chosen from within the group.

- The subgroups should report their results to the main meeting, so the underlying principle of openness is not violated.

If a meeting is extremely controversial, it may be appropriate to meet with leaders of the various interests several weeks in advance to discuss the meeting format. If the key actors have been consulted, it is harder for groups to claim later that they have been slighted or ignored.

When going into a large meeting where strong antagonism is anticipated, there will be a need to set ground rules for participation. Examples include time limits on speakers, the order in which speakers will be heard, and limits on the topics to be discussed. In a large meeting, a ground rule such as a five-minute time limit may be necessary to guarantee everybody a chance to speak; but it may

---

Principles of effective meeting leadership

The participants "own" the meeting. The fundamental premise of effective meeting leadership is that of democracy itself: all power derives from the consent of the governed. Put another way: people accept meeting leadership because it is in their interest to do so. To accomplish anything in a meeting there must be some structure. Limits need to be set on topics, procedures must be established for recognition of speakers, and so forth. As long as the leader provides this structure in a manner that the participants consider equitable and reasonable, it is in their interest to cooperate. If challenged, the leader will usually be supported by the rest of the audience. However, if the structure is not considered equitable or reasonable, the leader's power is diminished and is subject to challenge. In contentious settings, the meeting leader may need to request consent for the agenda and ground rules from the participants as the first order of business.

Lead the process, not the content. The meeting leader should concentrate on providing an equitable meeting process and avoid assuming the role of an advocate or participant by commenting on the content of the meeting. If the agency needs someone to be the "expert" on the topic being discussed, this should be someone other than the meeting leader.

Avoid power symbols. Large numbers of experts, thousands of dollars of displays, or costly maps and graphics all communicate that government and the people leading the meeting are more important than the public. This can breed resentment and antagonism.

be challenged by an organized group in an effort to win advantage for their position. The chair of the meeting should explain the ground rules to the meeting participants and then give the reasons for using them.

One of the disadvantages of large public meetings is that only a limited number of those present actually speak. The result is that the feelings of a number of attendees are never known. This problem can be minimized by providing a response form or hand-in workbook to everybody who attends a meeting, inviting their written comments. While not everybody will hand in a written comment, a significant percentage will, increasing your sense of confidence that the feelings and concerns of the total audience have been identified.

If the audience size is not too large, consider keeping a summary of comments on flip chart paper, posted on the wall. Even if the audience is too big to see the comments as they are written, they can review them on the wall afterwards. The value of recording on flip charts is that people can see that their comments were received. Also, it's easy to have the flip chart sheets typed up as a record of the meeting.

Guidelines for conducting workshops

Workshops are usually small meetings which are designed so that participants actually perform assigned tasks, generating a group "product." Some uses of the workshop format could include:

- Selecting a public participation program from among various options
- Reviewing a plan, or developing a single, mutually acceptable plan
- Defining issues or problems, possibly determining rank order
- Developing alternative solutions to a specific problem
- Reviewing the operational results of a plan that has been implemented
- Presenting a technical study and reviewing its implications
- Identifying the scope of a study
- Developing a list of the critical impacts that must be considered in evaluating alternatives.

Workshops are particularly useful when dealing with complex topics because they provide time for detailed consideration and a high level of interaction.

The number of participants in a workshop depends on your situation. As a general rule—and this doesn't apply only to workshops—the optimum number of participants for an effective meeting is 5 to 7 people. However, the need to have all interests represented usually means that most workshops will have as many as 20 to 25 participants. Even with larger numbers, however, some people may feel excluded. Two methods which can be used to prevent this problem are

- *Repeat meetings.* A workshop format can be developed which can be repeated as often as necessary, allowing opportunities for everyone who wishes to participate to go through the same experience.
- *Daytime meeting/evening meeting.* One approach to the problem of people feeling excluded is to conduct the workshop during the day, followed by an evening meeting at which everybody gets a chance to review the product generated during the day.

The following steps are useful in designing a workshop or other interactive meeting:

1. *Identify the desired product.* Identify precisely what the product is that should result from the meeting, such as a set of alternatives, a list of impacts to be evaluated, and so forth.
2. *Identify the resource information the public will need.* Identify information the participants will need in order to complete the desired product. This information should be written in simple, understandable language and presented in a format which makes it easy to find and grasp, so that the least amount of meeting time is spent locating needed information. This material might be incorporated into a small workbook which contains group or team assignments, exercise instructions, resource materials, and any hand-in response forms.
3. *Select or design a series of activities which will result in the desired product.* In some cases, there may be previously used meeting formats which will result in the desired product. If not, design a set of activities which will produce the needed materials. The usual technique is to write simple, clear instructions for group activities and give the groups substantial responsibility for both how the activity is completed and the product which is produced. The series of activities could incorporate small group processes such as brainstorming or nominal group process (discussed below).
4. *Design a simple mechanism for evaluating the product.* Once participants have worked together, they still need to evaluate what they have accomplished or to place some priority on what they think is most significant. Without an opportunity to evaluate, participants may feel restricted by the meeting format or feel that all points covered during the meeting are receiving equal weight. This evaluation mechanism could be a hand-in

response form, a straw vote, or a weighted vote to establish priorities.

Using structured small group processes

There are a number of small group processes which can improve group effectiveness in one way or another. Two of the most frequently used small group techniques are brainstorming and nominal group process.

Brainstorming. Brainstorming is a technique for increasing the number and creativity of ideas expressed in a group. In brainstorming, everyone in the group is encouraged to come up with as many ideas as possible, including "way-out" ones. Usually these ideas are recorded on a flip chart or blackboard. No evaluation is permitted until everybody is completely out of ideas. Brainstorming provides a "psychologically safe" climate in which people feel free to participate without fear of being judged, and this helps groups "break out" of the obvious solutions and push for more creative ones. It also greatly increases the number of solutions generated. While brainstorming may effectively generate a large number of ideas or alternatives in a hurry, other techniques must be used for evaluation.

There are also more "advanced" versions of brainstorming in which additional techniques are employed, using different types of analogies to increase group creativity.

Nominal group process. Nominal group process is a technique to help groups generate and prioritize a large number of ideas. It has also been successfully used for consensus formation. The nominal group process is based on research suggesting that people generate more ideas working by themselves, but in the presence of others.

The procedure for nominal group process is as follows:

1. *Opening presentation.* After an initial presentation describing the nominal group process, the audience is broken into small groups of 6 to 9 participants.
2. *Discussion leader and recorder.* Each group is assigned a discussion leader and a recorder. Prior to the meeting, these staff people will have put up a minimum of four sheets of newsprint, and also have ready a supply of felt-tip pens, scratch pads, pencils, and index cards.
3. *Introductions.* The discussion leader will introduce himself/herself and invite everyone in the group to do the same.

4. *Posing the question.* The discussion leader will then present the question to be answered. It will be carefully worded in order to draw out the specific information desired. The question will be written at the top of one of the flip chart sheets.
5. *Generating ideas.* Participants are provided with paper and asked to write down all the answers they can think of to the questions posed. These notes are for their own use only and will not be collected.
6. *Recording ideas.* Each person is then asked in turn for one idea. The idea will be summarized by the recorder on the newsprint, as accurately as possible. No discussion is permitted, except that people may suggest alternative wording to the recorder. The discussion leader will keep going around the room, one idea per person, until the group is out of ideas. Anyone can say "pass" without giving up his or her turn on the next round. The process continues until everyone is "passing." Participants are not limited to the ideas they have written down but can share new ideas that have been triggered by others' ideas. Alphabetize the items on the list: A–Z, AA–ZZ, etc.
7. *Discussion.* Time is then allowed for discussion of each item, beginning at the top of the list. The discussion should be aimed toward understanding each idea, its importance, and its weaknesses. While people may criticize an idea, it is important that they simply make their points and not get into an extended argument. Move rapidly through the list, as there is always a tendency to take too long on the first half of the list, not leaving enough time to do justice to the second half. This activity usually takes a minimum of about forty minutes, and can be permitted to take considerably more time if desired.
8. *Selecting favored ideas.* Each person then picks the ideas that he or she thinks are best. Instructions should be given to select a specific number, such as the best five, or the best eight. These ideas should be written on index cards, one idea per card. Participants may prefer just to write the letter of the item on the list (A, F, BB, etc.) or a brief summary, so that they do not have to write out the entire idea.
9. *Ranking favored ideas.* Participants then arrange their cards in preferential order, with the ones they like the most at the top. If they have been asked to select eight ideas, then they put an "8" on the most favored idea, and number on down to a "1" for their least favored idea among the eight selected.
10. *Scoring.* A score sheet should then be posted which contains a list of all the alphabet letters used on the lists of ideas. Then the participants call off the items they selected, and the points assigned to each, e.g., "G—eight points, L—seven points, A—

six points," etc. When all the scores have been shared, tally the score for each letter of the alphabet. The highest-scoring item receives the number one ranking, and so forth. Post the rankings for the top 5 to 10 ideas, depending on where a natural break occurs between high scores and low scores.

11. *Discussion of results.* The participants may then want to discuss the results. Depending on the time remaining in the meeting, this discussion may be brief or lengthy.

12. *Reminder of subsequent analysis.* Participants should be reminded that staff will conduct a detailed analysis of all items, not just the ones receiving high ranking. Depending on the decision-making process, they should also be reminded that this analysis could result in a considerable change in the ranking of items.

Designing and conducting open houses

An open house might be used instead of a public meeting as a consultative technique. Some public participation practitioners feel that it can be more constructive than a public meeting. A great number and diversity of interested people can obtain information and register their views in an informal and relaxed manner.

An open house is designed to follow 7 to 10 days after a publication has provided people with the basic information on the subject and an opportunity to reply with little effort. This could be a display advertisement or tabloid insert in the local newspaper with a tear-off coupon; or it could be a brochure, distributed by householder mail, with a prepaid reply postcard.

During the period following the publication, people have an opportunity to follow media coverage of the issues, discuss the issues with neighbors, and become more prepared to make the best use of the open house.

During an open house, citizens can drop in at a central facility during announced hours to view displays, ask questions, or discuss issues with staff. The open house is usually located in a building such as a library, school or church, and runs from 2 to 9 p.m. so that it is accessible to mothers with small children, teenagers returning from school, and adults, before or after supper. Visitors may come at any time and stay for as long as they like.

A series of display panels, arranged on easels in a rough circle, presents the purpose of the project, the study team, various aspects of the issues, evaluation criteria, alternative solutions, etc. Often a diagram on one panel is followed by a short text explanation on the next so the visitor can obtain a grasp of the whole project without being led by the hand through the display. An automatic slide presentation with a 3- to 5-minute cycle is useful to present visual aspects of the subject. Don't provide chairs, because that will inhibit the desired flow.

A table with handout material is usually provided. Coffee and doughnuts or sandwiches may be available. The primary characteristic of an open house is a free-flowing conversation directed by the visitors. People can come whenever they wish, stay as long as they wish, and address any topics that interest them in any order they choose. In many cases, individual problems can not only be raised but actually resolved. For example, someone with questions about how a proposed action affects his or her individual property can get an answer.

An open house can be effectively combined with a public meeting or other activities. For example, an all-day open house might be followed by a public meeting held the same evening. The open house would provide information to the public, then in the evening the public could give reactions back to the agency.

A variation on the open house is to invite interest groups to set up booths, so that citizens can walk around the room and get a sampling of the opinions of all the major actors. In several cases, the open house has even been expanded into a "fair," with recreational and social activities as part of the program, along with food and beverages.

The systematic gathering of informed public response is a vital feature of the open house. Staff, wearing name tags which also indicate their subject matter expertise, carry pads on which they record individual comments, concerns, questions and suggestions. Where staff cannot provide immediate answers, they note the name, address and phone number for later follow-up. Visitors are most appreciative when staff undertake to refer to the relevant organizations questions or concerns which are not part of their project.

While an open house is free to enter, visitors must "pay" to get out—by completing a short response form indicating reactions to the issues raised during the open house. This generates quantitative data such as weights on evaluative factors or ranking of alternatives. Background data obtained, such as geographic location or occupation, enables crosstabulation.

Staffing can usually be lighter during the day than in the evening. It is important to manage so as to avoid overcrowding.

After one or more open houses, it is important to

1.   Have a debriefing meeting with the staff to obtain their reactions, insights and suggestions.
2.   Analyze the response and make it available (a) to the decision-making group and (b) to the local media in a news release so residents will know the sentiments of the community at large.

3. Provide answers to questions recorded at the open house and forward requests for action to other organizations.

1. Most of the material in this section is adapted from James L. Creighton et al., *Advanced Course: Public Involvement in Water Resources Plan-ning* (Fort Belvoir, VA: U.S. Army Institute for Water Resources, 1977), 245–253.

PART 4

Working with the Public

Solving Community Problems by Consensus

Susan Carpenter

The complexity of today's community issues and the number and diversity of people who expect to participate in making decisions make it difficult for communities to solve problems using only traditional ways of doing business. The days when a handful of people, often from one sector of the community, could determine and implement a solution are gone. When a few decision makers try to sell their solution, the consequences are often no action—or worse, a new round of controversy. As the number of people who expect to have a role in making a decision grows and the complexity of issues increases, so must the range of tools for making decisions.

Ways to handle community issues

A local government manager has several choices when it comes to dealing with a community issue. Below are five common ways to respond to a community problem.

Do it yourself. A manager is paid to make sure things get done. When the demand to do something about a community issue arises, it is quite natural to pull staff together, come up with a reasonable, professional solution and offer the solution to the community. This response is effective as long as no other group in the community has another idea about how the problem should be handled. The do-it-yourself approach is dangerous if the manager needs the support of the community to implement a plan or program.

Reprinted by permission of the Program for Community Problem Solving, Washington, D.C. Adapted from *MIS Report* 21, no. 10 (1989), published by ICMA. Sponsored by six national organizations, including ICMA, the Program for Community Problem Solving seeks to help communities develop a civic culture that nurtures and supports inclusive and collaborative decision making processes. It serves as a clearinghouse for information on written resources, consultants, success stories, and technical assistance.

Stake out a position. Community agencies or organizations are likely to be asked where they stand on a community problem. Groups are frequently pressured into taking positions prematurely before all the issues and all the concerns of citizens are known. Once positions have been taken they become difficult to retract or even modify without losing face.

Set up a committee. Setting up a committee is a common way to address an issue. While most committees have good intentions, membership on conventional committees is often limited to people who are comfortable with one another. Parties who might make others uncomfortable are not included. If public input is sought at all by the conventional committee, it is late in the process, after a draft plan has been crafted. The results of conventional committee efforts are frequently proposals that, at best, receive limited support from the broader community and, at worst, generate conflict.

Consult and decide. Sometimes a manager decides to consult with all major interest groups before making a decision. He or she approaches each group separately, finds out the concerns of each group, and seeks suggestions for ways to address the issue before making a decision about how to proceed. Initially, citizens are pleased to be consulted, and the manager is satisfied that useful information has been gathered and that with it an even better decision can be made.

Much to the manager's surprise, the elegantly crafted solution is rejected by everyone, not because the solution is inherently unreasonable, but because the citizens did not have the benefit of hearing what other groups needed and did not participate directly in developing the solution.

Bring groups together to reach a consensus. A fifth problem-solving option is to identify major groups affected by an issue and bring representatives of those groups together to plan and to participate in a program that seeks a solution using a consensus decision-making process. In a consensus program parties work together to identify issues, to educate each other about their respective concerns, to generate options, and then to reach agreements that all sides can accept. This does not mean that all sides will be equally enthusiastic about a solution; rather, parties will recognize that it is the best solution available.

A successful consensus program can be more work to coordinate than other approaches, but will result in a workable solution that all parties can accept—implementation will not be impeded by a dissatisfied interest group. For example, Atlanta, Georgia, was finding it difficult to balance economic development with the preservation of historical landmarks and culture. Several controversies highlighted the need for a more systematic and consistent approach to resolving historic preservation issues. Representatives from city government, downtown business interests, and preservation advocates formed the Historic Preservation Task Force. The task force recommended a mediated negotiation as a means of resolving the controversies. A team of mediators was brought in to work with the task force to select representatives for a policy steering committee and a resource group. With the help of the resource group, the steering committee examined issues in depth and produced a statement of goals and a general outline for a historic preservation program. Parties then met in plenary sessions, caucus meetings, and working groups to develop a detailed description of Atlanta's new historic preservation program. An implementation strategy was also incorporated into the negotiated text.

Thinking about consensus programs

Consensus programs have a number of distinct advantages, several identifying characteristics, and a variety of goals. There are also times and situations when seeking consensus is appropriate, and times and situations when it is not appropriate.

Advantages of using a consensus program

Education.   A consensus program provides opportunities for parties to learn directly from one another. Education provides the basis for crafting workable and acceptable alternatives.

Better decisions.   Groups that have an opportunity to learn about each others' views and interests can create solutions that reflect the concerns of other parties as well as their own.

Acceptance of the outcome.   Parties that have worked together to understand the issues and have developed solutions using consensus will see the reasoning behind a recommendation or solution. Seldom will they challenge the results of a program.

Faster implementation.   Parties will not block implementation if they understand that a plan reflects their interests. Parties in a consensus program frequently make commitments to participate in the implementation.

Characteristics of a consensus program

Participation is inclusive.   Major parties, including those who disagree, are identified and brought together to discuss an issue and to reach agreements.

Parties are responsible for the success of the program.   Participants accept the responsibility for making the process work. They help plan the program and then continue to offer suggestions to make it effective.

People are kept informed.   Participants seek to keep their own constitutents and the general public informed as a program proceeds.

A common definition of the problem is used.   Parties discuss and agree on a constructive definition of the problem.

Parties educate each other.   In face-to-face sessions, parties spend time educating each other about the history and context of the problem, their perceptions and concerns about issues, and their views of ways to address the problem.

Multiple options are identified.   Participants seek a range of options to satisfy their respective concerns, rather than asserting single positions.

Decisions are made by consensus.   Parties do not vote; rather, they modify options until everyone thinks the best decision has been reached. Voting creates winners and losers. Losers can challenge the outcomes and impede implementation.

Parties are responsible for overseeing the implementation of solutions.   Too often, parties work together to identify solutions and then never see their agreements implemented. Part of an effective process includes parties' identifying methods for implementing solutions and then working together to monitor the implementation.

When to use a consensus process.   Consensus programs are used to enhance the work of existing organizations when broad-based community support is needed for the implementation of solutions. Consensus programs are appropriate ways to address community problems when

- An issue is complex
- Many parties are involved
- No one agency or organization has complete jurisdiction over solutions to the problem
- The issues are negotiable
- Parties are willing to participate.

When not to bring groups together.   Consensus programs are not appropriate for all community issues. It may not be in a community's interest to bring groups together when one or more of the following conditions apply.

The community faces an emergency.   Consensus programs are not used when quick action is required; for instance, when public health or safety is endangered.

The timing is not right.   Consensus programs are not appropriate when relevant information will not be available for several months, an important political election is several months off, or there is not enough time to achieve consensus given mandated deadlines.

A principle is the focus of the problem.   Occasionally a community issue focuses on a basic difference of values. Room for accommodation does not exist. Abortion is one such issue. While the central issue of abortion is not appropriate for a consensus program, factions can discuss acceptable rules for conducting demonstrations and cooperate on family planning education programs.

Legal clarification is needed.   Sometimes a group (a city council or constitutency group) will seek a legal judgment to clarify a rule or regulation before it decides whether to initiate a consensus program.

The community is so polarized that productive face-to-face discussions are not possible.   Occasionally an issue becomes so controversial that parties find it difficult, if not impossible, to work together. While face-to-face meetings may not be effective, shuttle diplomacy between parties by a mediator can help resolve differences.

One or more groups is not willing to participate.   A group may feel it has enough power to select and implement a solution without the assistance of other parties.

The level of concern is not great.   Changing a community's garbage pickup schedule may affect everyone but may not be high on people's list of concerns.

Goals for consensus programs.   Consensus programs can be used to achieve different goals. Three categories of goals for which consensus programs can be used are described here.

Developing community visions and goals.   Communities use consensus programs to bring together participants who reflect the community's diversity and engage them in a process that develops a shared vision and shared goals. For example, Roanoke, Virginia (population 100,600), wanted to develop a visionary plan that would protect neighborhoods while fostering economic development. The goal of Roanoke Vision was to design a comprehensive development plan that (1) revised land development regulations, (2) improved administrative procedures, (3) devised partnership approaches, and (4) determined planning and development actions. A planning team staffed the process, and a 25-member Roanoke Vision Comprehensive Plan Advisory Committee was established. Members were broadly representative of public and private interests. Roanoke's citizens were invited to examine the four areas and develop specific recommendations. An important component of the program was the development of a clearly defined vision for the community's future through the use of facilitated neighborhood meetings and media events, including a telethon-like TV show. In addition to a comprehensive plan, other outcomes of the program included a new set of zoning laws compatible with the plan and the establishment of neighborhood boards to enable each neighborhood to develop its own plan to become part of the comprehensive plan.

Achieving consensus on a public issue.   A community facing a major problem, such as economic stagnation, high unemployment, or siting a needed facility, can use a consensus program.

Resolving a public controversy.   A community embroiled in a controversy can create a consensus program to identify issues, clarify interests, and craft agreements that all sides can support. Litigation used to resolve a community dispute is expensive and time consuming, and frequently addresses procedural issues without resolving basic substantive concerns. Parties find, to their surprise, that a well-structured consensus program can help them back off from stated positions and refocus their discussions on their real interests. The result is workable solutions.

Three ways to structure a program

Consensus programs may be organized in a variety of ways. Three basic models for structuring a program emerged from a study of dozens of effective case examples. They may be described as the committee/task group model, the negotiating team model, and the conference/task group model.

Committee and task groups.   The most commonly used model for structuring a community consensus program is a committee combined with task groups or subcommittees. The committee may have anywhere from 10 to 60 members, and it represents the different interest groups concerned about a problem. The committee agrees on procedures, identifies issues, gathers information, generates options, and develops recommendations or reaches agreements.

Task groups are established by the committee to gather information on specific issues, to identify related concerns, or to develop alternative strategies to solve a problem. Task groups broaden participation and expand the resources available to the program. Task groups can be organized around substantive topics identified by the larger committee, or they can be set up to cover geographic areas, such as neighborhoods. Some programs put together task groups that reflect different roles: decision makers, technical resource people, and the general public. Individuals invited to join a task group contribute their expertise and experience on a specific topic without having to invest the time to participate in the larger program. Task groups report their results to the committee.

The committee may use one set of task groups to help it research information and identify issues to be addressed, and then establish a new set to help it generate solutions; or it may retain the same task groups through an entire program. A committee should be large enough to permit the representation of different groups and small enough to make decisions. For example, Lincoln/Lancaster County, Nebraska (population 210,000), was experiencing a slowed economy and growing polarization among different community groups. The city of Lincoln, the University of Nebraska, and the chamber of commerce jointly sponsored a retreat to introduce the concept of strategic planning to 90 opinion leaders from a broad section of the community. Following the retreat, a 13-member organizing committee was established to develop a strategic planning process for the community. Under the name "StarVenture," a 23-member coordinating committee was selected and charged with

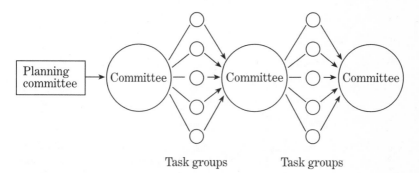

Task groups   Task groups

Figure 1. Committee and task group model.

overseeing the process. The process involved four phases: (1) *Issue identification* to determine what issues citizens felt were important to the quality of life in Lincoln/Lancaster, (2) *research* using task groups to conduct external, internal, and comparative analysis of their community, (3) *strategy selection* to assess possible strategies for feasibility, and (4) *implementation* to review plans, monitor progress and update goals. Twelve specific action strategies were adopted for implementation.

Negotiating teams.   Representatives in a consensus program can be organized into teams. Each team decides on its goals and interests and functions as a unit during problem-solving sessions. Negotiating teams work well when the number of teams is small—three to five is a reasonable number—and when each team has well-defined and compatible interests. Negotiating teams were used by the Kettering Foundation when it developed its Negotiated Investment Strategy to bring federal, state, and local levels of government together to coordinate their investments in communities.

Team members need time before sessions to talk among themselves about how to proceed and time to go back to their respective constituents to report the progress of the discussion and seek input from people not at the table. Negotiating teams can also choose to use smaller working groups to explore an issue in depth or develop

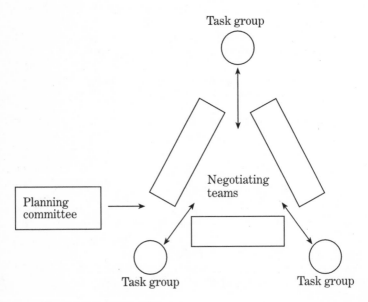

Figure 2. Negotiating team model.

and refine options and iron out differences. Working groups may consist of representatives from the teams, or their membership may be expanded to include non-team individuals.

In Bridgeport, Connecticut (population 366,100), a study placed the problem of unemployment in the community in the context of a thriving state economy that was suffering a substantial worker shortage. The nonprofit organization that conducted the study began exploring the possibility of bringing community representatives together to discuss the study findings and develop responses. An outside facilitator was brought in to help develop representative negotiating teams, to organize overall participation strategies, and to facilitate sessions among teams. Four interest group teams were created representing the city, the business community, the state, and the general public. The teams worked separately and together to identify problems and obstacles to solutions, to generate alternatives, and to create a consensus agreement that included strategies to educate and employ 500 welfare recipients. Implementation roles were specified for each interest group. The business team agreed to dedicate 500 jobs over a three-year period and provide on-the-job support. The state agreed to improve job readiness and ensure that barriers to employment (the lack of support services, such as child care and medical benefits) were removed. The city agreed to join the state in providing education, training, and support services. The community agreed to assist with the provision of services and outreach and to support other groups working with welfare recipients.

Conference and task groups. A third model features a large conference that convenes interested citizens around a community problem, followed by task group work and later by additional conferences. A conference may be open to any citizen or may be attended only by invited citizens. The advantage of a conference model is that it enables many more people to become involved face-to-face in a program. Conferences are a good forum for providing information, identifying issues and concerns, and gathering suggestions for alternative solutions. Conferences are not a good format for reaching consensus agreements. Generally, conferences identify issues that become the basis for organizing working groups. The composition of working groups can be by self-selection, or groups can be formed by a program's steering committee. Working groups report their results to a second conference held usually six to twelve months later. Conference participants discuss working group reports and proposals and then suggest future directions for the program, including the tasks of the same or new working groups. Additional conferences are held as needed.

The conference and task group format was used in Boston's Challenge to Leadership program. The Greater Boston, Massachusetts, area (population 4,500,000) was enjoying economic prosperity, but segments of the population were not benefiting from the general economic and social vitality. Community leaders, led by a prominent religious figure, began discussing these issues and out of their discussions came a request for a community conference. Three hundred and fifty community, business, and government leaders gathered to identify smaller, more workable problems and specific gaps in existing services. From the early stages on, consensus was used to reach agreements. Six priorities were established at the first conference: education, health, housing, strengthening civic virtue, improving public communication, and increasing regional cooperation. Task forces were established to broaden participation and address the six priority areas. At the second conference task forces presented 20 proposals, some of which included specific commitments for action from local organizations. At a third conference task forces reported on the status of existing concerns, identified new issues, and invited volunteers to sign up to work on the new issues. Among the initiatives undertaken as a result of the conferences were a program to build 300 affordable homes by 1989 and an effort to increase available day care by 500 slots. The Metropolitan Area Planning Council panel of experts on information technology was

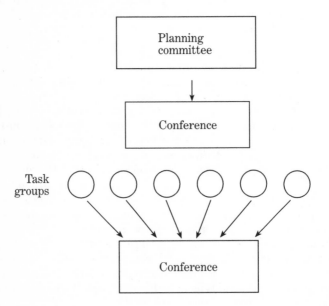

Figure 3. Conference and task group model.

assembled, a directory of minority experts and leaders in the community was created, and a television series was developed to educate people about the needs of the community and encourage volunteerism.

Summary

The call for cooperation is coming from all sectors of society and is being directed toward scores of tough issues facing communities. A community's ability to foster effective cooperation will depend on both its motivation to do so and its skills in bringing diverse groups together to establish common goals and initiatives.

To create a quality program that produces results in a timely fashion, community leaders must pay attention to how a program is structured, who is involved, and how the program is managed. The knowledge and skills needed to design and run an effective community consensus program are important tools for people who are concerned about solving community problems.

A Generic Design for Public Involvement Programs

Desmond M. Connor

Some public programs are designed by the initiative of activist interest groups with the proponents, governmental or corporate, in a reactive mode. In other cases, the threat of a problem leads an agency to issue a news release and sets off a chain reaction of further responses. In either case, the process is haphazard and the outcome very uncertain.

In the course of twenty-one years of full-time professional practice in public involvement and the completion of some 235 projects, I have developed a generic model for public involvement that includes four basic components: social profile, responsive publication, open house, and planning workshop. This article describes those basic components in detail, as well as six additional techniques that can be used to support the four basic components.

Social profile

Rationale. Many projects become controversial because proponents have failed to develop a systematic understanding of the residents of a community or area. A sound social database is the essential foundation for planning and managing subsequent activities. Proponent staff who are newcomers to a community or area obviously need to gather information about its residents. Those who have lived in a community all their lives will invariably perceive it from their own position in the social structure and will automatically have blind spots which can prove fatal.

Reprinted by permission of the author. This article was originally delivered as a paper at the annual conference of the National Association of Environmental Professionals in Raleigh, NC, 26 May 1993.

Methodology. We first review and make a content analysis of non-reactive sources; e.g., the last year of the local weekly newspaper, local histories, aerial photograph series, government reports. This provides initial information on key leaders, active organizations, major issues, attitudes to growth, and knowledge of—and attitudes toward—the proponent and its proposals and communication channels. One day is usually allocated to this work.

We next interview 12 to 15 key informants—people who have long residence, high contacts with parts of the population and secure positions. These include leaders of community groups and business organizations, clergy, government officials, a public health nurse and others. Rather than use a questionnaire, which often keeps out as much information as it gathers, we explore a list of key topics. We consider that we have established reality when we obtain concurrence from three independent sources; i.e., one written and two informants. Elected representatives are usually interviewed, if necessary, toward the end of this process. Five days are usually devoted to face-to-face and telephone interviews.

If a proponent is not yet known in the community and needs to remain unrecognized, data gathering is constrained, but not impossible. Certain people act as a community's "windows on the world" and are accustomed to providing information to researchers who cannot disclose the identify of their client.

Report. The social profile takes the form of a 25- to 30-page report with chapters on local history; industries and occupations; development issues; organizations and leadership; communication channels; knowledge of and attitudes toward the client, industry, and project; public affected; and observations and conclusions. There are 3 to 4 standard subheads for each chapter. The type of informants used is indicated, but not their names. A draft of the report is often reviewed by several of the principal sources. Four days are allowed for report preparation.

Expertise. The social profile is usually prepared by an experienced person with a master's degree in applied sociology, anthropology or community organization, preferably someone indigenous to the community or area. We have been able to identify such people even in small, remote communities. A passable social profile can also be assembled by several long-term residents of a community if they have different backgrounds to offset their inevitable individual blind spots; a high school civics class can also take this on as a shared project.

Time. The profile usually takes 10 working days to prepare. For an urgent project, we sometimes carry out the fieldwork and then prepare a two-page, point-form outline under the above chapter heads. This is usually sufficient to enable plans to be made and a publication to be drafted; the full report is then completed later.

Conclusion.   The social profile is often the most cost-effective expenditure in a public involvement program; without it, money spent on publications and meetings may be ill-founded and ineffectual.

Responsive publication

Rationale.   Effective public involvement programs cannot rely on the media to inform the public about a project; if you want it said right, you have to say it yourself. Before any type of meeting with the public occurs, it is essential to provide all those interested with relevant information in print in an understandable form in the comfort and security of their own homes. The recipients can then absorb it with a minimum of anxiety and at a time convenient for them. Print also has the advantage of permanence. Many readers will obtain all the information they feel they need through a publication and will not be forced to attend a meeting in order to obtain it.

Successful public participation is based upon informed public response. All communications thus need to incorporate a response mechanism; e.g., a tear-off coupon in a display newspaper advertisement or a reply-paid postcard in a brochure. These provide essential insights into the levels of support, indecision and opposition, the reasons for each and their geographic distribution.

Many residents who have a low level of interest and energy for this issue will read a publication, respond by mail, and follow subsequent media coverage but will not attend meetings or take a more active role except to reply to a telephone survey later in the program. However, they are usually the largest public—and they can all vote.

Methodology.   A question-and-answer format, based on issues and language discovered through the social profile, is important, as is a simple and direct style of writing. Check the "fog index" (percentage of words with three or more syllables, excluding proper and place names) of your draft text and compare it with what your public usually reads. (The fog index of a rural weekly is often about 6, an urban news magazine 10 to 12 and a planning or engineering report 20.)

The responsive publication must recognize perceived negative aspects of a proposal and deal with these directly. Any attempts to whitewash what some of the public see as problems will destroy credibility. In most situations, the general public may be divided into three components—those already in favor, who need little attention; those opposed, who are unlikely to change their minds through direct proponent action; and a large body of currently indifferent, skeptical or otherwise uninvolved who should be, in my view, the main focus of the public involvement program.

If one or more newspapers cover the main publics you wish to reach, a display advertisement is usually an economical way to reach most people; it also encourages letters to the editor, news coverage and editorials. A brochure distributed by mail can be targeted to a specific area by the selective use of postal walks; a reply-paid postcard usually results in a higher response rate than a tear-off coupon in a newspaper. Check postal regulations for paper weight, size of card, etc.

Report.   A short report is prepared with tables indicating the nature of the response with a breakdown by area. Some 85% of respondents will provide their name, address and telephone number for follow-up; 10% will add letters, diagrams, etc., relevant to the project. A content analysis of qualitative responses, combined with the quantitative data, guides the next steps in the program. The report is often combined with the responses to the open house.

Expertise.   Professional writing skills are needed to prepare effective publications but input from the social profile and the technical specialists is essential. Some technical staff are reluctant to part with their jargon, so diplomacy is needed to avoid a test of wills. Drafting an introductory brochure with an interdisciplinary group at the start of a project can be a major team-building experience.

Time.   In one case, four senior managers sat down with a practitioner and drafted an entire brochure in four hours; in another recent experience involving an engineering firm and a city department, approval for a brochure took two weeks. We usually allow two professional days to prepare and publish a responsive publication.

Conclusion.   The responsive publication enables a project team to speak clearly and directly to its publics and receive an equally clear and direct response. It provides a concise outline of key issues to the general public as a foundation for future activities. However, 5 to 20% of readers will want to obtain further information, ask questions or make suggestions; some form of meeting is thus required. The publication usually advertises one or more open houses a week later.

Open house

Rationale. The traditional public meeting, which often seems like the last of the blood sports, frequently generates a high level of anxiety, reinforces opposition groups and generates more heat than light on the subject. As a result of many such experiences, the open house, modeled on its real-estate analogue, was developed in the early 1970s. Open house visitors are free to determine at what time they visit (typically from 2 to 9 p.m.), how long they stay, and what questions they ask. By contrast, the typical public meeting fixes these elements and demands a three-hour or more commitment. In an open house, all are invited to complete a short questionnaire, often similar to the response element in the responsive publication; more than half usually do so. In a customary public meeting there is no definitive way to know what listeners think. The character of an open house is typically conversational, while a public meeting is often confrontational; this may sell newspapers, but it seldom solves problems.

Methodology. A dozen display panels with text and relevant graphics to summarize the main elements of a proposal are arranged on easels in a circle in some locally valued social space; e.g., church hall, library, school. Informal lettering in primary colors ensures that the nonverbal message ("This project is in an early development stage. Your comments and suggestions are invited and can be incorporated into the design still") reinforce the text and oral messages from the open house staff.

Staff are selected to be able to deal with three types of issues: policy, project management, and specific content, e.g., environmental concerns. A six-hour training session before the open house is required of all who will staff it. The agenda includes

- A summary of key issues from the social profile
- A review of early responses to the responsive publication
- A review of recent media coverage
- The identification of 25 questions likely to arise (it is also necessary to ensure that staff can give the short answer to all questions)
- A video on how to deal with hostile visitors
- The assignment of staff to teams and shifts (e.g., Team A, 2–5 p.m. and 7–9 p.m.; Team B, 5–9 p.m.).

Six proponent staff are usually required—two who can deal with policy issues, two involved with project management and two specialists dealing with the main issues, e.g., environmental concerns. The public involvement person is primarily concerned with process and ensuring that as many as possible complete the exit questionnaire. Usually all elected representatives for the area (local, state/provincial and federal) are invited to a sandwich lunch with no media present so that sensitive topics can be addressed; all open house staff usually attend the lunch. A short debriefing meeting after each open house is important to identify lessons learned and recommendations for the next open house.

While some people advocate holding open houses in shopping malls, our experience has been that better results occur when visitors come specifically for this occasion. Busy shoppers, laden with purchases and distracted by their children, cannot give their full attention to the issues and the answers provided.

Report.   An analysis of the exit checklists completed by visitors provides further insights into the reasons for the public's support, indecision and opposition, suggestions for alternative solutions to issues, etc. When responses from the responsive publication and the open house are sorted alphabetically, and handwriting compared for those without names and addresses, duplicates can be eliminated and a more accurate total response figure results.

Expertise.   Applied social science skills are useful in arranging the open house, monitoring the process and counselling staff, especially those who may experience difficulties with the public.

Time.   To organize the open house, provide training for its staff, manage the event and analyze and report the results takes about six professional days for an initial open house and two more for any additional open houses in the same series.

Conclusion.   The open house enables proponent staff to respond appropriately to the diverse publics for a proposal and develop linkages with visitors for future activities. When a regulatory body insists on traditional public meetings, we hold an open house from 2 to 7 p.m. and start the public meeting in the same location at 7:30 p.m. with a brief report on the usually positive open house. Typically 100 to 125 come to the open house and about the same number to the public meeting, which is often over by 9 p.m.[1]

Planning workshop

Rationale.   Organized groups play vital roles in shaping and managing the functions of a community, so it is essential to involve community groups in resolving community issues.

Such groups often possess valuable assets: specialized information, historic data, a high level of energy to pursue their values, experience in resolving previous issues, the power of numbers and the respect of many in the general population. In many cases, larger general-interest groups support a proposal which is opposed by one or more smaller special-interest groups. A workshop enables community leaders to take care of business as informed peer group pressure leads to workable compromises on key issues.

Methodology. Key organizations are invited to send one representative each to a one-day planning workshop, usually about two weeks after an open house. The agenda often includes

- A review of the proposal
- A question-and-answer period
- A review of public response to publications and open houses
- A second question-and-answer period
- Identification of remaining issues to be resolved.

After lunch, a problem-solving process is applied to each remaining issue (e.g., what, why, how, who, when?), so that steps will be taken to deal with each by a given time. The workshop adjourns with an evaluation about 3 or 4 p.m. Most participants prefer to have the planning workshop on a Saturday so they don't lose a work day. The rationale for the workshop and an agenda accompany the initial invitation to participate. Some 12 to 15 participants is an upper limit; often small local groups will let a larger umbrella group in their field speak for them.

Report. Detailed minutes are taken during the workshop and are distributed to all within a week. Participants need to know that they have been heard; the proponent is kept accountable in this way.

Expertise. The workshop leader needs to possess strong professional group skills. Trust levels may be low initially. The project manager is a major resource person to the workshop; but because the project manager is a task leader, he or she should definitely not serve as a process leader.

Time. Selecting and inviting participants, organizing and leading the workshop and preparing detailed minutes requires about four professional days.

Conclusion. The planning workshop is an important and often an exciting and creative technique as part of an overall participative program. In many cases, a co-management process, linking the community and the proponent, can emerge from a series of planning workshops.

Program design

For a simple project, these four techniques—social profile, responsive publication, open house, and planning workshop—can form the core of an effective program. A major planning project, however, often requires a three-stage process: introduction, alternative generation, and evaluation and recommendation. In this case, the last three techniques—responsive publication, open house and planning workshop—are repeated at 3- to 6-month intervals depending on the timing of the technical work program. (See Figures 1 and 2.)

Cablevision panel

Rationale.   In many situations, more than 20% of the adult population are functionally illiterate, 10% have limited mobility due to age or disability and perhaps 10% of households are single parents. Since these people are not served easily by print media or meetings, a cablevision panel is one effective way to reach them. A few 20-second radio spots and notices in the local newspapers, especially as part of a display advertisement, will boost the usually limited audience of a cable channel.

Methodology.   A 20-minute panel discussion by three resource people who will be staffing the open house, followed by a phone-in segment to complete the hour, is a useful program format. The station will usually repeat the program at several different times of day to make viewing more accessible. If scheduled between the

Stage	Technique	Elapsed time
Introductory	Social profile	3 weeks
	Responsive publication	1 week
	Open house	1 week
	Planning workshop	2 weeks
Alternative generation	Responsive publication	1 week
	Open house	1 week
	Planning workshop	2 weeks
Evaluation and recommendation	Responsive publication	1 week
	Open house	1 week
	Planning workshop	2 weeks
	Final report	2 weeks

Figure 1. A three-stage process for public involvement.

distribution of the responsive publication and the open house, it can increase attention to the former and raise attendance at the latter. There is typically no charge by the station for airtime or production costs.

Report.   A review of the number and nature of phone calls to the program can help those who will staff the open house to prepare for certain issues.

Expertise.   The cablevision station will usually supply an independent moderator for the panel and production expertise. The proponent supplies the panelists, typically with policy, project management and technical competence appropriate for the proposal, as discussed for the open house.

Time.   To organize and produce a cablevision program usually requires two days of professional time.

Conclusion.   The cablevision panel is a useful supplementary technique which reaches usually neglected segments of the population at minimum cost.

Meetings with organizations

Rationale.   While the traditional public meeting often generates more heat than light, meetings with the members of organizations which have a shared perspective on the proposal can be useful, especially *after* an open house.

Figure 2. Budget components.

To provide some idea of comparative costs, the following are estimates of current Canadian costs:

Social profile	$6,000 plus travel costs
Responsive publication	$3–5,000 depending on space costs or press run
Open house	$6,000 for the first in a series
	$2,000 for next in same series
Planning workshop	$4,000
Telephone survey	$6,000 (N=300) plus long distance charges

Thus the initial cycle is likely to cost about $25,000, a second cycle some $20,000 and the third cycle with a telephone survey and final report about $30,000. A three-cycle program is thus in the range of $75,000 to $100,000 Canadian.

Methodology. A more positive experience is likely if the proponent is invited as a guest of the organization, if one of its senior officers acts as chair of the meeting, if those invited are all members of the organization and if the agenda and use of space are designed for effective communications.[2] Copies of the responsive publication, or some adaptation of it, may be useful as an initial handout. If possible, a response form similar to that used at the open house should be circulated at the end of the meeting so that informed public response can be identified.

Report. Minutes of the meeting should be taken and the response forms summarized.

Expertise. An experienced and competent chair, provided by the host organization, will be important.[3]

Time. Preparing for, attending and reporting on the meeting will require about two professional days.

Conclusion. A series of meetings with relevant organizations can extend the level of public information and informed response for a proposal. This is particularly useful if some key publics appear to be missing in replies from the responsive publication and the open house.

Reference center

Rationale. The reference center provides interested professionals with an appropriate means to access technical reports and databases so that their comments and suggestions can be gathered early in the planning process. This small but important public needs more information than can be provided by responsive publications, open houses and planning workshops. If their concerns and suggestions can be tapped early, they can be incorporated productively into the planning process rather than appear for the first time at a concluding hearing when probably little positive use can be made of them.

Methodology. While proponents are reluctant to make many copies of expensive technical reports for "the public," a few copies placed on the reference shelf of the local library can enable some key people to access the information cost effectively. Alternatively, these documents can be made available to visitors at the proponent's office at certain times; in this case, some evening or weekend access will be required for professionals who are at work during office hours. The reference center needs to be advertised in publications and at open houses.

Report.   An introductory note can encourage readers to call a staff member with questions or comments; a sign-up sheet can be provided to gather readers' names, addresses and phone numbers for follow-up, and a brief report can be prepared.

Expertise.   Even in small communities there are residents or visitors with relevant specialties at the graduate level. Recruiting these people as potential supporters is a survival skill; ignoring them is a recipe for disaster.

Time.   A reference center can often be established in less than a day.

Conclusion.   The reference center is valuable not only for interested professionals but also as a resource for reporters to help ensure more informed coverage. Informed opposition is often easier to deal with than uninformed opposition, which results when proponents limit the distribution of information.

Telephone survey

Rationale.   The preceding techniques provide ways for the various interested publics to obtain information and express their views, but tell nothing of the elusive silent majority. Only through the telephone survey can a statistically valid cross section of the population be interviewed and its sentiments identified. While decision makers respect the views of activists, most also need to know the positions of the silent majority before they feel comfortable casting their vote on a major issue.

Methodology.   The technology for valid and reliable survey research is well established. A relatively small sample, e.g., 300 interviewees, if selected by a random procedure, will yield results accurate to $\pm 6\%$, 19 times out of 20. The questionnaire typically asks

- Whether respondents are aware of the issue
- Whether, after listening to a balanced description of the issue and a proposed solution, respondents are in favor of the proposal, opposed to it, or undecided
- Why they hold the position they do.

In addition, the survey requests demographic information such as gender, age, education, occupation, and location. Market research firms are usually contracted to conduct the interviews about one week after an open house when, with media coverage of the issue, public awareness is at a maximum. In larger cities, a monthly or quarterly omnibus survey enables proponents to ask a question or two on a regular basis and track public opinion at a modest cost.

Report. Market research firms, using trained staff and computer programs, typically produce a summary report with many statistical tables.

Expertise. Some knowledge of survey research methods is required to draft the questionnaire, contract for services and interpret the final report.

Time. To carry out the above tasks takes about two professional days.

Conclusion. The telephone survey is an essential element at the conclusion of a public involvement program to identify and assess the views of the general public before a final recommendation or decision is made about a major issue.

Media relations

Rationale. The media play a vital role in both shaping and reflecting the views of the general population. It is therefore essential to understand the various media in a community, assess their coverage and credibility and note their performance concerning the issue at hand and the proponent. In some cases, an uninformed and overworked reporter or a long-standing dispute between an editor and the proponent can prevent effective coverage of a new proposal unless this issue is addressed at the outset.

Methodology. While careful cultivation of the media can result in useful news coverage, the growing number of crusading, investigative reporters and the independence of the headline writer from the reporter frequently result in treatment which a proponent will label negative. As crisis-manager Jim Lukaszweski notes, you need to talk directly to those directly affected by a proposal.[4] The only way for an organization to ensure that a message is delivery fully, clearly and on schedule is to buy space or time and say it itself. Additional news coverage is then an appreciated bonus; any errors or omissions can be corrected by a short, direct letter to the editor, which will usually be published.

Senior staff of the proponent should receive training in how to handle a media interview, especially by the electronic media. Media deadlines and other constraints on time and space must be understood and respected to encourage useful coverage. Since a skeptical reporter can set the tone at a news conference and result in critical treatment by all present, a series of one-to-one meetings with reporters can often generate better results.

Report.   A news-clipping file should be kept chronologically and a content analysis carried out to identify major themes covered by each paper or station and the number of column inches or minutes of coverage per week or month. This can help guide future publications and perhaps point to the need to meet with reporters or editors.

Expertise.   Some knowledge of media relations is obviously useful both in terms of strategy and daily operations; e.g., treat every microphone and camera as "live."

Time.   During a one-month cycle of response publication, open house and planning workshop, we allocate no more than two days to media relations.

Conclusion.   The media are at best "fair weather friends" and at worst spoilers with their own agenda to foster controversy as a means to boost circulation and audience share, treating the proposal and the proponent as an entertaining spectacle.

Informal consultation

Rationale.   The formality of planning and public involvement events discourages many citizens, especially those with less education. These events also leave lengthy gaps in communication which ongoing informal contact with some key nodes on the community grapevines can help overcome. In this fashion, new ideas can be solicited and trial balloons tested quickly and inexpensively.

Methodology.   Informal participation encourages active fieldwork to meet with residents on their own turn, ask questions, listen, observe the social environment and test possible solutions to problems at an early stage. Key contacts can be identified initially during the preparation of the social profile and expanded through replies to the responsive publication and at the open house. A mix of face-to-face meetings and telephone calls is useful.

Report.   A daily log of contacts and key ideas should be kept for later reference.

Expertise.   Good facilitator skills are essential for informal consultation.

Time.   In an ongoing planning process, two to five days per month should be allocated to informal consultation.

Conclusion.   Especially in small, low-income and ethnic communities, informal consultation provides essential links to key networks in the community and provides continuity between major involvement events.

1. For further insights into public meetings, see Desmond M. Connor, "The Public Conversation and Other Ways to Improve Public Meetings," *Constructive Citizen Participation* 20, no. 3 (1992): 3–6.
2. See Desmond M. Connor, *Constructive Citizen Participation: A Resource Book*, 5th ed. (Victoria, B.C: Development Press, 1994); "The Public Conversation"; and "Career Development and Manpower Planning for Public Participation," in *Constructive Citizen Participation* Part III, 6–8.
3. E. Mina, "Get Ready for the Hot Seat!" *Constructive Citizen Participation* 19, no. 1 (1992): 5–6.
4. J. E. Lukaszweski, *Influencing Public Attitudes* (Leesburg, VA: Issue Action Publications, 1992).

Crafting the Language of Consensus

——————— Gerald W. Cormick

Many alternative dispute resolution processes are based on achieving mutual agreement among the participants. "Mutual agreement" assumes that all parties are supportive of decisions reached, as contrasted with procedures whereby a decision is achieved through a voting process (resulting in "winners" and "losers") or through some individual or body making a unilateral decision (such as a designated decision maker or through administrative or judicial proceedings).

Mutual agreement is often characterized as "consensus." Any form of negotiation—buyer-seller, labor-management, plaintiff and defendant in a civil suit, etc.—is essentially a consensus process: that is, if the parties fail to reach an agreement, no joint conclusion to the effort is reached. Where negotiations fail to result in such a mutual or consensus agreement, the parties revert to other processes. The buyer turns to another seller; labor and management have a strike or lockout or submit their differences to an adjudicatory body; and the plaintiff and defendant seek a judicial determination.

A consensus process is qualitatively different from other processes, and a critical element in that difference is the ability of any single interest to prevent a mutually acceptable outcome. Each defined participant has an effective veto. This requirement that unanimity be achieved is often viewed as an impractical or unreasonable test. However, experience suggests that the use of consensus

Reprinted by permission of Plenum Press from *Negotiation Journal* 7, no. 4 (1991): 363–368. The article is based on materials developed by the author for the British Columbia Round Table on the Environment and Economy, 8 April 1991.

can be both necessary and practical in resolving public interest conflicts.

In developing a forum for the settlement of economic/environmental conflicts, unanimity or, conversely, granting a "veto" to each participant, has important benefits. The veto "levels the playing field." For a defined period of time on the issues that the participants have agreed to address, they participate as equals. If, for example, the process included taking a vote, the participants would necessarily be concerned about how many participants were on "their side" as a condition of whether they would participate. The reality of consensus and ability to exercise a veto also tends to encourage a process whereby each of the participants has a concern for, and self-interest in, crafting a solution that meets the needs of the other interests, rather than merely seeking to gather adherents to their side of the issue. The number of adherents to a particular position, if short of unanimity, does not constitute consensus and agreement. Experience clearly indicates that where participants in negotiation processes have the security that they will not be overwhelmed by "numbers," they are more likely to search for and consider areas of accommodation and innovative solutions. The consensus process mirrors the situation that has resulted in the need for such a dispute settlement process: a single group or key individual can often effectively block either indefinitely or for extended periods the resolution of an issue.

Some definitions

A number of specific parameters of consensus are critical to the effective use of the process, and any group using the process should explicitly address and reach a common understanding on them as a precondition to using a consensus process. The realities of each situation will and should result in differing provisions being established.

Defining the entities necessary for a consensus.   An important initial issue in developing a working definition for the use of consensus is to be clear on the entities that must be in agreement. This does not lessen the requirement of unanimity but defines when it is achieved. Generally, two approaches are used: (1) Each individual participating in a process must support any agreement, or (2) caucuses or organizations of individuals must support the agreement. Determining which method or which combination of them is appropriate depends on how the participants are structured.

Defining consensus as the agreement of all individuals is likely to be appropriate in situations where disputes are relatively unstructured and few formal organizations are involved. Fairly simple language can serve to provide this definition; for example, "Consensus is defined as general agreement of all members of the Task Force." (This language was developed by the twenty-five–member Thurston County [Washington] Waste Water Management Plan Task Force, which was established to reach agreement on the configuration of an expanded waste water treatment facility and related issues.)

Where clearly defined organizations exist or the participants can be clustered into defined areas of interest, it may be appropriate to define consensus as the unanimous agreement of larger entities. Such definition is likely to require considerable discussion and needs to be clearly stated.

For example, in a dispute involving the determination of regulations relating to the exploration and development of offshore oil resources along the California coast, the parties organized themselves into five "negotiating teams" or "interest caucuses": federal government (consisting of five agencies); state government (consisting of the governor's office, two agencies, and the State Coastal Commission); local government (consisting of a number of counties, cities, and air quality districts); industry (a number of major oil companies and their industry association); and environmentalists (a coalition of local, state, and national environmental organizations). They defined consensus for their purposes this way:

> The negotiating committee will operate by consensus. "Consensus" is defined as agreement of the five negotiating teams, as conveyed by their negotiators.
>
> Each negotiating team shall represent the concerns and positions of its interest caucus. It is the responsibility of each negotiating team to ensure that any position taken or agreement reached has maximum assurance of broad acceptability to the caucus it represents.

In a similar situation, negotiators were seeking to reach agreement on how to address the impacts of noise from operations at Seattle-Tacoma International Airport in Washington State. Six caucuses were defined by the participants: impacted communities, air industry, airport users, Air Line Pilots Association, Federal Aviation Administration, and the Port of Seattle (the airport operator). They established the following definition of consensus:

> The explicit concurrence of the six caucuses participating in the mediation process, as conveyed by Mediation Committee Members. Each caucus is responsible for determining its own process for deciding whether or not to participate in a consensus.

Defining "consensus" as agreement between caucuses or teams requires fewer affirmative responses to achieve unanimity. However, it shifts some of the responsibility for achieving consensus to the individual participating teams. The teams themselves will use a variety of decision making rules to reach internal positions, including hierarchical authority, voting and reaching their own internal consensus.

The concept of the "package." Environmental/economic disputes are characterized by a complex set of issues relating to criteria for making choices, physical actions, undertakings regarding future impacts, and various forms of mitigation and compensation. A consensus is reached when the participants reach agreement on a set or package of provisions that addresses the entire range of issues. The participants may be more or less supportive of any single element of an agreement but must be able to support the total package. It is important to recognize this concept in the consensus definition. For example, consider the way this was handled by the parties to the previously cited offshore oil negotiations:

> All positions and agreements on specific issues or sets of issues are tentative and may be modified until there is consensus agreement on a total acceptable package addressing all issues.
>
> Each interest caucus shall ratify or decline to ratify the final document as a whole at the end of the process.

Failure to make explicit this understanding can detract from the willingness of the participants to explore possible areas of agreement and to reach tentative agreements with the understanding that these may be modified at a later point in the interest of crafting a total "package" agreement acceptable to all.

From enthusiastic support to veto: When is it a consensus?   It is sometimes said of negotiations that "if everyone is unhappy, it must be a good compromise." While this may be sufficient in some situations, many solutions to complex disputes may require the active support of participants to ensure that the actual implementation process proceeds. Clearly, a veto exercised by a defined entity in consensus signals disagreement. However, because the participants are dealing with a number of issues, it is likely that within the overall package, on an item-by-item basis, their support will range from enthusiastic to lukewarm to "willing to live with it." However, it is important that the level of support for the total package or agreement be sufficient to ensure its implementation.

Can there be less than "100 percent agreement"?   It may be appropriate to craft provisions to enable the participants to achieve consensus even in the absence of total agreement or consensus on every issue. Indeed, in some cases, the participants may not be able to reach closure because of the need for additional information or because of other factors. In determining how best to incorporate the possibility of less than 100 percent agreement on all issues, it is important that the participants address several concerns: for example, they should

1. Create clear, specific provisions to deal with less than 100 percent agreement, including provisions to describe and record the lack of agreement
2. Resist using those provisions as a way to avoid difficult choices (for example, agreeing on all the easy issues and "punting" on important but difficult ones)
3. Avoid defining lack of agreement as "how many for and how many against."

Appropriate language (developed by the Waste Water Management Plan Task Force) that recognizes and addresses such concerns might be as follows:

The goal is to reach consensus on as many issues before the Task Force as possible.

In the absence of consensus, any Task Force report will describe areas of agreement and disagreement; agreeing on where they disagree as well as where they agree. Every effort will be made to clearly and fairly state all points of view.

Disagreements will not be presented in terms of the members for or against, but rather in terms of where disagreements lie.

There will be a single final report encompassing both agreement and any disagreement, not majority and minority reports.

In the offshore oil negotiations, a similar provision was crafted by the parties:

The participants may agree to a consensus that includes all but a few specified provisions of a proposed rule. If this is the case, they will be explicit as to remaining areas of disagreement and how they will address those differences.

Negotiation participants may determine that, while they intend to use the consensus process as their operative procedure, there are certain defined areas where a lack of consensus will lead to an alternative decision-making process without resulting in the collapse of the entire effort. Such areas might include administrative or procedural issues such as where meetings are held, some budgetary matters, and other issues that may arise but are not central to the substantive purpose of the process. For example, the British Columbia Round Table on the Economy and the Environment considered a provision based on the following language:

Failure to agree on administrative issues (as defined) would result in a vote (of at least two-thirds majority) or a designated individual or group of individuals (such as an administrative subcommittee) making the determination.

The veto and the responsibility of the negotiator. With the "power" of the veto the negotiator also has the responsibility to exercise that power responsibly. Since participants may be unfamiliar with the consensus process it may be useful to explicitly recognize mutual expectations regarding how participants will exercise the veto. One of the impacted communities participating in the Seattle-Tacoma International Airport negotiations adopted the following provisions for their internal consensus process:

Should only one or a very few participants be in the position of preventing a consensus being reached, they shall have the responsibility to either show why they are differentially impacted by a situation or that the matter is one of such principle that they must prevent consensus. If they are unable to demonstrate one of these conditions, they will be expected to abstain from opposing or support a consensus.

Where a participant agrees to support or not oppose a consensus under this provision, the other participants have a responsibility to note the cause(s) for concern raised and make an explicit effort to address them and/or prevent their arising.

An additional provision considered in another situation suggests that a participant be able to garner the support of at least one other participant for the proposition that exercising the veto is appropriate under the above criteria, whether or not that participant agrees on the substance of the matter under consideration. This would not be an absolute requirement but, rather, a guideline for participants in considering whether they are appropriately exercising the veto.

The role of deadlines in achieving consensus. Simply stated, consensus processes are not always successful in resolving disputes, and provisions must be made for terminating the process. On the one hand, the difficult choices that are often required in reaching consensus are unlikely to be made unless a real deadline exists. Conversely, it may be difficult for the participants to declare or admit failure and return the dispute to other decision-making procedures.

It is often useful to define more than one deadline. Where a single point exists at which agreement is either achieved or the process is terminated, the tendency is for complex decisions to be left to just before the deadline when "agreements" are reached without the careful consideration they may deserve. Conversely, with only a single deadline, a failed consensus process may be maintained far beyond its useful life because no clear way of discontinuing the effort has been established and no participant wishes to bear the potentially negative consequences of unilaterally terminating the process.

Language that provides for more than one deadline is relatively simple to craft, but the deadlines need to be real and to require mutual effort to extend or override. Examples of such language include:

The Negotiating Committee shall review the progress being made every third negotiating session and decide by consensus whether or not to continue the negotiations (Offshore Oil Mediation).

The Mediation Committee shall establish interim dates at which time it shall evaluate progress and by consensus agree whether or not to continue. The target for developing substantive options and conclusions is June 30, 1989. At that time the Mediation Committee shall make a substantive progress assessment and determine whether or not it is necessary and productive to continue the mediation process. If the process is continued, a date for concluding the process shall be established (Seattle-Tacoma International Airport Mediation).

In deciding whether to undertake a consensus process, a sponsoring entity may also establish a set of deadlines for assessing whether the process is appropriate and for reaching agreement among the participants on a set of ground rules prior to discussion of the substantive issues in dispute.

Conclusion

In summary, the consensus process provides a necessary set of procedures and standards that provide the essential foundation for reaching mutually supported settlement of disputes. Adjudicatory or voting processes are antithetical to the very nature of the consensus process. When voting takes place, "winners" and "losers" are explicitly defined. This can lead to lessened support for implementation of solutions—and even to the "losers" preferring that implementation fail.

As with any other processes, consensus-based processes can—and, at times, should—fail. Where consensus fails, participants will have recourse to other alternatives for making decisions, including administrative, legal, and political forums, the alternative forums which provided the impetus for disputing parties to seek mutually agreeable solutions through a consensus process.

Seven Cardinal Rules of Risk Communication

Vincent T. Covello and Frederick W. Allen

Editor's note: Change can bring risk—both real and perceived; and the perception or presence of risk can be a major source of conflict. Whether the concern is the location of a substance abuse clinic, a change in police patrolling practices, a new industry coming to town, or a previously unidentified natural or technological hazard, local government managers are often called upon to explain or describe the parameters of risk. The rules that follow will help managers carry out this role openly and confidently.

There are no easy prescriptions for successful risk communication. However, those who have studied and participated in recent debates about risk generally agree on seven cardinal rules. These rules apply equally well to the public and private sectors.

Although many of the rules may seem obvious, they are continually and consistently violated in practice. Thus, a useful way to read these rules is to focus on why they are frequently not followed.

1: Accept and involve the public as a legitimate partner

A basic tenet of risk communication in a democracy is that people and communities have a right to participate in decisions that affect their lives, their property, and the things they value.

Guidelines. Demonstrate your respect for the public and underscore the sincerity of your effort by involving the community early, before important decisions are made. Involve all parties that have an interest or a stake in the issue under consideration. If you are a government employee, remember that you work for the public.

Reprinted from a pamphlet published in April 1988 by the U.S. Environmental Protection Agency, Washington, D.C.

If you do not work for the government, the public still holds you accountable.

Point to consider. The goal of risk communication in a democracy should be to produce an informed public that is involved, interested, reasonable, thoughtful, solution-oriented, and collaborative; it should not be to defuse public concerns or replace action.

2: Plan carefully and evaluate your efforts
Risk communication will be successful only if carefully planned.

Guidelines. Begin with clear, explicit risk-communication objectives—such as providing information to the public, motivating individuals to act, stimulating response to emergencies, or contributing to the resolution of conflict. Evaluate the information you have about the risks and know its strengths and weaknesses. Classify and segment the various groups in your audience. Aim your communications at specific subgroups in your audience. Recruit spokespeople who are good at presentation and interaction. Train your staff—including technical staff—in communications skills; reward outstanding performance. Whenever possible, pretest your messages. Carefully evaluate your efforts and learn from your mistakes.

Points to consider
1. There is no such entity as "the public"; instead, there are many publics, each with its own interests, needs, concerns, priorities, preferences, and organizations.
2. Different risk-communication goals, audiences, and media require different risk communication strategies.

3: Listen to the public's specific concerns
If you do not listen to people, you cannot expect them to listen to you. Communication is a two-way activity.

Guidelines. Do not make assumptions about what people know, think, or want done about risks. Take the time to find out what people are thinking: use techniques such as interviews, focus groups, and surveys. Let all parties that have an interest or a stake in the issue be heard. Identify with your audience and try to put yourself in their place. Recognize people's emotions. Let people know that you understand what they said, addressing their concerns as well as yours. Recognize the "hidden agendas," symbolic meanings, and broader economic or political considerations that often underlie and complicate the task of risk communication.

Point to consider. People in the community are often more concerned about such issues as trust, credibility, competence, control, voluntariness, fairness, caring, and compassion than about mortality statistics and the details of quantitative risk assessment.

4: Be honest, frank, and open

In communicating risk information, trust and credibility are your most precious assets.

Guidelines. State your credentials; but do not ask or expect to be trusted by the public. If you do not know an answer or are uncertain, say so. Get back to people with answers. Admit mistakes. Disclose risk information as soon as possible (emphasizing any reservations about reliability). Do not minimize or exaggerate the level of risk. Speculate only with great caution. If in doubt, lean toward sharing more information, not less—or people may think you are hiding something. Discuss data uncertainties, strengths and weaknesses—including the ones identified by other credible sources. Identify worst-case estimates as such, and cite ranges of risk estimates when appropriate.

Point to consider. Trust and credibility are difficult to obtain. Once lost, they are almost impossible to regain completely.

5: Coordinate and collaborate with other credible sources

Allies can be effective in helping you communicate risk information.

Guidelines. Take time to coordinate all interorganizational and intraorganizational communications. Devote effort and resources to the slow, hard work of building bridges with other organizations. Use credible and authoritative intermediaries. Consult with others to determine who is best able to answer questions about risk. Try to issue communications jointly with other trustworthy sources (for example, credible university scientists, physicians, or trusted local officials).

Point to consider. Few things make risk communication more difficult than conflicts or public disagreements with other credible sources.

6: Meet the needs of the media

The media are prime transmitters of information on risks; they play a critical role in setting agendas and in determining outcomes.

Guidelines. Be open with and accessible to reporters. Respect their deadlines. Provide risk information tailored to the needs of each type of media (for example, graphics and other visual aids for television). Prepare in advance and provide background material on complex risk issues. Do not hesitate to follow up on stories with praise or criticism, as warranted. Try to establish long-term relationships of trust with specific editors and reporters.

Point to consider. The media are frequently more interested in politics than in risk; more interested in simplicity than in complexity; more interested in danger than in safety.

7: Speak clearly and with compassion

Technical language and jargon are useful as professional shorthand. But they are barriers to successful communication with the public.

Guidelines. Use simple, nontechnical language. Be sensitive to local norms, such as speech and dress. Use vivid, concrete images that communicate on a personal level. Use examples and anecdotes that make technical risk data come alive. Avoid distant, abstract, unfeeling language about deaths, injuries, and illnesses. Acknowledge and respond (both in words and with actions) to emotions that people express—anxiety, fear, anger, outrage, helplessness. Acknowledge and respond to the distinctions that the public views as important in evaluating risks, e.g., voluntariness, controllability, familiarity, dread, origin (natural or manmade), benefits, fairness, and catastrophic potential. Use risk comparisons to help put risks in perspective; but avoid comparisons that ignore distinctions that people consider important. Always try to include a discussion of actions that are under way or can be taken. Tell people what you cannot do. Promise only what you can do, and be sure to do what you promise.

Points to consider

1. Regardless of how well you communicate risk information, some people will not be satisfied.
2. Never let your efforts to inform people about risks prevent you from acknowledging—and saying—that any illness, injury, or death is a tragedy.
3. If people are sufficiently motivated, they are quite capable of understanding complex risk information, even if they may not agree with you.

PART 5

Proactive Strategies for Long-term Success

A Proactive Approach to Organizational Conflict

Ozzie Bermant

If one were to do a free-association exercise with the word *conflict,* by far the most frequent responses would be negative. *Danger, fighting, pain, stress,* and *fear* might be some of the common, instinctive reactions. A few people might come up with an opposite view, like *opportunity, progress,* or *solutions.* This article describes a way to encourage a more positive view of conflict by treating it as a resource rather than as a burden.

Disputes in organizations—and elsewhere—are usually perceived as something to get through and forget. Pay the money, fire the employee, beat your competitor, divide the property—and get on with life. Even alternative dispute resolution (ADR) programs often emphasize procedures to resolve conflicts without necessarily concerning themselves with avoidance or prevention. If, however, we assume that conflict is a resource, then the question becomes how to use that resource. What does the dispute tell management about the organization? How can management use this information to help minimize the negative effects of future disputes? (See Figure 1.)

This article falls into two parts. The first part, which describes a framework for proactive conflict management, offers recommendations that can be used in any of three situations: when you are helping to resolve a conflict; when you are designing a conflict management system; or when you are a party to a conflict. The second part of the article offers guidelines to those who find themselves in the role of change agents for the improvement of conflict management processes in their organizations.

Ozzie Bermant is Director of the Concordia Systems Group, Potomac, MD.

An outline of a proactive system

Some organizations conduct annual planning sessions to look at where they are, where they want to be, and how they are going to get there. A proactive system for conflict management applies the same broad concepts to the condition of *relationships*. Although the following discussion focuses on intraorganizational conflict, the process described can be applied to individuals or groups outside the organization as well.

Diagram relationships and the current state of conflict

1. List all the relationships that might affect the performance of a department. Indicate the degree of interaction, the impor-

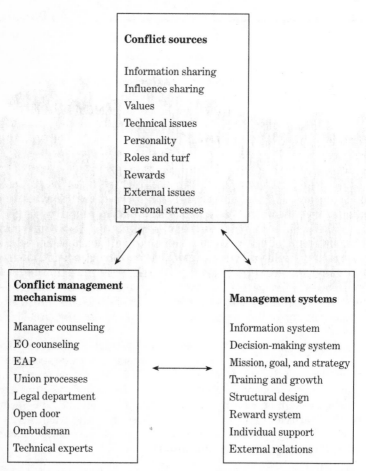

Figure 1. Organizational conflict connections.

tance of the relationship, its quality, and the level of conflict. This can be done in tabular form (indicating "high" to "low") or graphically. (The graphic could depict the department at the center, with lines radiating out to other departments or individuals, the thickness of the connecting lines could denote the frequency of interactions; a dotted line could indicate troubled relations; a red line could draw attention to critical relationships.)

2. Take a first cut at establishing priorities. Which relationships are the most important to work on first?

3. For the high-priority relationships, describe the current state of disagreement: What has transpired so far? What has been communicated? What are the demands of each party? Describe perceived or actual threats to the organization (psychological, physical, economic, reputational) if the conflict is not resolved.

Classify the basis of the disagreement[1]

1. Is this an information conflict? (That is, does it originate from lack of information, hoarding of information, misinterpretations, inaccurate information?)

2. Does the conflict stem from personality differences? (Is stereotyping involved? Contrasting styles? Poor communication? Petty annoyances?)

3. Is the conflict about value differences? (Do ideology, standards, ethics, or worldview come into play?)

4. Is the conflict structural? (Does it center on issues of power or control, turf, or role definition? Does it stem from procedures, physical or time constraints, allocation of resources?)

If there is more than one basis for the dispute, weigh the relative importance of each.

Develop a vision.   What do you want the relationship to look like, and by when do you want it to look like that?

Determine what you need to know that you don't yet know.   What information do you need before deciding how to proceed? Do you need expert advice or to consult with other parties?

Review the available strategic choices for dealing with the difference.   Develop a rationale for each one, then choose from among the following strategies:

1. Avoid it: Let it go, either temporarily or permanently.

2. Force it: Impose your own solution, through litigation, force, or persuasion.

3. Accommodate: Agree to the other party's demands.
4. Compromise: Look for a solution in which both parties give up some of their demands.
5. Collaborate: Commit to finding a new framework for creative solutions, possibly expanding the solutions beyond the bounds of the current disagreement.

Make an initial, first-cut decision on a choice of strategy.

Consider other things and choose a strategy

1. Time and cost issues:

- What is at stake? (Money? A little or a lot?)
- How important is it that something be done now?
- What are the relative costs of each strategy?
- Are the resources (time, money, skills, leadership) available to pursue the strategy?

2. Power issues:

- What historical, legal, or administrative factors are at play?
- What are the sources of available power, and what kinds of power are available (e.g., knowledge, resources, influence, position)?
- What are the external alliances or pressures that may come into play?
- Is power balanced or imbalanced? Are there likely shifts in the power balance or alliances?
- How is power now being used?

3. What are the available alternatives? What's the worst thing or best thing that can happen?

4. Relationship issues:

- Is this an ongoing relationship that will be important in the future?
- What is the current level of trust between the parties?
- How is the conflict affecting others in the organization?

5. Are there compatible or interdependent interests?
6. Is precedent setting an issue?
7. Will the parties agree to start the process?
8. What degree of control do the parties have to implement a solution?
9. What are some other likely future results? Is a judicial ruling needed?

Now make a final decision on the strategic approach.

Final preparation for the negotiation

1. Describe the dispute and the known positions of all parties, including both agreed-upon and contested facts.
2. Develop the latest view of your own interest-based vision.
3. Develop the latest view of the other party's interest-based vision.
4. Look for known rules, regulations, and standards.
5. Consider options, cost, and benefits.
6. Put yourself in the other party's place: figure what their best and worst alternatives are, how they can get what they want, what their options are.
7. Determine the probable limits of what you—and the other party—will accept.
8. Find out who is going to negotiate and what they are like; learn about their strengths, foibles, and styles.
9. Develop a disclosure plan: what will you reveal, and when?
10. Avoid the trap of false assumptions about your power or lack of it.

Use the results: Inform your organization. Create feedback mechanisms to inform the relevant management systems in your organization.

1. First, decide where in the organization the information about the dispute should be channelled, then determine whether or not the conflict is worthy of deeper analysis and possible system changes.
2. Determine how to address the cause of the dispute, thereby reducing the cost or frequency of future similar disputes.
3. Determine what changes, if any, need to be made in the dispute management mechanisms.

If relationship analysis and planning is done on a regular basis, then the management of differences will become useful and effective, and will no longer be considered an experience to be feared.

Fifteen canons of dispute resolution leadership
The following is a list of nostrums for those who find themselves anointed as change agents for the improvement of conflict management, whether it be the introduction of new processes or the reorientation of old ones.

1: Be wary of the bearers of canons, aphorisms, maxims and precepts. Bearers of advice (and gurus in general) often have a hidden desire to have people kneel at their feet while they proclaim the wisdom of the ages. This can often be an unpleasant experience for the kneelers, and isn't always as thrilling for the gurus as they thought, especially when the kneelers return bloodied and unsuccessful after following the guru's advice.

2: Use ADR to get ADR.   Face it: promoting ADR is in itself a conflict management exercise. Using consensus-building methods, interest-based bargaining, principled negotiation, and rational and empathetic techniques will move the process more securely ahead than relying on management dicta. The way you promote ADR will be a model for the ADR you get.

3: Use power and rights also.   Face it: you may need more than logic, rationality, and goodwill to get things started in resistant situations. A little pressure from the right folks, a little emphasis on the potential penalties for delay might encourage reluctant participants. Does this sound like the end justifies the means? Well ... maybe sometimes it does. Development of the political domain is no sin.

4: Make a plan, not a straitjacket.   Sometimes wonderful things can happen that weren't planned. Sometimes just setting some general goals and letting people take it from there can give better results than a highly structured process. In most cases it is advisable to allow for both planned and "open" or "nonscripted" approaches. There is no single best way to get a result.

5: Co-opt the culture before trying to convert it.   This means you have to work with what you've got. This is especially true if you are a small minority in a neutral or strange environment. As Gerald Weinberg, writing about cucumbers in a barrel of brine, has said, "It is more likely for cucumbers to be pickled than for brine to be cucumbered."[2] Use the bureaucracy; don't fight it.

6: Deal in the coin of the realm.   First, know what the coin of the realm is in any situation. Is it money? Power? Recognition? Position? Influence? Efficiency? Quality? Peace and quiet? Excitement? Present your vision and then describe and plan for the benefits using the coins that people recognize and value. In most cases, more than one type of currency will be needed.

7: Make it like a campaign.[3]   Formulate your strategy as if this were an election campaign—but no dirty tricks, of course. This includes the possibility of forming coalitions, using effective sound bites and media resources, both direct and indirect communications, image building, and targeted marketing.

8: Use your wide-angle lens to spot and feed the hungry beasts. There are many beasts to be fed in an organization. The Rational Beasts of dollars and common sense and technology; the Cultural Beasts of history and tradition; the Political Beasts of loyalty, networks, and alliances; the Personal Beasts of success, advancement, nonrational emotions and cupidity. They each present opportunities and pitfalls. For example, paying attention to the bottom line alone may win favor with some, but ignoring the opinion leaders and trendsetters may result in some scuttling surprises.

9: Be certain that certainty is certainly uncertain. Most managers and executives pursue certainty; they want to be sure that any investment they make is a sound one, with predictable results. They also realize, down deep, that this rarely happens, that uncontrollable forces change results, sometimes for the better and sometimes for the worse. Change agents should sell a *process* toward a vision rather than the certainty that the vision will appear next Tuesday at 3 PM.

10: Don't confuse system design and implementation with stretch socks. One size does not fit all. Be careful about picking up someone else's plan and process, even if it worked well elsewhere. Look for standard, repeatable elements that suit your own situation; modify them as needed, but sequence events in a customized way. Don't reinvent unnecessarily, but rearrange to suit.

11: Don't confuse

- Slogans with visions
- Visions with plans
- Plans with programs
- Programs with results
- Results with completion *or*
- Training with capability.

Assessment and development are never completed. Of course, slogans and visions may, in some cases, be the coin of the realm. Then the change agent will need to spend more time as an agent of reality and be a purveyor of dreams about the benefits of using other kinds of currency.

Training mediators does not automatically result in having competent mediators. Invest in monitoring, continued education, evaluation, recordkeeping, and the review of written agreements.

12: Don't get stuck in one role. ADR change agents may see themselves as evangelists, trainers, managing directors, moles, mediators, arbitrators, gurus, buffers, apologists, recordkeepers, or just as people going through the motions until the next fad comes along. It is dangerous to assume only one role; the person who is most flexible about taking on different roles will be the most powerful change agent.

13: If you've got a funny bone, use it!   Telling jokes is very risky; but a natural, lighthearted intervention can relieve tension and help break through an impasse.

14: Get out of it if you're not with it.   The most effective role a change agent can play is that of role model. If you don't believe in the values that underlie ADR, then you're in the wrong business. If you don't "walk the talk" of participative problem solving, nonjudgmental processes, and respect for individual feelings and aspirations, credibility and program success will be impaired.

15: Look for trouble.   Opportunities abound in every organization for helping to resolve internal and external problems, to the benefit of individuals and the whole. Be proactive: Search for those opportunities.

1. C.W. Moore, *The Mediation Process* (San Francisco: Jossey-Bass, 1986).
2. G. Weinberg, *The Secrets of Consulting* (New York: Dorset House, 1985).
3. This idea is borrowed courtesy of Dr. Len Hirsch, Institute for Strategic Management, Washington, D.C.

Developing a Comprehensive Internal Dispute Resolution System

Douglas H. Yarn

There is a long tradition of using extrajudicial means to resolve workplace disputes. In the typical model, parties agree to use a formal adjudicative grievance procedure with arbitration as a last resort. Unfortunately, these procedures are designed to respond only to mature disputes and tend to focus on rights and power rather than on the parties' interests. By the time a dispute has matured, positions are entrenched, disruption has occurred, and the fiscal and emotional costs of resolution are higher.

More recently, private corporations have been experimenting with informal, conciliatory dispute resolution mechanisms to resolve internal problems at an earlier stage and minimize workplace disruption. Mechanisms such as conciliation and mediation focus more on interests than on rights and allow the disputants an opportunity to collaborate on a mutually acceptable solution.

In some organizations, formal and informal mechanisms are being combined to provide comprehensive internal dispute resolution (DR) systems delivering both adjudicative and conciliatory processes as needed. As employers beset by the same range of workplace grievances and disputes experienced by any private employers, local governments should evaluate the effectiveness of their current dispute management and resolution systems. This article provides an example of how such an evaluation was conducted within a local government.

Case background

In late fall of 1992, the municipal government of a city in a South-eastern state adopted an ordinance prohibiting discrimination against and harassment of local government employees on the basis of race, color, sex, religion, national origin, citizenship, age, or disability. The goal was to eliminate prohibited discriminatory or harassing behavior and thereby improve morale and reduce the potential for damaging litigation.

Unfortunately, the only mechanism in place to handle discrimination and harassment complaints was the existing formal grievance procedure. Under that procedure (hereinafter referred to as the general procedure or system), an employee was expected to lodge a formal complaint with his or her supervisor. A decision unsatisfactory to the employee could be appealed at successive levels of the organizational hierarchy until it reached the grievance review panel. Sensing the inadequacy of the general system, the city council directed the city manager to institute new policies and procedures—including a process for investigation and response—for the specific purpose of handling employee complaints under the ordinance.

Within a week, the manager approved an outline of the Procedure for Carrying out the Prohibited Discrimination and Harassment Ordinance (hereinafter referred to as the special procedure or system). Drafted by a local attorney with considerable knowledge and experience in alternative dispute resolution (ADR), the procedure responded to the ordinance's mandate by having employee liaisons carry out its provisons.

The employee liaisons would be responsible for receiving complaints under the ordinance. After undertaking a formal investigation, the liaisons could proceed with informal mediation or formal steps toward resolution. The procedure outlined some aspects of the formal procedure by which the liaisons would report their findings and recommendations to the director and department head, who would then decide the best way to remedy the situation. Affected parties would be notified and given an opportunity to appeal—first to the assistant manager and then to the manager for a final decision.

The manager appointed two employee liaisons: a white female from the human resources department and a white male from physical services. The liaisons were selected on the basis of the manager's assessment of their "people skills" and the high regard in which they were held by other employees. They were expected to continue their normal duties as well.

By early 1993, the employee liaisons had received numerous complaints under the ordinance and encountered a number of problems in implementing the procedures. The sheer number of complaints and the processing time required, particularly for the formal investigative process, were interfering with their regular duties. The lack of racial diversity among the liaisons was put into question. Complaining employees and the liaisons themselves were confused as to whether they were advocates for the complainant, the government, or neither. Department heads were suspicious of the liaisons' motives, and some complaints involved the liaisons' own departments. Many employees wanted the problems solved confidentially and informally, but the liaisons did not know how far to intervene informally, and the procedures seemed to require an investigation before informal mechanisms were employed. The extent of confidentiality and protection from reprisal was unclear. Most notably, employees began converting all their standard grievances (e.g., promotion, benefits, and discipline complaints) into discrimination and harassment complaints.

Faced with these difficulties, the city asked the American Arbitration Association (AAA) to review the special procedure and help in its implementation.

Evaluating the DR system

Comprehensive internal DR systems provide anyone within an organization a range of both conciliatory and adjudicative DR mechanisms with which to resolve complaints, grievances, and other workplace problems. Once in place, the comprehensive DR system identifies and resolves disputes earlier and at less overall cost to the organization and to the employees involved; it also helps prevent similar disputes from arising in the future.

DR systems provide specially trained individuals who function as complaint handlers or "internal ombudsmen" or "ombuds." As defined by the Ombudsman Association, an internal ombuds is a neutral, impartial manager or administrator whose office is outside ordinary line management. The ombuds may provide confidential and informal assistance to anyone within the organization to resolve work-related complaints. He or she may serve as counselor, go-between, mediator, fact-finder, or as a mechanism for systems change.

Most reevaluation of DR systems is sparked by a crisis or demand on the existing system; this case was no exception. After reviewing the ordinance, examining the pre-existing general procedures and the ordinance's special procedures, and interviewing the employee liaisons, it was clear to the AAA that a more unified, comprehensive system was needed. The AAA initiated a series of facilitated, structured work sessions involving the manager, two assistant managers, the local government's legal counsel, the personnel director, and the employee liaisons. By engaging these primary players in an analysis of the current system and in the development of a more comprehensive system, the AAA could better identify the problems and create a system that had the full support of management. In the first meeting, the participants discussed the problems experienced by the employee liaisons and agreed to rethink the entire system.

To evaluate the system, the AAA facilitator set out to compare the characteristics of the existing system to those of an effective, comprehensive, internal DR system. The sections that follow trace the comparison.

Does it provide a full range of DR mechanisms?   A comprehensive DR system should provide a full range of DR mechanisms, from active listening to formal decision making or adjudication. To paraphrase Maslow, if all you have is a hammer, then every problem becomes a nail. Complainants' needs can vary significantly, depending on their personalities and the nature of the dispute; instead of trying to force all complaints through the same process, a comprehensive DR system tries to provide the optimal process for the particular problem—fitting the forum to the fuss rather than fitting the fuss to the forum. The accompanying sidebar details the full range of DR mechanisms.

The participants concluded that the city actually had two DR systems—the pre-existing general procedure for general employee grievances, and the new special procedure for discrimination and harassment complaints. The general system had very limited adjudicative mechanisms; the special system had fact-finding, mediation, and decision making, but was dominated by the adjudicative mechanisms. Neither system had a full range of mechanisms.

Is it accessible?   A comprehensive DR system should be easily and universally accessible. Full and equal access legitimizes the system. Accessibility involves five interrelated characteristics: availability, knowledge, confidentiality, protection from retaliation, and impartial aid.

Availability.   The system should be open to all employees without restrictions.

The city's special system for discrimination and harassment complaints was open only to employees with discrimination and harassment complaints. Because employees perceived it as having a wider range of mechanisms and because the employee liaisons were perceived as more helpful and accessible than the general system, employees were converting general employment grievances into racial discrimination or sexual harassment grievances in order to access what was perceived as a better system.

Knowledge.   Potential users should be aware of the existence, purpose, functions, and availability of the system.

A range of dispute resolution mechanisms

A full range of DR mechanisms (listed in increasing order of cost) might include

1. *Active listening.* The system provides an opportunity for employees to talk about problems and express feelings. This function legitimizes and shows respect for the complainant's emotions, while not necessarily validating the complaint.

2. *Appropriate self-help.* The system provides ways for complainants to solve the problem themselves, without external intervention. For example, the system could provide access to facts, policies, or institutional history that may help the complainant understand and evaluate the situation. It could provide an impartial third party with whom the complainant could discuss various ways to resolve the problem without direct assistance and from whom the complainant could receive impartial feedback on the possible results. The system could provide for informal information gathering by an impartial third party who may recommend to the complainant an approach to solve the problem.

3. *Conciliation or shuttle diplomacy.* The system provides an impartial third party who opens channels of communication on the issues, reduces the level of hostility, and arranges negotiations between the complainant and the co-worker or supervisor who is the perceived source of the grievance. In lieu of face-to-face negotiations, the third party can serve as a "go-between" or shuttle diplomat.

4. *Intermediation.* The system provides an informal, impartial intermediary who facilitates face-to-face, private discussions in which the two parties try to create their own resolution.

5. *External mediation.* The system provides formal mediation with a professional mediator not affiliated with the organization.

6. *Fact finding or investigation.* The system provides for formal or informal fact finding or investigations by an impartial party, internal or external to the organization. The fact finder might be authorized to make recommendations on the best way to resolve the problem.

7. *Authoritative decision making or adjudication.* The system provides for authoritative decision makers, internal or external to the organization, to impose solutions to resolve problems.

Mechanisms 1 through 5 are "conciliatory," interest-based mechanisms allowing the disputants themseves to make voluntary behavioral adjustments or shape mutually acceptable solutions based on their interests. Mechanisms 6 and 7 are largely "adjudicative," requiring a third party or management to assess the situation and impose a solution.

The employee liaisons met with most departments to explain the existence and availability of the special system, so the majority of employees had some general knowledge of that system. However, the broad availability of the special system had not been impressed upon middle and upper management. In addition, higher levels of management, particularly department heads, were suspicious of the employee liaisons and were not informed as to how the special system could benefit their departments.

Confidentiality and protection from retaliation. The system should guarantee confidentiality to all who approach off the record. This encourages employees to bring their complaints into the system and candidly discuss the problem. In many cases, they are looking for ways to solve a problem without direct confrontation or further deterioration of the work environment. Because employees sometimes fear retaliation from co-workers or supervisors who are the source of the complaint, there should be strictly enforced policies against retaliation.

The city's special system provided for the confidentiality of fact-finding reports and directed the employees involved to keep the matter confidential. However, the procedures required fact-finding reports on every complaint to be issued to the affected department heads, and thus did not protect information from exposure to superiors. In addition, there was no express policy to protect complainants from retaliation.

Impartial aid. The system should provide designated, trained, impartial third parties or neutrals, both internal and external to the organization, to aid in the resolution of the problem. In addition to helping the complainant understand the workings of the system, these neutrals are essential to almost every aspect of the system itself. Neutrals serve as sounding boards, active listeners, information resources, informal and formal fact finders, counsellors, go-betweens, intermediaries, mediators, and arbitrators.

Impartiality of third parties generates trust in the system. Impartiality can be achieved through the use of external neutrals or through the creation of an office of neutrals (full- or part-time employees) devoted exclusively to DR mechanisms and outside the standard organizational structure. There should be more than one neutral, so that a complainant who perceives one neutral as partial or biased can choose from among others. Gender and racial diversity among the neutrals is an important legitimizing factor.

In order to maintain trust in their impartiality, neutrals who engage in confidential informal activities such as counselling, conciliation, and mediation should be different from those who engage in more judgmental, formal mechanisms, such as fact finding or arbitration. Although neutrals engaged in any DR activity should be impartial, the role of confidential listener and counsellor is inconsistent with the adjudicative role of the formal fact finder. Internal ombuds in most organizations perform only the conciliatory functions, although they sometimes conduct informal fact finding in which no recommendations are made.

In the city's special system, employee liaisons provided aid through the informal mechanisms and conducted formal fact finding with recommendations. Although they had good natural skills, the liaisons lacked the training and experience necessary to effectively employ a range of DR mechanisms. In addition, they had other full-time duties within the government and could not therefore be independent of the organizational hierarchy.

Are the mechanisms primarily client driven?   A comprehensive DR system should be client driven, providing DR options at the choice of the complainant. Once the complainant understands the various mechanisms available in the system, he or she can make informed choices on the basis of personal preference for resolving the problem. The system should also provide "loopsback" and "loopsforward" so that the complainant can move among different DR mechanisms as preferred.

The city's general system had only one mechanism; therefore, it could not provide options. In the city's special system, once the complainant had initiated a complaint, he or she had no control over the mechanisms employed in the resolution of the problem. On paper, a complaint would automatically initiate formal fact finding, and the fact finding report was automatically submitted to decision makers for formal action. Mediation was at the discretion of the employee liaison. Under both the general and special systems, the complainant could stop the DR mechanisms only by withdrawing the complaint. In practice, the employee liaisons were trying to modify the written procedures by experimenting with various informal mechanisms before initiating formal fact finding.

Will it produce constructive organizational change?   An effective comprehensive DR system will lead to constructive changes in the organizational culture. A newly instituted DR system with a range of accessible, client-driven mechanisms will become a lightning rod for all the festering problems in the organization. An initial deluge of activity is a healthy sign that the system is needed; however, employees will continue to use the system only if it is taken seriously by management and produces significant evidence of constructive change. Thus, a comprehensive DR system should provide appropriate feedback to management, which in turn can respond with general structural changes in policy, organization, or corporate culture to prevent problems from arising in the future.

Since the special system was new and had yet to completely process a case, there had not been any evidence of management's support for the system or of the system's ability to resolve complaints. Functionally, city management was privy to all formal grievances in the general system and to all fact finding reports in the special system. There was no process in either system, however, that would track and identify recurring complaints and systemic problems. Nor had management expressly recognized how the systems could signal the need for long-term organizational change.

Redesign and implementation tasks

By combining conciliatory and adjudicative DR mechanisms and appointing the employee liaisons to serve in the role of internal ombuds, the city had created a rudimentary framework for a DR system. Fortunately, the drafter of the original special procedures had ADR expertise and had created a well-reasoned, functional document upon which to build. As written, the adjudicative mechanisms required little revision. However, the system was limited to only one class of complaint, failed to provide a full range of conciliatory DR options, and poorly defined the roles of the employee liaisons with respect to those options.

In subsequent facilitated meetings, city management concluded that the city needed a single, unified, and comprehensive DR system for all employee grievances, including those involving discrimination and harassment. They adopted additional conciliatory DR mechanisms and agreed to modify the procedures so that the complainant, in consultation with the liaison, could choose between conciliatory and adjudicative tracks and switch processes as needed. They adopted a strategy to more effectively communicate information about the system, approved an explicit policy prohibiting retaliation, and created more expansive rules on confidentiality. Most important, they clearly defined the functions and roles of the employee liaisons by limiting them to the conciliatory functions. They provided for liaison training and for external formal mediators and fact finders. They agreed that the position of employee liaison should be independent of line management. Finally, they adopted a liaison-run tracking and reporting system to monitor the trends in complaints.

Over the next several months, the procedures were substantially rewritten to reflect these changes. The liaisons were trained in mediation and conflict resolution skills. Forms were developed for information management and procedures adopted to keep records and ensure their confidentiality. General information fliers and informational materials specifically for complainants were created. In addition to a procedural and operating manual for the employee liaison office, a small library of resources on intraorganizational dispute resolution and discrimination and harassment complaints was established.

To date, the city has yet to formally adopt or implement the comprehensive system. Good implementation will require council and employee involvement and broader management consultation. Some anticipated problems include funding separate employee liaison positions. Larger local governments are more able to create such positions. Some options for smaller local governments include training a number of current, full-time employees to undertake the ombuds functions or using outside neutrals (volunteer and paid) as needed. Outside neutrals would, of course, need training and a good understanding of the local government's organization and policies (retired employees are a good source). Management in this case has yet to identify external neutrals in the immediate community for the formal functions of mediating and fact finding. One option is to use nonprofit providers of such services, such as the AAA.

Conclusion

Local governments should take a hard look at how employee complaints are handled and whether their DR systems are as efficient and effective as possible. Such an examination will lead many local governments to adopt more flexible and comprehensive models. In this case study, once management was exposed to the range of possibilities and potential, it opted for a more comprehensive system.

References

Center for Public Resources, *Corporate Dispute Management* (New York: Matthew Bender, 1982).

Roger Fisher, William Ury, and Bruce Patton, *Getting to Yes: Negotiating Agreement Without Giving In* (New York: Penguin, 1991).

William L. Ury, Jeanne M. Brett, and Stephen B. Goldberg, *Getting Dis-pute Resolved: Designing Systems to Cut the Costs of Conflict* (San Francisco: Jossey-Bass, 1988).

The following associations are good sources for additional information and assistance:

American Arbitration Association, 140 West 51st St., N.Y., N.Y. 10020–1203 (or one of the AAA regional offices).

The Ombudsman Association, P. O. Box 7700, Arlington, VA 22207.

Unlocking Gridlock: Establishing a Regional Network of Local Consensus Councils

Bruce Levi and Larry Spears

The critical importance of basic agreements to our public life—agreements that result from our leaders' capacity to deliver fundamental decisions about where we are going or what we are going to do—is certain. All local governments need the capacity to say yes—to establish a consensus and to act on behalf of citizens. Yet far too often, the policy processes of government offer a multitude of diverse interests the right to say no.[1] Neither the "yes" nor the "no" may understand what underlies the other position. This makes concerted action quite difficult; gridlock can result.

Equally disturbing is the impact on the increasing fragmentation of our society—fragmentation that isolates one person from another and disconnects citizens from their leaders and government. There seem to be fewer places where people can gather to share focused conversation on public issues and fewer opportunities for people to have meaningful conversation with others with whom they may not otherwise come in contact.[2]

The key to unlocking local government gridlock is consensus councils, a process infrastructure for public policy consensus building. These consensus councils can be in place, working, and ready as an institutionalized means of developing agreement among local stakeholders on difficult issues of public policy. The consensus council is designed to supplement current public policy processes in ways that increase the decision-making capacity of local leaders and decrease the fragmentation among citizens and leaders.

The consensus council provides process assistance; the participants develop the products. In other words, the consensus council is a tool for assisting citizens to be a think tank—to participate, think, and express their ideas in a forum that connects leaders and citizens in important discussions about public policy.

A practical step to unlocking gridlock

The future is a network of cooperating, local consensus councils established in each region to supplement and support democratic processes. North Dakota's private and public leaders recognized this new reality (see sidebar). They created the North Dakota Consensus Council, an institutional "umbrella" for consensus processes that address the restructuring and services of government and other important, intractable issues of public policy on a statewide basis.[3] While the North Dakota Consensus Council is a model for *statewide* public policy consensus building, the premises and unique features of the consensus council are applicable to *local* public policy consensus building.

The important characteristics of each *individual* consensus council that serves a local community include the following:

- A *continuing structure* for consensus-building processes that lasts and builds a tradition of nonpartisan, competent assistance to leadership
- A *trusteeship* of diverse public and private leaders to identify the major intractable public policy issues and supervise accountability for the capacity and creativity of the consensus processes

---

The North Dakota Consensus Council: A statewide model for local application

With a population of 650,000, North Dakota is like a medium-sized city with its population dispersed over 70,000 square miles. The North Dakota Consensus Council, Inc., is a private, nonprofit corporation founded by a partnership of North Dakota's private and public leaders. The consensus council provides statewide institutional capacity for supplemental consensus processes in support of traditional public policy processes. The consensus processes are used to develop basic public agreements on major issues of government structure and policy to position the state for effective governance in the future. A board of directors composed of public and private leaders provides a trusteeship form of supervision of the consensus processes. The consensus processes include forums for discussion and study among leaders of diverse viewpoints, supported by nonpolarizing methods for connecting citizens to leaders, and preparation of documents that articulate the resulting agreements and provide mechanisms for implementation. The participants in the consensus processes identify the methods for citizens and leaders to work together to monitor or assist in implementation.

- *Adaptive modeling* of consensus processes to fit the unique circumstances of each issue and include all important stakeholders
- *Support for leaders* of diverse viewpoints in exploring intractable issues
- A process for *citizen conversations* about important values and priorities in the presence of local leaders.

A consensus council providing a continuous structure for consensus-building processes strengthens a local community's capacity to build mutual agreements that survive changes in political administrations. This cultural change can position a community for sustainable leadership and development.

The important characteristics of a local government *network* of consensus councils to serve a transboundary region include the following:

- Visible ownership of interlocal or regional problems by local public and private leaders
- A practical mechanism for joint trusteeship among consensus councils to identify regional public policy issues as consensus subjects and to allocate resources
- Practical mechanisms for consensus councils (e.g., shared resources and forums) to address regional problems
- Development and preservation of a pool of personnel skilled in transboundary problem solving
- Enhanced citizen conversation and participation regarding basic values and priorities
- Encouragement of positive public attitudes.

The unique features of a consensus council

A supplement and support for traditional public processes, not a replacement.   The established public policy processes of local government provide the center for historic continuity in public decision making. Nothing about consensus processes will change that. Consensus processes are designed to help the political process work better, not to replace it. The goal is to assist leaders and citizens in developing agreements that are pragmatic, long lasting, economical, and easier to implement through the political process.

This supplemental consensus building is accomplished through an infrastructure of credible, neutral forums for discussion among leaders and meaningful citizen participation. Leaders do not lose responsibility or authority for making decisions. Leaders gain authority by encouraging participatory processes that form the basis for wise, fair, stable, and efficient agreements. The limitations or requirements of law are respected, and all due process and equal protection obligations can be fulfilled. All agreements are subject to ratification, and any participating leader can withdraw or veto any document or agreement that fails to meet necessary interests.

A sustained model, not an episodic one.   Much of the collaborative problem solving that occurs in this country happens on an ad hoc basis: an urgent issue or a crisis encourages a political leader or the parties to a conflict to develop a collaborative process for resolving the problem after all else has failed. The consensus council, in contrast, provides a sustained, credible organizational structure and resources that are ready when public policy issues are ripe. A sustained model has the benefit of creating a "culture of consensus building"—the public expectation that consensus processes will be used whenever there is difficulty in reaching a solution through the traditional public policy process.

A private-sector placement for public purposes.   A consensus council should be placed in the private sector. It can be effectively created as a corporation, whose governance by a trusteeship of private-sector leaders and public leaders enhances its independence and credibility. In addition, a private corporation can attract the balance of private and public funding needed to maintain that independence and credibility.

A public trusteeship governance.   A consensus council provides private and public leaders with the opportunity to develop a new supervisory rule as trustees of consensus processes without abandoning their institutional, partisan leadership roles in public life. For example, the governing board of directors of the North Dakota Consensus Council, Inc., reflects a wide spectrum of the major viewpoints among the leadership of the state.[4]

The role of a trustee governance in setting the agenda is essential. The trusteeship is *not* oriented to existing, immediate crises that are solvable through traditional processes but to deeper, historically intractable, long-term issues that span administrations and political offices (e.g., judicial reform, civil service structures, social services, nonprofit-sector health). Over time, this agenda-setting function will encourage early intervention in emerging problem areas.

The agreements and implementation mechanisms generated by each consensus process are not submitted to the governing board for their approval. The counsel does not endorse the specific recommendations of the forums it supports, nor does it engage in public advocacy on the issues that are subjects of consensus services. Thus, the individual members of the governing board remain free in any other public capacity to advocate for or against legislation

Premises of a consensus council

Consensus processes can be a valuable means to achieve public goals. The intractability of complex public policy issues can be frustrating. Some important public policy issues cannot be resolved adequately in the more familiar processes of government because of the ability of more interests to say no. The resolution of public policy issues that incorporates interests of diverse important viewpoints with fairness, efficiency, and stability is possible and practical with procedural assistance, a neutral location, and nonpartisan staff support.

A trusteeship of public and private leaders can endow supplemental consensus processes with permanence and continuity. Public and private leaders with diverse viewpoints can ensure the credibility, creativity, and competence of the consensus process without influencing or being held responsible for supporting the specific products of the process. This sustained, trustee model brings continuity to the consensus processes.

A private-sector corporation, linked to government, can provide a sustained location for consensus processes. A private-sector location provides visible independence and flexibility, ensuring the neutrality and credibility of the consensus process *outside of* government, while maintaining these processes as a resource *for* government.

Supplemental consensus processes for assisting public decision making are necessary to support changing notions of citizen participation and public leadership. Citizens want to help frame the issues, identify core values, identify priorities among values, suggest means for approaching problems, and propose solutions. Citizens do not insist on making the final decision, but they do increasingly insist on their perspectives being considered in the solution.

Notions of leadership are also changing. Leaders are developing new skills to arrive at solutions to difficult public policy issues. In consensus processes, the focus is not so much on leaders as it is on leadership, with leadership defined as a variety of shared activities among both leaders and citizens needed to move forward on an issue.

Leaders in consensus processes can provide citizens with meaningful ways to participate in decisions that affect their lives. The traditional, noncollaborative methods of writing letters and visiting leaders are not enough to capture the wisdom or beliefs of citizens. The participation of citizens must be authentic. Through the consensus process, citizens communicate their views by interacting in the presence of leaders.

Citizen participation in decision-making processes is important for leaders. While leaders are generally good listeners, our public policy institutions have not developed many new methods for hearing people in an accurate and efficient way.

Latent shared interests and agreements exist. Digging beneath the surface of positions on issues can uncover common underlying interests, values, and beliefs. These are opportunities that can be identified, "built," and strengthened through consensus processes.[1]

Consensus building requires resources. Resources include time; a location conducive to exploration of new or half-formed ideas; representation of diverse viewpoints; skilled process assistance from persons without policy commitments in the subject area; and staff assistance for the provision of nonpartisan analysis, research, and document preparation.

Principled and practical agreements last. An agreement based on principles identified and articulated by the participants provides justification that can sustain the policy direction. Agreements supported by written principles of implementation diminish occasions for misunderstanding and increase the confidence of all constituencies.

Cumulative agreements create a positive public environment. Cumulative agreements on major, previously intractable issues create a critical mass of consensus thinking, generate a positive public and political environment, and release creative energy to address new problems.

Consensus processes can result in significant savings in time, expense, and relationships. Consensus processes can provide models that institutionalize processes for resolving routine policy issues; minimize the resource impacts of public policy conflict; and strengthen relationships between parties.[2]

Leaders and citizens can see the benefits of supplemental consensus processes and can recognize these processes as a natural component of the public policy process. With the success of consensus processes over time they may become a natural part of the way public policy concerns are resolved.[3]

1. See Roger Fisher and William Ury, *Getting To Yes: Negotiating Agreement Without Giving In* (New York: Penguin Books, 1981), 75.
2. Kristen L. Dillon, *Statewide Offices of Dispute Resolution: Initiating Collaborative Approaches to Dispute Resolution in State Government* (National Institute for Dispute Resolution, 1993), 5.
3. See David Mathews and Noelle McAfee, *Community Politics*, 2d ed. (Dayton, OH: The Kettering Foundation, n.d.). This book discusses alternative perspectives on how communities can work together.

or specific public policies derived from the consensus processes of a consensus council. Because specific agreements do not divide the board, they can continue to provide credible oversight, lending legitimacy to the council in the eyes of citizens and other leaders.

Connecting citizens to leaders.　Citizen participation is the essence of democracy. Although there is a tradition in this country of active citizen involvement in the political process, this tradition is at risk.[5] The problems with our political system run much deeper than low voter turnout. Citizens are not apathetic about public life; instead, they feel disconnected from their communities and from their public officials, and they perceive that public processes fail to address important issues in an appropriate manner.[6]

Many of the consensus processes used by consensus council forums include community meetings and other tools for connecting citizens in meaningful public dialogue with leaders. These tools tap the felt need of citizens to participate in decisions that affect their lives by focusing on identification of fundamental values and value priorities in the presence of leaders who can then bring these ideas to the consensus process. Conversation among citizens in the presence of leaders is the way we can be sure that we have made up our collective minds, that we have understood and accepted the cost and consequences of our choices.

Staff services.　Careful planning and staff resources are critical to the success of a consensus process. The role of a consensus council's small, nonpartisan staff is to serve the board and the consensus processes. The staff supervises the ongoing documentation and evaluation of council programs; coordinates the planning and implementation of the consensus programs; and provides nonpartisan analysis, research, documentation, and drafting assistance on request.

Although the council's policies may allow staff to participate in the legislative hearing process by providing explanation and background materials on the genesis and development of agreements, staff do not advocate on behalf of any proposal that results from a consensus process. This advocacy function is left to the participant leaders in the consensus process. Staff should also be encouraged to provide explanatory information, participate in discussions, and make presentations to any other person or organization about the work of the consensus council.

A regional future

The future of local government is regional.[7] Local government will be focused on "problem sheds" that, like watersheds, cross political boundaries. Regional problems include transportation, law enforcement, social services, the nonprofit sector, public health, and education.[8] In the future, the jurisdictional integrity of separate units of local government will depend on the structures and processes they provide for addressing regional problems.

Vigorous local governments, creating consensus councils and linking them in a network, protect themselves by effectively addressing regional problems and building local agreements. By filling the vacuum that would otherwise be occupied by state government, a network of consensus councils can be an essential tool of local governments against state preemption. In addition, a network of local consensus councils provides opportunities to leverage local government resources. The network can provide the basis for cooperative initiatives to address regional public policy issues and fundamental infrastructure issues. Finally, the consensus council initiative increases the power of local governments by ensuring that they retain the initiative to address local issues, thereby increasing the practical power of local citizens and their views and allowing the details of agreements to be consistent with local culture and expectations.

An example of what local governments can accomplish through networking is the North Dakota Local Government "Tool Chest." In 1990, The North Dakota Consensus Council convened a Local Government Negotiation. Participants included the North Dakota Association of Counties, North Dakota League of Cities, North Dakota Township Officers Association, North Dakota Recreation and Park Association, the governor's office, and legislative leadership. Together, they assessed the needs of local governments and developed a set of tools to enable citizens and local governments to reorganize local government structure and services to meet local needs. This effort reflected a major change in state policy from state prescription to providing generic tools for local initiatives. The Tool Chest was approved by the North Dakota Legislative Assembly in 1993, with the combined support of all participants.

Conclusion

As local units of government collaborate with the private sector in establishing consensus councils and link them in networks, benefits will result:

- The existence of the network encourages the development of crossboundary collaborations in shared problem areas.
- Shared experiences in one problem area develop confidence and skills to address new issues.
- Shared experience develops teams with improved skills for participating in assisting and supporting consensus processes that produce practical results.

- Public attitudes change positively as hope is reinforced in regular, concrete ways.
- Public opinion toward consensus building processes helps build a public culture that unlocks public policy gridlock.

1. Alan Ehrenhalt, *United States of Ambition: Politicians, Power, and the Pursuit of Office* (New York: Random House, 1991), 40.
2. Richard C. Harwood, *Meaningful Chaos: How People Form Relationships with Public Concerns* (Dayton, OH: The Kettering Foundation, 1993), 37–39.
3. See Bruce Levi and Larry Spears, "North Dakota: Building a Consensus on the Future," *Intergovernmental Perspective* (Winter 1993): 35. The North Dakota Consensus Council, Inc., is organized as a 501(c)(3) organization. Financial resources for Consensus Council programs are provided by major foundations, including the Northwest Area Foundation, the Otto Bremer Foundation, and The William and Flora Hewlett Foundation; public contracts; and the private sector and individuals through the Friends of the North Dakota Consensus Council. For fur-

ther information, contact the North Dakota Consensus Council, Inc., 1003 Interstate Avenue, Suite 7, Bismarck, ND 58501-0500, (701) 224-0588, FAX (701) 224-0787.
4. The governor always has the opportunity for *ex officio* membership on the Board of Directors.
5. National Commission for the Renewal of American Democracy, *The Portland Agenda: Principles and Practices for Reconnecting Citizens and the Political Process* (Washington, D.C.: National Association of Secretaries of State, 1993), ix.
6. *Ibid.*
7. Neal R. Peirce, "The Metropolitan Perplex: City Boundaries are Widening in Missoula, Montana, and Elsewhere," *Nation's Cities Weekly*, 20 December 1993.
8. S. Smith and M. Lipsky, *Nonprofits for Hire: The Welfare State in the Age of Contracting* (Cambridge: Harvard University Press, 1993).

For Further Reference

Conflict and dispute resolution

Axelrod, Robert. *The Evolution of Co-operation.* New York: Basic Books, 1984.

Bickmore, Kathy; Prill Goldthwait; and John Looney. *Alternatives to Violence.* Akron, OH: Peace GROWS, Inc., 1984.

Boulding, Elise. *Building a Global Civic Culture: Education for an Interdependent World.* New York: Columbia University Teachers College, 1988.

Boulding, Kenneth. *Conflict and Defense.* New York: Harper & Row, 1962.

Brett, Jeanne M. "Negotiating Group Decisions." *Negotiation Journal* 7, no. 3 (July 1991): 291–310.

Carpenter, Susan L., and Kennedy, W. T. D. *Managing Public Disputes.* San Francisco: Jossey-Bass, 1988.

Coates, Dan, and Steven Penrod. "Social Psychology and the Emergence of Disputes." *Law and Society Review* 15, no. 3/4 (1980–81): 655–680.

Coser, Lewis A. *The Functions of Social Conflict.* Glencoe, IL: The Free Press, 1956.

Deutsch, Morton. *The Resolution of Conflict: Constructive and Destructive Processes.* New Haven, CT: Yale University Press, 1973.

Dunlop, John T. *Dispute Resolution.* Dover, MA: Auburn House Publishing Company, 1984.

Felstiner, W.; R. Abel; and A. Sarat. "The Emergence and Transformation of Disputes: Naming, Blaming, and Claiming ..." *Law and Society Review* 25, no. 3/4 (1980): 631–654.

Filley, Alan. *Interpersonal Conflict Resolution.* Glenview, IL: Scott, Foresman & Co., 1975.

Folberg, Jay, and Alison Taylor. *Mediation: A Comprehensive Guide to Resolving Conflicts without Litigation.* San Francisco: Jossey-Bass, 1985.

Frost, Joyce, and William Wilmot. *Interpersonal Conflict.* Dubuque, IA: William C. Brown, 1978.

Galtung, Johan. "Is Peaceful Research Possible? One Methodology of Peace Research." In *Peace Research, Education, and Action.* Copenhagen: Christian Ejlers, 1975.

Goldberg, Steven; Eric Green; and Frank Sander. *Dispute Resolution.* Boston, MA: Little, Brown, and Co., 1985.

Gray, Barbara. *Collaborating.* San Francisco: Jossey-Bass, 1989.

Himes, Joseph S. *Conflict and Conflict Management.* Athens, GA: University of Georgia Press, 1980.

Johnson, David, and Dean Tjosvold. "Constructive Controversy: The Key to Effective Decision Making." In *Productive Conflict Management,* edited by Dean Tjosvold and David Johnson. New York: Irvington Publishers, 1983.

Mann, Leon, and Irving Janis. "Decisional Conflict In Organizations." In *Productive Conflict Management*, edited by Dean Tjosvold and David Johnson. New York: Irvington Publishers, 1983.

Minahan, Ann. " 'Martha's Rules': An Alternative to Robert's Rules of Order." *Affilia* (summer 1986): 53–56.

Pruitt, Dean, and D. Syna. "Successful Problem Solving." In *Productive Conflict Management*, edited by Dean Tjosvold and David Johnson. New York: Irvington Publishers, 1983.

Pruitt, Dean, and Jeffrey Rubin. *Social Conflict*. New York: Random House, 1986.

Sander, Frank E. A. "Alternative Methods of Dispute Resolution: An Overview." *University of Florida Law Review* 37 (winter 1985): 1–18.

Sandole, Dennis, and Ingrid Sandole-Staroste, eds. *Conflict Management and Problem Solving*. New York: New York University Press, 1987.

Schellenburg, James A. *The Science of Conflict*. New York: Oxford University Press, 1982.

Smith, Kenwyn K. "The Movement of Conflict in Organizations: The Joint Dynamics of Splitting and Triangulation." *Administrative Science Quarterly* 34 (1989): 1–20.

Steiner, Claude M. *The Other Side of Power*. New York: Grove Press, 1981.

Tjosvold, Dean. *Managing Conflict*. Minneapolis: Team Media, 1989.

_____. *The Conflict-Positive Organization*. Reading, MA: Addison-Wesley Publishing Co., 1991.

Tjosvold, Dean, and David Johnson. "Introduction." In *Productive Conflict Management*, edited by Dean Tjosvold and David Johnson. New York: Irvington Publishers, 1983.

Van Ness, D. "Pursuing a Restorative Vision of Justice." *New Perspectives on Crime and Justice* (February 1989): 17–30.

Zehr, Howard, "Justice: Stumbling toward a Restorative Ideal." *New Perspectives on Crime and Justice* (February 1989): 1–15.

Multicultural issues

Chalmers, E., and Gerald Cormick. *Racial Conflict and Negotiation*. Ann Arbor, MI: Institute of Labor and Industrial Relations, 1971.

Gulliver, P. H. *Disputes and Negotiations: A Cross-Cultural Perspective*. New York: Academic Press, 1979.

Hewitt, Roger. *White Talk Black Talk*. New York: Cambridge University Press, 1986.

Kreider, William. *Creative Conflict Resolution*. Glenview, IL: Scott, Foresman and Co., 1984.

Samover, Larry A., and Richard E. Porter. *Intercultural Communication: A Reader*. Belmont, CA: Wadsworth Publishing Co., 1972.

Walton, Richard. *Interpersonal Peacemaking: Confrontations and Third-Party Consultation*. Reading, MA: Addison-Wesley Publishing Co., 1969.

Negotiation

Asherman, Ira, and Sandra Asherman. *Negotiation Source Book*. Amherst, MA: Human Resource Development Press, 1989.

Bascow, Lawrence S., and M. Wheeler. "Negotiation: A Look at Decision-Making." Chapter 2 of *Environmental Dispute Resolution*. New York: Plenum Press, 1985.

Bellow, Gary, and Bea Moulton. *The Lawyering Process: Negotiation*. Mineola, NY: Foundation Press, 1981.

Bramson, Robert M. *Coping with Difficult People*. New York: Ballantine, 1981.

Edwards, Harry T., and James J. White. *The Lawyer as a Negotiator*. St. Paul, MN: West Publishing Co., 1977.

Fisher, Roger, and William Ury. *Getting to Yes*. Boston: Houghton Mifflin Publishing Co., 1981.

Greenhalgh, Leonard. "Relationships in Negotiation." *Negotiation Journal* 3, no. 3 (1987): 235–243.

Jandt, Fred E. *Win/Win Negotiation: Turning Conflict into Agreement*. New York: John Wiley & Sons, 1985.

Kennedy, Gavin; John Benson; and John McMillian. *Managing Negotiations.* Englewood Cliffs, NJ: Prentice-Hall, 1982.

Lax, David, and James Sebenius. *The Manager as Negotiator.* New York: The Free Press, 1986.

Maddux, Robert. *Successful Negotiation: Effective "Win/Win" Strategies and Tactics.* Los Altos, CA: Crisp Publications, 1988.

Nierenberg, Gerald I. *The Complete Negotiator.* New York: Berkeley Books, 1986.

———. *Fundamentals of Negotiation.* New York: Hawthorn Books, 1977.

Pruitt, Dean. *Negotiation Behavior.* New York: Academic Press, 1981.

Raiffa, Howard. *The Art and Science of Negotiation.* Cambridge, MA: Harvard University Press, 1982.

Rubin, Jeffrey A. "Negotiation: An Introduction to Some Issues and Themes." *American Behavioral Scientist* 27, no. 2 (1983).

Wall, James. *Negotiation Theory and Practice.* Glenview, IL: Scott, Foresman and Co., 1985.

Williams, Gerald. *Legal Negotiation and Settlement.* St. Paul, MN: West Publishing Co., 1983.

Zartman, I. William. "Common Elements in the Analysis of the Negotiation Process." *Negotiation Journal* 4, no. 1 (1988): 31–43.

Zartman, I. William, and Majorie Berman. *The Practical Negotiator.* New Haven, CT: Yale University Press, 1982.

Mediation

Allison, John R. "Five Ways to Keep Disputes Out of Court." *Harvard Business Review* (January/February 1990).

Auerback, Jerold S. *Justice without Law.* New York: Oxford University Press, 1983.

Barletti, M. D., and E. Stork. "Hands-On Mediation Training in a Private-Practice Setting." *Mediation Quarterly* 8, no. 3 (spring 1991).

Berkovitch, Jacob. *Social Conflicts and Third Parties.* Boulder, CO: Westview Press, 1984.

Brutsche, Steve. "Mediation Cross-Examined." *Texas Bar Journal* (June 1990).

Carlson, Eugene. "Mediators Are Flourishing on Anti-Litigation Sentiment." *Wall Street Journal,* 9 September 1991.

Cloke, Kenneth. "Conflict Resolution Systems Design: The United Nations and the New World Order." *Mediation Quarterly* 8, no. 3 (summer 1991).

Cobb, S., and Rifkin, J. "Practice and Paradox: Deconstructing Neutrality in Mediation." *Law and Social Inquiry* 16, no. 1 (1991).

Curriden, Mark. "Big Fees Are Giving Lawyers a Black Eye." *Atlanta Journal/Constitution,* 9 September 1991.

———. "Indigent Defendants Get Poor Legal Aid, Chief Justice Says." *Atlanta Journal/Constitution,* 15 June 1991.

Dworkin, J.; L. Jacob; and E. Scott. "The Boundaries between Mediation and Therapy: Ethical Considerations." *Mediation Quarterly* 9, no. 2 (1991).

Fine, Erika S., and Elizabeth Plapinger. *ADR and the Courts: A Manual for Judges and Lawyers.* New York: Butterworth Legal Publishers, 1987.

Fisher, Roger. *International Mediation: A Workshop Guide.* New York: International Peace Academy, 1978.

Fisher, Roger, and Scott Brown. *Getting Together: Building a Relationship that Gets to Yes.* Boston: Houghton Mifflin Company, 1988.

Folberg, Jay, and Alison Taylor. *Mediation: A Comprehensive Guide to Resolving Conflicts without Litigation.* San Francisco: Jossey-Bass, 1984.

Gergen, David, and Ted Gest. "Ruling on Quayle v. Lawyers." *U.S. News and World Report,* 26 August/2 September 1991.

Haynes, John, and Gretchen Haynes. *Mediating Divorce.* San Francisco: Jossey-Bass, 1989.

Kessler, Sheila. *Creative Conflict Resolution: Mediation.* Atlanta, GA: Institute for Professional Training, 1978.

Kolb, Deborah. *The Mediators*. Cambridge, MA: MIT Press, 1983.

Kressell, Kenneth; Dean Pruitt; and Associates. *Mediation Research*. San Francisco: Jossey-Bass, 1989.

Marshall, Tony F. "The Power of Mediation." *Mediation Quarterly* 8, no. 2, (winter 1990).

Moore, Christopher W. *The Mediation Process: Practical Strategies for Resolving Conflict*. San Francisco: Jossey-Bass, 1986.

Pollock, E., and M. Geyelin. "Law Firms Promise to Encourage Litigation Alternatives for Clients." *Wall Street Journal*, 21 October 1991.

Richman, Roger; Orion White; and Michaux Wilkinson. *Intergovernmental Mediation: Negotiation in Local Government Disputes*. Boulder, CO: Westview Press, 1986.

Rogers, Nancy H., and Richard Salem. *A Student's Guide to Mediation and the Law*. New York: Matthew Bender & Co., 1987.

Rogers, Susan J. "The Dynamics of Conflict Behavior in a Mediated Dispute." *Mediation Quarterly* 18 (winter 1987).

Rubin, Jeffrey, ed. *Dynamics of Third Party Intervention*. New York: Praeger Publishers, 1981.

Simon, Stephanie. "Joint Custody Loses Favor for Increasing Children's Feelings of Being Torn Apart." *Wall Street Journal*, 15 July 1991.

Singer, Linda R. "The Quiet Revolution in Dispute Settlement." *Mediation Quarterly* 7, no. 2 (Winter 1989).

Ury, William. *Getting Past No*. New York: Bantam Books, 1991.

Volpe, M. R., and C. Bahn. "Resistance to Mediation: Understanding and Handling It." *Negotiation Journal* (July 1987).

Welton, Gary; Dean G. Pruitt; and Neil B. McGillicuddy. "The Role of Caucusing in Community Mediation." *Journal of Conflict Resolution* 32, no. 1 (March 1988).

Wilkinson, John H. "Mediation Law: ADR Is Increasing Efficiency, Averts Litigation in Many Cases." *The National Law Journal* (4 April 1988).

Communication

Bandler, Richard, and John Grinder. *Reframing: Neurolinguistic Programming and the Transformation of Meaning*. Moab, UT: Real People Press, 1982.

Breslin, J. "Breaking Away from Subtle Biases." *Negotiation Journal* 5, no. 3 (1989).

Folger, Joseph P., and Marshall Scott Poole. *Working through Conflict*. Glenview, IL: Scott, Foresman and Co., 1984.

Gordon, Thomas. *Leadership Effectiveness Training*. New York: Wyden Books, 1978.

Henley, Nancy A. *Body Politics*. Englewood Cliffs, NJ: Prentice-Hall, 1977.

Katz, Neil H., and John W. Lawyer. *Communication and Conflict Resolution Skills*. Dubuque, IA: Kendall/Hunt Publishers, 1985.

Tannen, Deborah. *That's Not What I Meant!* New York: Ballantine Books, 1986.

————. *You Just Don't Understand*. New York: Ballantine Books, 1990.

Organizational conflict management

Bazerman, Max H., and Roy J. Lewcki, eds. *Negotiation in Organizations: The Social Psychology of Conflict, Coalitions and Bargaining*. San Francisco: Jossey-Bass, 1980.

Belasco, James A. *Teaching the Elephant to Dance: Empowering Change in Your Organization*. New York: Crown Publishers, 1990.

Benfari, Robert. *Understanding Your Management Style*. Lexington, MA: Lexington Books, 1991.

Blake, R., and Mouton, J. "Lateral Conflict." In *Productive Conflict Management*, edited by Dean Tjosvold and David Johnson. New York: Irvington Publishers, 1983.

Bolman, Lee, and Terrence Deal. *Modern Approaches to Understanding and Managing Organizations*. San Francisco: Jossey-Bass, 1984.

Brown, Bert. *Managing Conflict at Organizational Interfaces*. Reading, MA: Addison-Wesley Publishing Co., 1983.

Douglas, Ann. *Industrial Peacemaking.* New York: Columbia University Press, 1962.

Hirschhorn, Larry. *The Workplace Within: Psychodynamics of Organizational Life.* Cambridge, MA: MIT Press, 1988.

Kindler, Herbert S. *Managing Disagreement Constructively: Conflict Management in Organizations.* San Francisco: Crisp Publishing, 1988.

Kolb, David A.; Irwin Rubin; and Joyce Osland. *Organizational Behavior.* Englewood Cliffs, NJ: Prentice-Hall, 1991.

Loden, Marilyn, and Judy B. Rosener. *Workforce America: Managing Employee Diversity as a Vital Resource.* Homewood, IL: Business One Irwin, 1991.

Pfeiffer, Jeffrey. *Power in Organizations.* Marshfield, MA: Pitman, 1981.

Schelling, Thomas C. *Strategy of Conflict.* Cambridge, MA: Harvard University Press, 1969.

Solomon, Muriel. *Working with Difficult People.* Englewood Cliffs, NJ: Prentice-Hall, 1990.

Tichy, Noel, and Mary A. Devanma. *The Transformational Leader.* New York: John Wiley & Sons, 1986.

Weeks, Dudley. *Conflict Partnership.* Orange, CA: Trans World Productions, 1984.

Wehr, Paul. *Conflict Regulation.* Boulder, CO: Westview Press, 1979.

Zander, Alvin. *The Purposes of Groups and Organizations.* San Francisco: Jossey-Bass, 1988.

Intergovernmental and public policy disputes

Baxter, Ralph H., and Evelyn Hunt. "ADR: Arbitration of Employment Claims." *Employee Relations Law Journal* (autumn 1989).

Bragi, Bob. *Working Together: A Manual for Helping Groups Work More Effectively.* Amherst, MA: University of Massachusetts, 1978.

Breger, Marshall J. "Realizing the Potential of Arbitration." *Federal Agency Dispute Resolution Arbitration Journal* (June 1991).

Brittin, Alexander J. "ADR in Government Contract Appeals." *Public Contract Law Journal* (winter 1990).

Carpenter, Susan, and W. J. D. Kennedy. *Managing Public Disputes.* San Francisco: Jossey-Bass, 1988.

Connor, Desmond M. *Preventing and Resolving Public Controversy.* Victoria, B. C.: Connor Development Services Limited, n.d.

Dilts, David A.; Amad Karim; and Ali Rassuli. "Mediation in the Public Sector: Toward a Paradigm of Negotiations and Dispute Resolution." *Journal of Collective Negotiation in the Public Sector* (winter 1990).

Drake, William, ed. *Regulatory Negotiation Issue.* Washington, D.C.: Dispute Resolution Forum, National Institute for Dispute Resolution, 1986.

Gottlieb, Henry. "Mediation Masterpiece: A State Mediator and a Federal Judge Have Helped Set a Precedent for Settling Complex Public Housing Battles." *New Jersey Law Bulletin* (29 August 1989).

Huelsberg, Nancy, and William Lincoln. *Successful Negotiating in Local Government.* Washington, D.C.: ICMA, 1985.

Kraybill, Ron. *Repairing the Breach: Ministering in Community Conflict.* Scottsdale, PA: Herald Press, 1980.

Laue, James H.; Sharon Burde; William Potapchuk; and Miranda Salkoff. "Getting to the Table: Three Paths." *Mediation Quarterly* 20 (summer 1988): 7–21.

McAdoo, Barbara, and Larry Bakken. "Local Government Use of Mediation for Resolution of Public Disputes." *The Urban Lawyer* 22, no. 2 (spring 1990).

National Institute for Dispute Resolution. *Paths to Justice: Major Public Policy Issues of Dispute Resolution.* Report of the Ad Hoc Panel on Dispute Resolution and Public Policy, January 1984.

Pops, Gerald M., and Max O. Stephenson, Jr. *Conflict Resolution in the Policy Process.* Department of Public Administration, West Virginia University, 1987.

Potapchuk, William, and Chris Carlson. "A Model for Using Conflict Analysis to Determine Intervention Techniques." *Mediation Quarterly* 16 (July 1987): 31–43.

Pou, Charles, Jr. *Federal Agency Use of ADR: The Experience to Date.* Center for Public Resources, January 1987.

Richman, Roger. "Environmental Mediation: An Alternative Dispute Settlement System." In *Conflict Management and Problem Solving,* edited by Dennis Sandole and Ingrid Sandole-Staroste. New York: New York University Press, 1987.

Sullivan, Timothy J. *Resolving Development Disputes through Negotiation.* New York: Plenum Press, 1984.

Susskind, Lawrence, and J. Cruikshank. *Breaking the Impasse: Consensual Approaches to Resolving Public Disputes.* Cambridge, MA: Schenkman Publishing Co., 1983.

Susskind, Lawrence; Lawrence Bacow; and Michael Wheeler, eds. *Resolving Environmental Regulatory Disputes.* Cambridge, MA: Schenkman Publishing Co., 1983.

Welsh, Nancy A. "Effective Alternatives to Court." *Urban, State and Local Law Newsletter* (Spring 1989).

White, Orion. *The Dynamics of Negotiation for Intergovernmental Mediation: Negotiation in Local Government Disputes.* Boulder, CO: Westview Press, 1985.

Systems design

Brett, Jeanne; Stephen B. Goldberg; and William Ury. "Designing Systems for Resolving Disputes in Organizations." *The American Psychologist* (February 1990).

Milhauser, M. S. "The Next Step in ADR: Building an Effective Dispute-Handling System within the Corporation." *Corporate Quarterly* 5 (October 1989).

Warfield, Wallace. "The Implication of ADR Processes for Decisionmaking in Administrative Disputes." *Pepperdine Law Review* 16 (May 1989).

Employee relations

Bakalay, Charles. "Alternative Dispute Resolution of Employer-Employee Disputes in a Non-Union Setting." *Arbitration Journal* 45, no. 3 (September 1990).

Baxter, Ralph, and Evelyn Hurst. "ADR: Arbitration of Employment Claims." *Employee Relations Law Journal* (autumn 1989).

Bureau of National Affairs, "Lawyers Say Use of Arbitration for Non-Union Employees Will Grow." *ADR Report* 4 (28 June 1990).

Csiernik, Rick. "Mediation and the Workplace: Creating Awareness with an Employee Assistance Program." *Mediation Quarterly* 8, no. 2 (winter 1990).

Lord, Mary. "How Nabisco Solved Its Labor Problem: New Mediation Efforts Pull the Company Closer." *U.S. News and World Report,* 20 May 1991.

Sherman, Mark R. "Streamlined Mediation: An Alternative to Litigating Discharge Disputes." *Arbitration Journal* (March 1991).

Skratek, Sylvia. "Grievance Mediation: Does It Really Work?" *Negotiation Journal* 6, no. 3 (July 1990): 269–280.

Ethics

Bush, Robert A. Baruch. *The Dilemmas of Mediation Practice: A Study of Ethical Dilemmas and Policy Implications.* Washington, D.C.: National Institute for Dispute Resolution, 1993.

"SPIDR's Ethical Standards of Professional Conduct." *Dispute Resolution Forum* (March 1987).

Walker, Gregg B. "Training Mediation: Teaching about Ethical Concerns and Obligations." *Mediation Quarterly* (spring 1988).

NORTH CHICAGO
PUBLIC LIBRARY

Practical Management Series

**Resolving Conflict:
Strategies for Local Government**

Text type
Century Expanded

Composition
EPS Group, Inc.
Hanover, Maryland

Printing and binding
R. R. Donnelley & Sons Company
Harrisonburg, Virginia

Cover design
Rebecca Geanaros